RELIGIOUS TRUTH

THE LITTMAN LIBRARY OF
JEWISH CIVILIZATION

Life Patron
COLETTE LITTMAN

Dedicated to the memory of
LOUIS THOMAS SIDNEY LITTMAN
who founded the Littman Library for the love of God
and as an act of charity in memory of his father
JOSEPH AARON LITTMAN
and to the memory of
ROBERT JOSEPH LITTMAN
who continued what his father Louis had begun
יהא זכרם ברוך

'Get wisdom, get understanding:
Forsake her not and she shall preserve thee'
PROV. 4:5

The Littman Library of Jewish Civilization is a registered UK charity
Registered charity no. 1000784

RELIGIOUS TRUTH
Towards a
Jewish Theology of Religions

◆

EDITED BY
ALON GOSHEN-GOTTSTEIN

London
The Littman Library of Jewish Civilization
in association with Liverpool University Press

The Littman Library of Jewish Civilization
Registered office: 14th Floor, 33 Cavendish Square, London WIG OPW

in association with Liverpool University Press
4 Cambridge Street, Liverpool L69 7ZU, UK
www.liverpooluniversitypress.co.uk/littman
Managing Editor: Connie Webber

Distributed in North America by Longleaf Services
116 S Boundary St, Chapel Hill, NC 27514, USA

First published 2020
First published in paperback 2024

© *the several contributors 2020; copyright in this collection*
the Littman Library of Civilization 2020

All rights reserved.
No part of this publication may be reproduced,
stored in a retrieval system, or transmitted, in any form or
by any means, without the prior permission in writing of
the Littman Library of Jewish Civilization

This book is sold subject to the condition that it shall not, by way
of trade or otherwise, be lent, re-sold, hired out or otherwise circulated
without the publisher's prior consent in any form of binding or cover
other than that in which it is published and without a similar condition
including this condition being imposed on the subsequent purchaser

Catalogue records for this book are available from the
British Library and the Library of Congress

ISBN 978–1–802071–91–7

Publishing co-ordinator: Janet Moth
Copy-editing: Agnes Erdos
Proof-reading: Mark Newby
Index: Chris Cecot
Designed and typeset by Pete Russell, Faringdon, Oxon.

Dedicated to the sainted memory of my teacher
Rabbi Gedalyahu Aharon Kenig

Committed to the pursuit of truth, he was able to accommodate the truth of others

◆

Preface

◆

FOR THE PAST TWENTY YEARS I have engaged in a two-pronged intellectual and theological journey. On the one hand, I have been cultivating resources for interreligious thinking and understanding through conferences, publications, and other educational resources. Some of these works have been published in a series entitled Interreligious Reflections, originally published by Lexington Books and now by Wipf and Stock. This work has been complemented by work in the field of theology of religions. This two-pronged approach stems from the recognition that one cannot engage in serious interreligious work without examining the foundations of one's own faith and how it relates to other faiths. As far as theology of religions goes (perhaps the same applies to other branches of theology as well), I would argue similarly that it requires serious interreligious engagement.

The present volume is part of a trajectory of work in the field of Jewish theology of religions. The first contribution to the field was in the 2012 publication by the Littman Library of *Jewish Theology and World Religions*, which I co-edited with Eugene Korn. I am delighted to continue the process of convening a conversation on these issues between leading Jewish thinkers in what feels like a homecoming, returning to Littman as a host for these conversations. (Other monographs have appeared in the meantime at Palgrave Macmillan, focusing on a Jewish view of Hinduism, and still others are in preparation.)

The focus of this volume on the problem of truth and how it figures in a view of other religions grows out of my own analysis of the key issues that a contemporary Jewish theology of religions must address. This analysis appears in my introductory essay to *Jewish Theology and World Religions*. An identification of one's religion with truth and the eventual view of other religions as being false, or possessing only partial truth, is an important challenge for a Jewish view of other religions. The present volume brings together scholars who collaboratively explore what truth means to contemporary Jewish thought and consequently to a contemporary Jewish theology of religions.

The project was launched in partnership with Yeshivat Chovevei Torah Rabbinical Seminary following its receipt of a grant from the Henry Luce Foundation. With the help of this grant, educational materials were developed and a summer school session took place in 2013, which brought together students of Chovevei Torah and Union Theological Seminary. Two sessions on the subject were held as part of the 16th World Congress of Jewish Studies. The present volume is based on the materials produced for this project. For various reasons, some of the essays initially prepared as part of the project are not published here, while two studies—those of Yehuda Gellman and Arthur Green—were solicited for this publication. Tamar Ross's essay, previously published in *Ḥazon Naḥum: Studies in Jewish Law, Thought and History Presented to Dr. Norman Lamm*, is reprinted here with permission of the Michael Scharf Publication Trust of Yeshiva University Press. In keeping with the original intent of this project, after the different views have been set forth, I attempt, at the end of the volume, to translate the various insights into a theological workshop for both the student and the religious professional, helping them gain a conceptual handle and enter their own theological process relating to a contemporary Jewish theology of religions.

I am grateful to the Henry Luce Foundation and Yeshivat Chovevei Torah, and in particular to Rabbi Dov Linzer, for their support and partnership in this project of religious reflection, which is germane to interfaith engagement. I am grateful to Reuven Goldfarb for his help in the final editing of the typescript for production. Connie Webber grasped immediately the significance of this volume and felt Littman would provide it with the best placement. I am convinced she is right and am delighted to be back at Littman and to be working again with Connie and enjoying her wisdom and support. I am also grateful to the wonderful team. Agi Erdos's edits improved the manuscript immeasurably. As one of the authors comments, he had, in many years of publishing, never experienced such an active, and able, editor who not only improved the text but actually improved the argument. Janet Moth ensured a smooth flow of data and communication at all stages with grace. A special word of thanks is due to Pete Russell for the cover design. His work does more than provide aesthetics for the book. It actually makes a theological statement. I would like to conclude this preface by expounding on what I see as the meaning of Pete's artwork.

Religious Truth does not take a position; it opens up a conversation. The conversation takes place in a particular context, that of Judaism and world religions. There are many ways of presenting the relationship between what truth means to/in Judaism and how it might relate to truth as found in other religions, peoples, and languages. Pete's artwork enriches our conversation by alluding to one possibility, one theologoumenon, found in rabbinic literature. Deuteronomy 1: 5 describes Moses as explicating the Torah to Israel. The word *be'er*, explicated, is glossed by the *midrash*, cited in Rashi as: 'He interpreted it in seventy languages.' This is one of several instances in which the Torah's interpretation, hence understanding, is understood by the rabbis by reference to seventy languages, an archetypal expression relating to the totality of human languages. By placing the word אמת, truth, on the front line of the image, and then offering translations of 'truth' in a variety of other languages, Pete alludes to this understanding. The midrashic idea provides us with a thought structure that can be extended and that is relevant to the project of religious truth and world religions. One possible way of interpreting the image is to consider a core revelation, a core truth, here captured in Hebrew, and a variety of translations by means of which it is extended beyond Judaism to other nations and peoples. These have a share in the truth and allow us to understand it more fully, to interpret it, through the diversity of languages and religions. Translation is an act of dialogue and enrichment by means of which understanding grows in a reciprocal movement that increases understanding. It is, in this reading, a key to interpreting and to understanding the truth of the Torah.

R. Nathan of Breslav, whom I quote in my essay, refers to the power of peace, more powerful than a limited truth that we might practise, that allows us to draw all seventy nations together. The coming together of the seventy nations (languages) fulfils the biblical prophecy: 'then I will restore to the peoples a pure language, so that all of them may call on the name of the Lord and serve Him with one accord' (Zeph. 3: 9). The image of the one word and its multiple translations recalls this hope of future unity in pursuit of purity and the common worship of the one God. May the present volume make a small contribution towards advancing harmony and understanding across the lines of religious diversity—a necessary step towards the fulfilment of this prophecy.

Thank you to all.

ALON GOSHEN-GOTTSTEIN
The Elijah Interfaith Institute

Contents

Note on Transliteration	xii
INTRODUCTION	
The Scope of Religious Truth: Project Overview	1
ALON GOSHEN-GOTTSTEIN	
1. Old-Fashioned Truth, Telic Truth, and Interreligious Understanding	29
JEROME YEHUDA GELLMAN	
2. History and Truth in Religion	47
STANISLAW KRAJEWSKI	
3. The Cosmic Eye and Its Pupil: Divine Perfection and the Mediation of Universal and Particular Truth in Rabbinic Theology	61
CASS FISHER	
4. *Da'at*: Universalizing a Hasidic Value	83
AVRAHAM YIZHAK (ARTHUR) GREEN	
5. The Truth Beyond and Beyond Truth: Religious Truth in Teachings of the Breslav Tradition and Their Contemporary Interreligious Application	107
ALON GOSHEN-GOTTSTEIN	
6. The Cognitive Value of Religious Truth Statements: Rabbi A. I. Kook and Postmodernism	133
TAMAR ROSS	
Religious Truth: A Process Summary	177
ALON GOSHEN-GOTTSTEIN	
Bibliography	189
Notes on the Contributors	197
Index	199

Note on Transliteration

◆

THE TRANSLITERATION of Hebrew in this book reflects consideration of the type of book it is, in terms of its content, purpose, and readership. The system adopted therefore reflects a broad approach to transcription, rather than the narrower approaches found in the *Encyclopaedia Judaica* or other systems developed for text-based or linguistic studies. The aim has been to reflect the pronunciation prescribed for modern Hebrew, rather than the spelling or Hebrew word structure, and to do so using conventions that are generally familiar to the English-speaking reader.

In accordance with this approach, no attempt is made to indicate the distinctions between *alef* and *ayin*, *tet* and *taf*, *kaf* and *kuf*, *sin* and *samekh*, since these are not relevant to pronunciation; likewise, the *dagesh* is not indicated except where it affects pronunciation. Following the principle of using conventions familiar to the majority of readers, however, transcriptions that are well established have been retained even when they are not fully consistent with the transliteration system adopted. On similar grounds, the *tsadi* is rendered by 'tz' in such familiar words as barmitzvah. Likewise, the distinction between *ḥet* and *khaf* has been retained, using *ḥ* for the former and *kh* for the latter; the associated forms are generally familiar to readers, even if the distinction is not actually borne out in pronunciation, and for the same reason the final *heh* is indicated too. As in Hebrew, no capital letters are used, except that an initial capital has been retained in transliterating titles of published works (for example, *Shulḥan arukh*).

Since no distinction is made between *alef* and *ayin*, they are indicated by an apostrophe only in intervocalic positions where a failure to do so could lead an English-speaking reader to pronounce the vowel cluster as a diphthong—as, for example, in *ha'ir*—or otherwise mispronounce the word. An apostrophe is also used, for the same reason, to disambiguate the pronunciation of other English vowel clusters, as for example in *mizbe'aḥ*.

The *sheva na* is indicated by an *e*—*perikat ol*, *reshut*—except, again, when established convention dictates otherwise.

The *yod* is represented by *i* when it occurs as a vowel (*bereshit*), by *y* when it occurs as a consonant (*yesodot*), and by *yi* when it occurs as both (*yisra'el*).

Names have generally been left in their familiar forms, even when this is inconsistent with the overall system.

INTRODUCTION

The Scope of Religious Truth
Project Overview

ALON GOSHEN-GOTTSTEIN

Why Truth?

There are various dimensions of religious thought that inform the attitudes of members of one faith tradition towards another. For Abrahamic faiths, and for some expressions of other faiths as well, truth is a central concern. Exclusivism is a common attitude of religions, affirming superiority, and very often also an attitude whereby the given religion considers itself to be in possession of an exclusive value, commensurate with its own stated ideals and worldview. This often amounts to a zero-sum game—my religion is in, yours is out. There is more than one way of affirming such an exclusivist stance. Much depends on how one understands the purpose of religion. If it is to offer salvation, then the exclusivist claim would be that my religion, or my path, provides salvation; yours does not. Exclusivist claims, the view that sees relations between religions as a zero-sum game, need not appeal to the notion of truth. There are other ways of justifying such an attitude, and in any event it is as much an attitude, a psychological-emotional-social construct, as it is a view, an opinion, a persuasion. Yet sooner or later this persuasion is couched in terms of truth, leading to the affirmation that my religion is true while yours is false, or at best partially true.

Truth seems to hold a deep fascination over the Abrahamic religious imagination. In the quest for ultimacy and affirmation of the fullness of relationship with God and the validity of one's faith tradition, one readily resorts to utilizing the language of truth and to its ensuing applications in relation to other faiths. There is something imprecise in how we use 'truth' in religious discourse. Properly speaking, 'truth' describes something in the metaphysical realm, has strong philosophical associations, and overall relates to a value of high abstraction. It assumes that the quest for truth and the avoidance of falsehood are primary concerns of the spiritual, perhaps more broadly the human, life.

It is telling that most of what is communicated by 'truth' can actually be communicated in other ways. Primary among them is the narrative that tells of a special relationship, a special vocation, a historical mission, and a view of the end of time. To speak of the special salvation offered by Jesus in terms of truth is, in some way, to overlay it with meaning taken from a different domain. To speak of Israel's special relationship with God as the truth of Judaism is an expression of devotion and commitment to a world-view, but also a confusion of categories. A philosopher in quest of truth would not immediately or intuitively recognize the contents of what we sometimes refer to as truth in the domain of religion as the same subject matter. Hence significant efforts have been expended by philosophers of religious persuasion throughout the ages to reconcile the internal reference to truth with broader canons of epistemology and justification as applied in the philosophical disciplines.

Perhaps it is good to recognize at the outset that when we speak of truth in a religious context, we may intend something specific that is different from what is meant by the philosopher. Perhaps if we could identify the contours of what is intended, it would be easier for us to relate truth as used by members of one faith to how it is used by those of another.

A personal incident comes to mind as I write these words. It goes back nearly half a century, and perhaps it requires that much time and perspective to make sense. I was a teenager, full of religious zeal, following my discovery of the living power of Judaism. I was engaged in studies at a yeshiva and in the academy. I recall a visit to the home of David Hartman, at the time a teacher at the Hebrew University and a member of our community. David asked what drove me in my religious quest. I replied it was a sense of having found the truth. David set forth to grill me on what that meant and attempted to extract from me a definition of religious truth, something he as a philosopher of religion could relate to. I was unable to provide an answer that was adequate for him. And I got precious little from that engagement, other than a sense of inability to communicate with him. Thankfully, the exchange did not touch whatever it was in the spirit that was alive in me. I could imagine that for other people under similar circumstances the consequences might have been more extreme.

Looking back upon this episode, one of my earliest encounters with a Jewish philosopher, I realize that, in fact, it summarizes the problematics of this volume, or, more broadly speaking, of reference to religion in terms of truth. What I sought to express was a religious feeling. It had elements of conviction, authenticity, dedication, absolute value, calling, engagement, and more.

It also included aspects of truth claims on historical or metaphysical grounds that I had adopted or accepted. All these somehow coalesced in the mind of the 16- or 17-year-old under the rubric of 'truth', which in turn could not withstand the scrutiny of the philosopher.

I find my exchange with David Hartman suggestive of two important features of reference to truth in religious discourse. The first is that there is a deep drive to speak of truth and that reference to truth seems to provide satisfaction to the believer, equip him or her with meaning, or perhaps it even offers justification. But it is also, in a significant way, a feeling, an attitude, an orientation. When I said I had found the truth, I was not sharing the fruit of a long philosophical or existential search. I was expressing an internal orientation that, more than anything, sought to affirm a sense of deep belonging and satisfaction in my new-found religious commitment. What I did, with however much or little help I drew from teachers who informed my thinking up to that point in life, was to implicitly appeal to a category that has some absolute value and to describe my religious reality in such absolute terms. Moreover, it seems that the appeal to such absolute valuation also functioned as a means of communication. I could tell Hartman that I had found the truth because I naively believed that this communicated something objective that he could relate to, and which allowed our conversation to advance. I probably did so because I had no way, or no confidence in my ability under the circumstances, to express whatever it was in my religious experience and subjectivity that was really driving me. I therefore appealed to truth as a code term for value, absolute meaning, and justification, one that had an air of objectivity and communicability. In fact, as this incident shows, it was a conversation-killer. No real understanding ensued. How could it when I communicated via a cover-up mechanism, rather than expressing what really made me tick? And how could it when I had, unbeknownst to me, moved into the technical field of philosophy, in which I was not properly equipped to express myself, let alone tackle Hartman's inquisitive mind and existential struggles?

What drove that 16-year-old to express his convictions in terms of truth still drives me. Yet I doubt that I would express myself in this language today. To a large extent, the present project is a way of working out an intuition I have regarding the notion of religious truth. I consider truth to be a heavily overrated category in religious discourse, beyond a narrow application that is philosophically motivated and therefore more rigorous. It is meaningful in terms of religious language and expression, but overrated in terms of its actual content, meaning, significance, and implications. One of those implications has to do with how members of one faith tradition relate to another.

A more considered use of truth can aid us in dismantling one of the biggest hurdles in terms of the psychology of religion and in the attitudes of religious communities to one another. I do not wish to claim that the challenges of religious truth can be solved simply by moving the discussion over from philosophy to psychology of religion, nor do I seek to empty truth of its content —philosophical, historical, or otherwise. But I think it is imperative to raise the question of what we mean when we speak of truth in a religious context.

The 16-year-old who was in conversation with the eminent philosopher had little interest in affirming the superiority of Judaism to other faiths. He was seeking to articulate something about his religious experience and his ongoing quest. But religious truth is not limited to internal discourse. It is also prominent in the discourse of how one religion views another. Its prominence there is in part reasoned; for the most part it is no more reasoned than my own appeal to truth was at the age of 16. If, on the internal front, truth-talk is ultimately harmless, ranging from a form of communal spiritual pep talk to the sincere devotional expressions of the faithful, in the context of relations with other religions (as well as of internal division) truth can play a much more sinister role. It can become something to die for, and, no less importantly—to kill for.

This does not mean that all talk about truth must be abandoned. But we must ask what we mean when we refer to religion itself (as distinct from specific acts or faith claims) as true. Truth must be queried, made precise, and understood, much as David Hartman sought to clarify my intentions over forty years ago. If its sense is clarified, it can play a constructive role in religious education, piety, and inspiration to the good. If its sense remains not well clarified, then it will continue to wreak havoc in relations.

The present collection of essays, then, is devoted to the challenge of making sense of religious truth. Its context is internal, but its horizons reach beyond Judaism. It is an attempt of a group of Jewish thinkers to consider what is meant by truth. The discussion stands independently and has merit even without the dimension of theology of religions. Indeed, the question of religious truth is just as relevant for issues of internal Jewish diversity. Some of the distinctions that allow us to consider how to relate to people of other religions in light of truth might equally well be applied to differences between varying approaches to Judaism, across denominational divides, and even within a given denomination. However, the impetus for the present volume grew from an attempt to make sense of how we, as thinkers working from within Judaism, appeal to truth as we view other religions.

The contribution of this volume is not to provide one single, agreed-upon answer to the challenge of religious truth within interreligious relations. Rather, it is the common effort to problematize, relativize, ponder upon, or otherwise attempt to understand what we mean when we speak of religious truth. The task at hand invites a dual perspective. On the one hand, reflections on what truth means to a religious tradition in general—in our case, Judaism. On the other hand, grounding this understanding within Jewish traditions. The former leans to the philosophical. The latter generates studies that engage particular thinkers or sources and is therefore more textual. Accordingly, the volume moves from more philosophical considerations, which illustrate a broader theory in relation to Judaism, to more specific textual studies, which seek to extrapolate a view of truth based on specific corpora or on the thought of specific individuals. As we move across the spectrum we encounter different dimensions and meanings of the very notion of truth, as it is variously applied to philosophical truth claims, historical factuality, and the encounter with spiritual reality, transformative consciousness, and the totality of being in the divine presence. The challenge and richness of the present project are due, in part, to the multidimensionality of the term and the problematics it engenders, and to the conscious decision regarding what aspect of truth is privileged and highlighted as we think of truth, both in and of itself and in terms of how it impacts a Jewish view of other religions.

Overview

Each of the essays presents us with a particular balance of philosophical understanding and traditional mooring. Each essay is relevant both to an appreciation of what constitutes religious truth and to the implications of such an understanding to a Jewish view of other religions, or to the possibility of interreligious understanding or collaboration. The sequence of chapters in the volume has a clear line of progression that moves from the more philosophical to the more textually or case-based essays. Accordingly, it opens with Yehuda Gellman's 'Old-Fashioned Truth, Telic Truth, and Interreligious Understanding'. Gellman offers a philosophical analysis of religious truth and his own defence of a correspondence-based understanding of truth. He explores the meaning of religious truth within the framework of a broader philosophical discussion that is not particular to Judaism. Judaism provides the specific instance for statements of broader context and appeal. This is followed by another philosophically oriented exploration of truth, offered by Stanislaw Krajewski in his 'History and Truth in Religion'. Rather than engage with the more theoretical question of what we mean when we speak of truth in a religious context, Krajewski tackles a specific challenge to truth within Judaism, but that challenge potentially applies to other traditions as well. Judaism is a textual tradition that makes appeal to historical reality. It is thus highly historical. What happens when factual certitude falters and we lose the safe moorings of faith in the plain sense of historical accounts that provide the basis for the religious life? Krajewski's efforts are an attempt to salvage or uphold a notion of truth in textual and historical matters, despite various uncertainties that we are confronted with. He also addresses the ultimate challenge of truth: identifying or pointing to the immutable element in religion—that which transcends the processes of change and growth that characterize everything, religion included. As the title of his essay, referring to both history and truth, suggests, Krajewski tackles the challenges that history poses to religious truth on multiple levels.

The other four authors in our volume approach the question of truth not from the starting point of theoretical considerations but rather from specific textual contexts. Cass Fisher studies rabbinic sources in detail and brings them into dialogue with broader philosophical concerns that pertain to universal and particular truth in his 'The Cosmic Eye and Its Pupil'. The fuller theoretical articulation of these concerns is found in the works of Mendelssohn and Rosenzweig, and Fisher discovers them also at the heart of midrashic thinking. Reflecting on God's perfection leads one to recognize God's universality, the potential to know God in ways that transcend the particularity of Judaism. This opens us up to the presence of a universal dimension that derives from God's being and his creative act and relationship to all, beyond the particularity of his relationship with Israel. Notions of particular and universal truth are thus refracted or approached through affirmation of God's perfection.

Arthur Green presents the teachings of a hasidic teacher, Menahem Nahum of Chernobyl, in his '*Da'at*: Universalizing a Hasidic Value'. Green focuses his attention on the notion of *da'at*, knowledge or consciousness, as it appears in Rabbi Menahem Nahum's classic *Me'or einayim*. He considers it the ultimate goal of the mystical life. Focusing on *da'at* provides a particular approach to the issue of religious truth. Here religious truth is viewed from the subjective and cognitive dimension, in terms of human consciousness and its ability to enter the reality of God. Green explores the relationship between this cognitive and conscious dimension of approach to God and the more objective dimensions of religion in relation to the notion of truth. His presentation takes up the problematic we have already encountered in Krajewski's essay—the problems raised by historical studies as they relate to the veracity of scriptural witness to events. From here the challenge extends into a variety of challenges, practical and moral, that arise once the literalist foundations of scriptural witness are undermined or weakened. Green offers us a turn to the subjective, the experiential, and the conscious as a means of safeguarding the foundations of truth, grounded in God, and the quest for *da'at*. The focus on God recalls God as the guarantor of a truth that transcends particularity in Fisher's preceding essay. One might almost discern a parallel between Green's appeal to *da'at* on metaphysical, cognitive, and mystical grounds and Krajewski's appeal to a kernel of historical truth in tradition. However, *da'at* is more than a kernel. In fact, *da'at* is the essence, the goal, and what counts most in the spiritual quest. Getting to the heart of things therefore allows us to rebalance perspective and to affirm that which matters most in religion, its ultimate truth, despite the weakening of the historical and other foundations of the religious system.

Like Green's piece, my own essay, 'The Truth Beyond and Beyond Truth', also tackles the notion of truth within hasidic literature. My study examines various aspects of the system of Breslav hasidism. It juxtaposes two stages in Breslav theology: the thought of its founder, R. Nahman, and that of his disciple, R. Nathan. For R. Nahman, truth is to be understood as a state of being in fullness, rather than as an affirmation of specific doctrines and faith tenets. In this, his reference to truth comes close to what Green presents as *da'at* in the *Me'or einayim*. Rabbi Nahman considers that this state of truth is the reserve of the few. Not all can attain truth, here conceived as the higher state of being in union with the One, the Good, and the True. Truth is a state of being with moral and existential expressions. Truth is rising to God himself. For R. Nahman, then, truth is not really identified with the stuff and ideas of religion, but with God himself. Only those who attain to God really attain to truth.

R. Nahman's disciple takes the argument a step further. For him, truth in this world is impossible. We cannot attain truth; hence, we must cultivate faith. Along with faith come humility and the efforts of peacemaking, which have as their foundation the recognition of our inability to attain truth. For both teachers, the approach to truth ultimately points to a way of being. For R. Nahman it is the way of being in God that constitutes truth, as it is attained by the few, the great masters. For his disciple, R. Nathan, renouncing truth in the cognitive sense leads to a way of being that prefers other values. Ultimately truth, in the sense of true opinions over which one would fight and argue, is more of a vice than a virtue. It is faith we must seek, not truth.

The volume concludes with Tamar Ross's 'The Cognitive Value of Religious Truth Statements: Rabbi A. I. Kook and Postmodernism'. The decision to include this essay, originally published two decades ago, was informed by the fact that it is one of the few essays that tackle the problem of religious truth in a broader theological context, and not simply with reference to one of the prevailing challenges, typically the challenge of the reliability of tradition or the confrontation with science. Ross makes us aware of the surprising anti-realist position of Rav Kook, wherein he is willing to consider various truth statements as not capturing truth fully and completely. She explores Rav Kook's position against the history of non-realism in Jewish tradition, but more significantly against the broader orientations of postmodern philosophy. In seeking to distinguish Rav Kook from postmodern thinkers, she allows us to appreciate the fine balancing act between the theoretical flexibility that allows him to adopt an instrumentalist view of truth statements and the relativism that characterizes postmodern philosophy. Rav Kook, then, offers an intriguing balance between non-realist understandings on the one hand and an ontological grounding of his spiritual life on the other, largely by virtue of his mystical experience and panentheistic world-view. This balance opens up promising avenues in a contemporary educational context, wherein one seeks to integrate willingness to adopt a view that does not rely on heavy ontological claims for grounding truth with religious fervour and devotion.

Surveying the range of issues and positions, we notice how far we have come and how diverse the contexts of and approaches to truth are—from Gellman's affirmation of the validity of truth claims to R. Nathan's renouncing the possibility of the common person attaining truth in a cognitive way, leading one to cultivate instead faith and humility, and to Rav Kook's willingness to forgo realist understandings of truth statements. The range points to the richness of the subject matter and to the multiple approaches to it, which in turn rely on diverse definitions and understandings. We must recognize that under the rubric of 'truth', different people refer to different issues and aspects of the religious and spiritual life. Truth serves as a kind of overarching concept by means of which these diverse issues can be brought under one conceptual framework. The different discussions, whether philosophical or textual, also allow us to develop an in-depth understanding of what truth means. Following this overview of what our volume includes, I would therefore like to point out additional insights and dimensions that emerge from our essays and which contribute to the riches of how we understand truth. I will not repeat or summarize the arguments beyond the terse descriptions above. What I would like to do instead is highlight thought strands in the chapters that enrich our understanding of truth and that are relevant to appreciating the author's view of how truth plays out in the interaction between religions and their believers.

Telic Truth and Interreligious Engagement

Turning, then, to the essays, I begin by noting some distinctive features of Gellman's exposition of religious truth. He distinguishes two kinds of truth: old-fashioned and telic. This distinction is important because it allows him to appreciate other religions independently of their classical truth claims. This dual perspective opens him up to engagement with and receptivity to other faiths. As concerns truth in the classical sense, Gellman affirms correspondence theory, in other words that there is something in the core beliefs of Judaism that describes reality as it is. He offers a series of fundamental beliefs that include God's existence, his loving relationship with the Jewish people, the unique divine sanction of Judaism, and the affirmation that Jews ought to follow Judaism. Every other religion, he claims, has at least one false core belief, or is mistaken in teaching that he (as a Jew) ought to follow it. Thus, to speak of religious truth in this sense is to affirm the correctness and factuality of core faith tenets as descriptive of objective reality.

Gellman introduces the notion of telic truth, from telos—goal—as a way of describing how religion achieves good ends that are laudable and even worthy of emulation, independently of its faith or truth claims. The true value of telic truth lies in the lives of religious individuals, who can serve as exemplars beyond the native faith community.

This dual perspective allows Gellman to engage with other religions with a balance that both affirms the uniqueness of Jewish faith as true, that is, its fundamental faith tenets corresponding to reality, and allows him to be receptive to those aspects of the other traditions that help believers achieve spiritual ends, such ends that he himself shares or can be inspired by.

I would like to highlight one more notion found in Gellman's essay. Interreligious engagement is a context in which beliefs are opened up to questioning through encounter with the other. At the same time that one receives inspiration from telic truths, one also confronts challenges to specific doctrines. Gellman describes his orientation as epistemological framework conservatism. To understand this, we recall that religions are composite systems that bring together multiple dimensions of life and tie together various strands of belief. Because aspects of belief are intertwined with one another, the default position is to uphold individual beliefs, as they form part of the broader fabric of the belief system. One should relinquish a belief only if there is a strong reason to give it up. Therefore, in entering into dialogue with a member of another faith, one need not be concerned with constant revision or justification of one's faith. Nevertheless, an openness to change must be maintained, to avoid religious dogmatism. Accordingly, the position adopted by Gellman is characterized as vulnerable apologetics, wherein faith is sustained and defended while remaining open to the possibility of change as a consequence of insights gained from the outside. Gellman shares with us instances in which he has had to revise his understanding of fundamental faith tenets, such as election or revelation, in view of strong arguments against extant conceptions. It is worth noting, however, that these arguments are not the outcome of the encounter with other religions, but of broader philosophical or religious sensibilities. In terms of method, encounter with the religious other could, in theory, lead to a redefinition or refinement of one's faith. Gellman's own witness on this matter, however, seems to be limited to the beneficial inspiration provided by telic truths of other religions.

Situating Truth Amidst the Changes of History

Following the theoretical discussions that consider truth in light of a correspondence theory, we note the particular application of this issue in Krajewski's essay to the problem of the historical truth of scriptural or traditional narratives. If events really happened, then they are appreciated in line with a correspondence theory of truth. If, on the other hand, they did not really occur and are only metaphorical, then in fact their significance falls in line with coherence theory, inasmuch as it confirms and upholds values already known and upheld by the tradition. True knowledge is a reliable relationship between knower and known, a set of reliable beliefs, and reliability gives justification for believing. The stronger the reliability of a relationship, the truer the knowledge is. Krajewski struggles with the problem of truth and history and seeks to avoid two extremes—textual fundamentalism and modern allegorization of all biblical stories. To this end he suggests a two-step process. In the first, one recognizes a historical kernel of truth in theory, even if one cannot always point to it. Here a correspondence theory is upheld. The second step is adopting an 'as if' mentality, wherein one reclaims a myth, even if broken, and treats it as if it were true. Even though Krajewski does not make the point explicitly, here he seems to be applying the alternative theoretical approach, namely, the coherence view of truth, thus striking a balance between the two.

This balance is appropriate for how he deals with conflicting truths, or rather the conflict of interpretations between different religions. While differing emphases in approaching the literalness of Scripture and its truth are also a matter of difference between believers of one faith, they take on particular significance when they divide different religions. Krajewski offers us two guidelines in dealing with such a situation. The first is to agree on the core of historical truth, even if one cannot define it. In terms of further application, one must respect the 'as if' dimension of the other tradition. This approach allows a multiplicity of narratives, even regarding what seem to be common stories. Accordingly, Krajewski is happy to accommodate Muslim celebration of the sacrifice of Ismail, recognizing it as a different story rather than a story that competes with the biblical Akedah. Because communities develop their stories around and beyond the kernel of historical reality, the attitude of acceptance that is extended within can also be extended without, thereby minimizing conflict.

This approach does not cover all circumstances. At times there are conflicts over the core of a faith and its story. One cannot allot the Gospel story and the Jewish polemical tractate *Toledot yeshu* the same status in a willingness to accommodate multiple narratives. Here Krajewski develops a notion of centre and periphery. Discernment of what lies at the centre of one faith and of the marginal place that the same story occupies in another, especially as it is grounded in polemics, provides a yardstick for avoiding conflict and hopefully relegating the marginal to the margins.

The structure of Krajewski's argument regarding a 'something' that is a residue of truth, even in the midst of various accretions and developments, parallels his strategy regarding another problem posed by history—recognizing that which is essential and unchanging in religion, even in the midst of the ever-changing reality of all life, religion included. Krajewski affirms a *belief* in eternal essence, even if it cannot be known within historical processes. In order to see meaning in the world, humans must reach beyond it, to the realm of transcendence. This affirmation exposes us to another dimension of truth than the one that can be verified by senses or by history. He does not apply this challenge to relations between religions, but rather focuses it on the question of the essence of Judaism and the various expressions it has taken through the ages. Yet the evolution of faith and the appeal to transcendence are significantly couched in human terms and hence could provide a point of commonality for different traditions. No tradition is exempt from the rule of history and change, even if it does not acknowledge it. In the quest for the beyond and the affirmation of an essence that transcends historical change, religions may be allies, partners on the road, rather than competitors for the one truth.

Universal Truth Derivative of Divine Perfection

Cass Fisher's reading of rabbinic texts is framed by a broader philosophical concern. A perfect God must necessarily be the God of all people, and as such it is inconceivable that human well-being would be dependent on a particular divine revelation. Fisher walks us through a range of rabbinic options. In the process, we put on different theological lenses. At times, God's perspective is at the forefront, in his particular relationship with Israel and in the revelations he has made to them. At other times, God's perfection is at the forefront, leading us to recognize that God is greater than a particular revelation. Consequently, he is known, approached, praised, and otherwise associated and in relationship with others beyond Judaism. Such associations constitute a form of approach to God, and as such are a dimension of religious truth that complements, or stands in tension with, the particular form of truth known in Judaism through God's particular relationship with Israel.

The issues of universality and particularity open us up to fundamental considerations of truth. The universal perspective assumes that, with all the privilege and special relationship that the people of Israel enjoy, theirs is not the only perspective or approach to God. As such, it assumes other potential channels of recognizing truth. Foremost among them is the association with nature and creation, as noted in rabbinic discourses and parables, where nature serves as the basic metaphor and matrix for establishing both a common ground with non-Jews and a parallel path. From some of the texts cited by Fisher, it seems that God has an ongoing relationship with others and that therefore access to him and knowledge of him are dependent neither on revelation nor exclusively on whatever degree of knowledge of God could be attained by the study of creation and by relating to God as creator.

All this is relevant to religious truth in several ways. First, it undermines a natural tendency that comes with revelation to regard it as the full and exclusive access to truth. Here Fisher's reliance on James Barr's reflections on natural theology as part of biblical theology is particularly helpful. Natural theology, in the sense that it is assumed that God is known also beyond a particular revelation, is itself part of the biblical heritage, that is: of revelation, and not something independent of it. This opens up both truth and revelation to broader understandings. Second, this recognition fosters an attitude of theological humility. Fisher does not apply this attitude, nor does he address the broader concerns of the universal and the particular to the relations between Judaism and other religions. But he does provide an important framing for such a discussion. A consideration of other religions could, perhaps ought to, take place within the arc of universal–particular, both seen in relation to God's perfection, which in turn entails and necessitates a broader approach to God and knowledge of him that are also beyond the confines of a particular revelation. This framing also has its limitations. It may or may not allow for multiple or competing claims of revelation, and it may lead to a strong emphasis upon creation as a means of knowing God. Yet these theoretical options still provide significant frameworks for appreciating other religions. In fact, they may be applied to many forms of world religions as they are, without the need for further adaptation. As Fisher teaches us, the relationship of the particular to the universal is not a formula but an arc, a point of tension, an ongoing creative and constitutive dynamic. This dynamic may, therefore, find varying expressions both within the rabbinic tradition, including within the particular school and sources surveyed by Fisher, and within different strands of Jewish thought as it has evolved through the ages. It suggests that a Jewish view of truth beyond Judaism, including other religions, is never a matter of yes/no, but rather a more nuanced quest for recognition and appreciation within the fundamental dynamic that seeks to balance God's universal perfection with his particular relationship with Israel.

There are several points at which Fisher's work can be brought into dialogue with that of the other authors. Gellman's discussion sought to articulate what are the fundamentals of Jewish faith. Fisher touches briefly on the question of the cognitive content of Judaism in his opening remarks. In one way, these comments echo the points made in the other essays. When the cognitive content of Jewish faith is seen in the framework of his overall argument, it raises the question of what faith content serves as common ground that bonds the particular and the universal, and which in turn could also be helpful in the conversation between Judaism and other world religions. While his initial statement is more philosophical in nature, the rabbinic sources he cites in the course of his presentation offer us important perspectives on how God's perfection allows us to recognize truth and relationality in other faiths, not only philosophically but also in ways such as prayer and other expressions of the relationship with the Divine.

It is perhaps also worth relating Fisher's work to the correspondence or coherence theories of truth. Fisher himself is not concerned with the status of truth and the kind of truth to which Jews and non-Jews have access. It seems his use of truth encompasses both senses. The basic perspective seems to be one that affirms a correspondence approach to truth. God is known in his perfection, and it is his perfection that provides the frame of orientation for seeking truth for Jews and for all. As such, all share in the objectivity of the reality of God and his creation. At the same time, Fisher, following Rosenzweig, also urges us to make truth more than an affirmation of objective reality. Truth has to be interiorized, made my own. Real truth is that which is imparted in my inner being in the here and now. This subjectivity of truth is ultimately of greater significance than the question of whether it is full and complete truth. The quest for 'my part' or portion of truth takes one from philosophical affirmation to the domain of praise, liturgical reality, and poetry and song, all of which give expression to a living relationship with God and to the subjective recognition of God.

If I read Fisher correctly, in light of his appeal to Rosenzweig, then truth is not a matter of who affirms correct beliefs. Some aspects of that are available to all. Rather, the attainment of truth is in the fullness of living a relationship with God and in the degree to which truth is internalized and interiorized. Perhaps herein lies the key to Israel's special relationship with God as a path that has made this dimension of truth real through millennia of intimate devotion. At the same time, the very foundations of both objective recognition of God's perfection and the subjective process of entering into that truth and living it from within make this dual approach to truth something that is not exclusive to Israel. God's perfection and the theological humility we are called on to have point us to the quest for discovering our own portion of the truth and in so doing make room for recognition of the same in the other.

Religious Truth and Mystical Consciousness

This serves as a good segue to Arthur Green's essay on *da'at* in the teachings of Rabbi Menahem Nahum of Chernobyl. If Fisher presented us with one constitutive tension around truth—the universal versus the particular—Green presents us with another—'concrete' religion versus mystical consciousness. The subjective processes of acquisition of consciousness and awareness are at the heart of the spirituality of this hasidic teacher. *Da'at* as interiorized consciousness that integrates the emotional reality of love and awe into the awareness of the Divine permeating all of life, and which infuses all actions—formal religious actions as well as daily life—with divine awareness, is distinct from affirmation of truth claims or statements. In fact, Green begins his presentation by juxtaposing the two. The juxtaposition is pertinent to our interests in that it is couched in terms of competing narratives, and hence truth claims, of different faiths, specifically the three Abrahamic faiths, with their diverging core narratives. Rather than explore the contrast between narrative and historical reality, which was at the heart of Krajewski's reflections, Green directly juxtaposes competing narratives, thereby pointing to the impossibility of truth on the narrative level, and by extension on the level of outer religious action. This tension is complemented by the difficulty the contemporary faithful have in accepting what Green refers to as the scaffolding of the religious system, which means any number of historical claims made by the tradition, whether concerning its own authenticity or with reference to truths narrated in Scripture. The problems of critical thinking, informed by contemporary scientific standards, which are presented by Krajewski also inform Green's perspective.

Green finds refuge, so to speak, in the turn to *da'at*. *Da'at* is an awareness of God that links one to the upper universe. It is a mystical awareness, an opening of the human mind that permits one to be united to the universal Self that fills the world. The content of *da'at* is what might be called 'cosmic consciousness', the awareness that the world is utterly filled with divinity and that this abundance is bound to its transcendent and mysterious source. *Da'at* is the subjective consciousness of the presence of God that is known to mystics in all religions. Mystics go beyond the stories and structures of their faith to discover the core spiritual reality of divine presence. These structures, the scaffolding if you will, of religion, are interpreted in light of this internal experience, which is the goal of the religious life and is what ultimately validates it. Green speaks of deeper meanings and eternal truths, a hint at the possibility of a truth beyond truth, a higher or fuller truth that transcends the competing truth narratives of religions in their diversity.

As presented thus far, Green's argument appeals to mysticism as a means of discovering the higher and ultimate truths within religious traditions. It seems to me, however, that he stops short of making the argument in full. In fact, in our conversation around the precise focus of his thesis, he conceded his own internal inhibitions in making the thesis as extreme or consistent as it might be, and in shying away from its full and radical implication. He was willing, however, for me to spell it out in the present analysis and to give his approval to this implication, though, significantly, not in the body of his essay. In what follows, I would therefore like to juxtapose the thesis that Green nearly states, and which he was willing to affirm as a kind of *torah shebe'al peh*, with the thesis he actually presents in the chapter.

The structure of Green's argument points from relative truth to absolute or higher truth, from truth in its diversity to truth in a unified sense, from the multiple and conflicting truths of conflicting narratives and practices to the unified truth that the mystic accesses and wherein he encounters mystics of other traditions as partakers of the same truth. According to this construct, the internal core of all religions is one, and it is here that religions meet. This is the real truth, to which the scaffolding of religion is but a preparation.

At various points, Green leads us in this direction, and yet, as I shall presently suggest, he ultimately shifts his thesis to a less radical affirmation. The claim for degrees of truth within religions and for the relationship of mysticism and the external dimensions of religion is one that can be made on phenomenological and historical grounds. R. Menahem Nahum of Chernobyl is presented as a member of a larger class, a Jewish genus of the broader species of mystics. The argument could, in theory, proceed along the following lines. Similar tensions between external and internal truths can be identified in other traditions. Characteristics of *da'at* could likewise be found in other traditions. This parallel would corroborate, on phenomenological grounds, the similarity of type and would allow us to make the evaluative judgement that, at their core, religions (all religions, or Abrahamic religions, as we might make the argument) are one. The inner mystical core would then have a relativizing effect on our religious traditions, pointing to their ultimate commonality and historical contingency, as well as to the absurdity of religious competition when all religions ultimately strive towards the same end and provide instances for its attainment. Perennialists and scholars of comparative religion such as Huston Smith would be very comfortable making this argument and could provide ample evidence for it. This line of reasoning would tackle the challenge of religious truth on a comparative, phenomenological basis and would then draw its conclusions regarding relations between faiths. One might even take the argument as a justification for a correspondence view of religious truth. The core mystical truth, attained through and within all—or the major—religious traditions, corresponds to the higher spiritual reality. Mysticism proffers a sense of reality to religious truth across traditions, providing also for the respective verification of parallel paths, culminating in one higher truth.

Green never goes as far as making this argument fully, though several of his formulations, especially in the introductory part of the essay, point in this direction. Whether he is more circumspect because his study is limited to one tradition or because he has reservations about the objective, correspondence-like implication of a perennialist position is something one can query. In order to appreciate where he does take the argument, I would like to contrast the appeal to truth with the appeal to wisdom.

As Green's argument unfolds, and as he draws conclusions from the textual resources he presents to his readers, he places the emphasis on how the vision of the centrality of *da'at* and its quest can be shared. Sharing of wisdom can take place despite differences in world-view. Even if we no longer partake of much of the faith content of the *Me'or einayim* on historical or other grounds, we can still benefit from R. Menahem Nahum's reading of Scripture, which is oriented to the present rather than to the past; to the individual, who must make Scripture his or her own, rather than to the neutral collective historical upholding of memory. There is a wisdom that can be communicated from the core of this experience and which remains relevant, despite changes in the content of faith. And precisely for this reason, it can also communicate across religious difference. This positions Green as a teacher who is willing to extend the wisdom of the *Me'or einayim* and make it speak also to the members of another faith tradition.

This is, in and of itself, no small feat, and one to which considerable efforts of justification have been devoted. We note multiple arguments throughout Green's essay that support taking the testimony of the *Me'or einayim* and making it relevant not only to the Jew and not only to the classically faithful Jew. Green describes himself as a non-literalist who stands in the tradition of neo-hasidism and therefore derives permission for this expansion of meaning from within this tradition. Various historical understandings of *da'at* contribute to its universal, in other words non-exclusively Jewish, application. These include the Jewish philosophical tradition and its universalizing understanding of wisdom and knowledge. The kabbalistic tradition and its grounding of knowledge and wisdom in the Godhead could equally provide such support. Green points to inconsistencies within the kabbalistic and hasidic world-view, where immanentist and panentheistic strands ought to have led to a universal application of wisdom, but failed to do so. A blind spot in hasidic and kabbalistic understanding leads those traditions to ignore the universal potential contained in the notions of the image of God and common descent from primordial Adam. One would have to account for such inconsistencies on historical rather than principled grounds, and see Green's neo-hasidic efforts as bringing the theoretical potential of the system to its logical conclusion, once freed from certain historical constraints. Ultimately, Green recognizes that the texts he studies address universal religious concerns. For this reason, they can be made to speak to an audience never intended by their author.

The emphasis on sharing the wisdom of the tradition with members of other faiths does shift us away from truth towards meaning, usefulness, and a more psychologically oriented application of the wisdom of past spiritual masters to our present-day life. Does the shift in emphasis from truth to applied wisdom actually betray scepticism concerning the metaphysical or philosophical implications of continued appeal to truth? This is an interesting question to ponder further. It does, moreover, have some consequences for Green's presentation.

The conclusion of Green's essay may betray why he stops short of drawing the full conclusions from the structure he has put in place. Situating himself in postmodern consciousness, he speaks of the primal Word, which transcends the specificity of all religious traditions. 'That Word, bursting forth from the primal point of universal wisdom with all the energy of the Big Bang, blows our self-protective modernist "shells" into tiny, scattered pieces, and permits us to again find broken sparks of divine light within all of being. From there we go back to the work of restoring them—and ourselves—to our single Source.' This powerful and evocative conclusion allows us a glimpse into Green's core theological project, as it extends also into interreligious work. He seems to apply the kabbalistic myth of broken vessels not only to Judaism but to all faiths as well. All traditions find themselves in a situation of broken vessels, where critical modernity has undermined the truth that they affirmed in the pre-critical state. Green assumes commonality in this historical condition and the applicability of this kabbalistic language not only to Jewish efforts but also to those of members of all religions.

Therefore, we must continue our quest to reconnect with the original and single source, and thereby restore ourselves and renew our traditions. In this process, human effort—the labour of restoration and the uncertainty that accompanies such restoration—would seem to have a prominent role, even if it is oriented towards the unifying source of universal wisdom. It is not only this supreme wisdom that relativizes religions; it is also their common brokenness and their common project of restoration. Perhaps herein lies Green's reluctance to affirm a parallel truth in different religions, opting instead for the common project of sharing wisdom in an attempt to regain the lost originary wisdom. If so, his reading extends his own historically situated position to mystics and teachers of other traditions, and he discovers a commonality not in the mystical reality that is found in the deeper and eternal truths of the religions, but in the quest for the remaking of religious sense in light of the teachings of the great mystics.

Religious Responses to the Unattainability of Truth

My essay on Breslav hasidism shares much with Green's view of the *Me'or einayim*. It too posits a tension between religion as manifest in actions and beliefs on the one hand, and, on the other, the dimension of ultimate truth, grounded in consciousness and a higher form of being. I too use this tension as an invitation to explore the question of truth in relation to Judaism and world religions. Like Green, I too seek to take teachings articulated in an internal context and to consider their internal coherence in a way that justifies their application to a view of other religions. While Green's sources did not explicitly address the question of truth, the Breslav sources I study do. In fact, my own study focuses on two formative stages in the history of this hasidic school and its construction of a notion of truth: the respective approaches of the teacher, R. Nahman, and of the disciple, R. Nathan, to truth, and their applicability to a view of other religions.

For R. Nahman, truth is not necessarily cognitive, a statement to affirm or a proposition to which one must assent. Grounded in existence itself, truth is to be considered a metaphysical way of being that has a moral and existential counterpart. Accordingly, truth is a total way of being, beyond the content of specific faith doctrines. Attaining truth involves gaining a state of being that transcends the created order. Truth is a sharing in God himself.

Such an understanding is full of potential for interreligious relations. It suggests that religion, my religion, is not to be automatically identified with 'the truth'. Rather, truth is a particular high point of the spiritual life, only attained by those who have reached the depths or heights of the spiritual life, or divine reality itself. While nothing is stated in relation to other religions, grounding truth in God, rather than in religion, does open up the possibility that this structure may be applied to all religions, not only to Judaism.

R. Nahman's use of truth does not include reference to the content of truth in the form of specific beliefs, positions, dogmas, and so on. He avoids the aspect of truth that is typically the focus of discussions of religious truth. It is R. Nathan who introduces this aspect of 'religious truth' into the discussion. R. Nathan develops a layered notion of truth, wherein absolute truth remains largely beyond reach as the individual makes his way through the complexities of the world of multiplicity. Only by going through the trials and tribulations of an earthly life can a higher kind of truth, possibly a synthetic and all-encompassing truth, be attained.

Truth in its unique sense cannot be known in our common reality. Metaphysical multiplicity translates into ideological pluralism. This does not mean renouncing the uniqueness of ultimate truth, but it does make it far less accessible. Ultimate truth becomes accessible only to masters who successfully traverse the multiplicity of reality, with its attendant imperfections and impurities. It thus becomes the lot of a very narrow group of individuals, *tsadikim*, who are able to reveal deeper unifying power within.

Once it is recognized that all truth escapes us and that really, within the realm of multiplicity, one cannot, with rare exceptions, attain it, then intention functions as a primary means of validation that provides meaning to one's quest for truth. It is much easier to recognize the honest intentions of members of other faiths than it is to admit the truth of their faith claims. A notion of truth that highlights intentionality is thus one that fills the void created by the affirmation that we cannot access truth.

All this leads us to R. Nathan's emphasis on tolerance and peace as core virtues that in practical terms should prevail over truth. The theoretical inaccessibility of truth is matched by the moral and social teaching that privileges peace and tolerance over truth. Consequently, R. Nathan critiques ideological controversy, based as it is on the supposed quest for truth, as a social vice that is of no benefit. In the axiological confrontation between truth and peace, peace wins hands down.

Both R. Nahman and R. Nathan provide us with approaches that can be translated to the concerns of truth and the interreligious situation. For R. Nahman, truth is grounded in the order beyond creation. As such it transcends all multiplicity, including the multiplicity of religions. Where through reflection and mystical experience one can rediscover this higher metaphysical ground is where religions can meet. For the rest, concerns for the content of belief captured as religious truth should be cast aside in favour of the concern for truthful living in daily relations.

R. Nathan offers us another lesson. For him, it is not the quest for the highest truth—the Truth beyond—that could provide the formula for interreligious harmony. Rather, it is the recognition that truth cannot be attained and that other values are superior to truth—are beyond truth. It is God's will that we live in peace and compassion with one another, and focusing on truth ultimately goes against the very foundations that make it possible for humanity to exist, imperfect as it is. God does not will truth, nor can we attain it. God's highest purpose, the ultimate truth, points to compassion and to peace as the guiding values of life, and consequently these should also govern interreligious relations.

It is worth reflecting briefly on the relationship between the two views of truth in Breslav hasidism and the two understandings of truth that have framed much of our discussion. If truth is something beyond cognitive affirmation, and all such affirmation is part of the relative order and its tendency to error, does this not make a correspondence view of truth impossible? If so, all truth statements are to be understood as coherence-based. All that we call by the name of truth is not, after all, real or absolute truth. It is, significantly, a matter of convention, convenience, or of limited and partial understanding. Perhaps, R. Nathan might argue, it is the very claim for objectivity and correspondence of one's beliefs to the truth of reality that is the vice that attaches itself to religious life and religious truth.

Could the metaphysical state of being, associated by R. Nahman with truth, be considered in light of a correspondence theory? I have suggested that Green's presentation of *da'at* could be read in this light, and one might make the same point with reference to R. Nahman. If so, the application of a correspondence view of truth would relate only to the higher state of consciousness of being in the Divine. What is striking for both master and disciple is the relative low value placed upon concrete beliefs. Because a higher truth is known in consciousness, there is a relativizing approach to the concrete truths typically associated with religion. Spiritual reality thus provides the most potent means of taking the sting out of truth claims, suggesting instead humility and peace as the ultimate virtues, which could then be applied in principle also to a view of other religions.

The Instrumentalist Approach of the Panentheist Mystic

Tamar Ross's essay is last in our collection not simply because her subject, Rav Kook, is the most recent author. What characterizes Rav Kook is his synthetic thought. His world-view encompasses and integrates perspectives that, for most of history, have been held in tension and conflict. The greatness of the soul, mystical experience, and pantheistic, or more correctly panentheistic, theological premises all contribute to a unique capacity to incorporate diverging views within one totality. Reviewing the themes that we have covered in our various essays, one can almost say that all our major themes are integrated in Ross's presentation of Rav Kook's approach to truth. This includes the alternative options of correspondence- and coherence-based theories. It includes the theoretical possibility, encountered most clearly in the Breslav sources, that truth is really beyond us. It includes the specific struggles with history, the reliability of biblical witness, and the various challenges of science to what Green has called the scaffolding of religion. Naturally, it also includes the tension between truth, conceived as a statement, a position, an assent, and truth as a dimension of being, a totality of consciousness, an entry into the Divine. Somehow Rav Kook is able to hold these various options and alternatives in balance, at times in tension, and to accommodate the differing positions within his broader view of the spiritual life and of the place of truth within it.

Ross never makes the following point explicitly, but I believe she takes it for granted and assumes it as a foundation for her attempt to reconstruct Rav Kook's views. Rav Kook is a spiritual giant with strong mystical experiences and a sense of first-hand insight into the core subject matter of the spiritual life. If we consider the *da'at* discussed by Green or the existential state described by R. Nahman as the locus of truth, we should begin with the recognition that Rav Kook speaks from 'that' place. Each of the three mystics reviewed in our volume expresses his experience and the consequences of the vision of reality he attains for the practice of religion. Each does so within the intellectual tradition to which he belongs and within the literary framework it provides. We have no way of affirming Rav Kook's subjective and mystical experience as compared to the other figures studied. But we can certainly recognize the impact and benefits of his experience, not only in his body of thought but also in the broader, probably unprecedented, expanse of thought upon which he brings it to bear. Therefore, the starting point of an appreciation of truth in the writings of Rav Kook must be some sense of direct, interior apprehension of the Divine. If one were to contest this as a starting point, one would, at the very least, have to acknowledge that the possibility or quest for such experience frames his horizons and allows him an approach to the question of truth that is particular.

In addition to the comprehensiveness of his approach, we must also consider that, unlike all the other sources studied in our volume—from the talmudic rabbis to Breslav—Rav Kook is in conscious dialogue with philosophy and epistemology within the Western philosophical tradition—one additional dimension that he integrates within his religious world-view. Therefore, complementing his internal religious experience and its relativizing potential in relation to beliefs and opinions held as the common stuff of religion is also his engagement with relativizing approaches grounded in philosophy. Tamar Ross makes us aware of his appeal to Kantian philosophy and its non-realist implications.

Rav Kook, as we learn from Ross, is, for an Orthodox thinker, surprisingly sceptical regarding the ability of any religious formulation to capture truth finally and completely. In his view, the ontological commitment of most religious truth statements is a relative matter. Ross points out the parallel with the perspectives of many mystics, ancient and modern, on this very point.

Rav Kook holds a non-realist position with reference to truth statements—because we are fundamentally unable to grasp truth as it is—making conventional faith and heresy equally removed from the reality of God. He recognizes divine reality as the base of our knowledge, as well as its ultimate goal. This already provides a kind of ontological anchoring for processes of truth acquisition. But precisely against this background, all the concrete positions that give content to religious faith are considered with remarkable flexibility and ease. Whether to believe in God as classically understood or to adopt a pantheist view; whether to believe in creation or emanation; whether to view the Torah literally over and against the findings of science; whether Torah from Heaven ought to be understood narrowly and literally or in some broader sense, and so on—all these are decided not on the basis of what is true, but according to what is most useful in an instrumental way. An instrumental approach means that truth does not matter, inasmuch as it cannot be attained. Consequently, one adopts the belief that leads one to a better life. Indeed, Rav Kook posits the moral dimension as the ultimate criterion. However, this dimension is more extensive than just the morality of governing a society; it touches the very fabric of creation and divinity itself. Thus, while Rav Kook speaks of instrumentality in moral terms, we are equally justified in relating to this morality in terms of the spiritual processes that upholding a position will lead to.

This, in turn, offers us a counterbalance to what might otherwise seem relativist, postmodern disregard for facticity of belief and its ontological grounding. There is particular value to certain truth positions not because they capture the ultimate truth adequately, but because adopting them will have an impact on the person that leads him or her towards a higher state of being. Truth may not be known, but it may be approximated, approached as the amplitude of divine perfection, into which one grows through the adoption of beliefs, practices, and orientating frameworks, provided by certain positions and truths.

Truth is instrumental to spiritual advancement, against the background of the impossibility of proper formulation of truth statements. It is this instrumentality that makes room for multiple positions, each of which may be appropriate for its context and helpful in its particular way. Here panentheism makes all the difference. Each of the varying and conflicting truth options ultimately partakes of God's reality, and God is found and accessed through all. A panentheistic position thus allows for relativism or a certain choice between multiple options that are simultaneously reduced to their instrumental spiritual value and upheld in terms of their absolute value, grounded in the Divine.

Rav Kook thus strikes a unique balance between theological leeway, based on the assumption that truth is beyond reach, and the recognition of ontological foundations grounded in God himself. This particular perspective allows him not only to accommodate diverse internal Jewish positions or to integrate general philosophical perspectives into his world-view. It also allows him to be 'easy' on points of conflict with science and biblical criticism, and on the many issues that confronted modernity in the early twentieth century and which in many ways continue to confront us even in what some consider a postmodern reality.

The instrumentalist perspective of truth brings us back to the opening essay by Gellman. Gellman distinguished between classical truth statements and telic truths, which are judged by their outcome and spiritual benefit in the lives of believers. His distinction was intended to open up the issue of truth to the realm of spirituality and to recognize the benefits of a spiritual life that are independent of specific positions taken in relation to matters of truth. What we find in Rav Kook is, if we will, a collapse of this distinction. All religious truth is telic truth. Religious truth, in the conventional sense, is there to help us attain the telos of religion, whether understood in terms of morality or in terms of growing closer to the true reality of God, which transcends particular formulations of truth. Seeing all truth statements as serving telic purposes helps relativize them. More importantly, it helps us realize that what counts most when we think of truth is not the correctness of positions but rather their consequences—moral and spiritual—in the lives of believers. And if the ultimate telos of the religious life is related to that higher dimension that I described above as *da'at*, or which Rav Kook describes in terms of proximity to God, then the ultimate test of various positions is in their ability to transport us to the divine realm, eventually transcending the very language or formulation through which these truths were grasped.

A non-realist, instrumental view of truth would seem to be coherence-based. Indeed, Rav Kook affirms the value of particular beliefs in terms of how they uphold the totality of the religious life. Yet, as Ross shows us, there is simultaneous affirmation of the correspondence of truth to the higher spiritual reality. Perhaps the paradox of Rav Kook is best summed up by the recognition that ultimately correspondence points to a dimension that is beyond language and articulation, making it real and aloof, fundamental to our being yet at the same time leading to enormous flexibility and adaptability. This is, then, the broadest and most encompassing view of truth, containing within it the various challenges and positions we have seen throughout our essays, all of which ultimately find their meaning in a dimension that transcends language and truth formulations.

Tamar Ross does not tackle the implications of her presentation to a Jewish theology of religions. I would like to offer some reflections based on her presentation. However, before offering these reflections—and some suggestions—I would like to consider how Ross's work could help us advance our thinking about Rav Kook's attitude to other religions, as it is known from other sources. The starting point of the following reflection is the identification of a profound tension, even contrast, in the writings of Rav Kook on other religions. In some of his writings, he emerges as a near-pluralist. Other religions, even the low religious life associated with pagan faiths, are of positive value—all the more so the faiths that are derivative of Judaism. Rav Kook is capable, in some of his works, of developing a pluralism of revelations, and in so doing offers us some of the most receptive and open moments of Jewish thought in relation to other religions. At the other end are numerous critical statements concerning other religions, particularly Christianity. The high metaphysical positioning that Rav Kook ascribes to Israel and the Torah may or may not be relevant to further intensifying this tension.

The question of Rav Kook's attitudes to other religions deserves a monograph-length study. Not only the complexity of his thought, but also the promise it holds for any subject, and especially for one that goes to the heart of the religious life, justifies much more than these brief remarks can sustain. Even though the issue of other religions and idolatry occupies considerable space in the corpus of Rav Kook's writings, it has received very little scholarly treatment, possibly because the question of attitude to other religions does not lie at the forefront of interest for those who delve into his thought. At this point in our study of the subject, I am therefore unable to offer one single explanation for the tensions and conflicts within his thought. Are they expressions of early and late Rav Kook? Do they reflect different audiences and literary contexts? Do they express varying philosophical vantage points? Are they the consequence of a moral critique of other religions, Christianity in particular, under specific historical circumstances, rather than a principled opposition to the validity of multiple spiritual paths? Do they express concerns that spill over from Rav Kook's care for *kelal yisra'el* and its well-being at a given point in time or beyond any particular time? Or perhaps Rav Kook himself struggled with this question, fundamental as it is to the very vocation of a religion, especially a religion that sees itself as possessing a universal message, as does Judaism. In the absence of a formulated theory by means of which to account for his overall approach to religions, let us consider how Tamar Ross's work can be helpful in advancing our thought on this matter.

By way of a preliminary suggestion, one may consider how the alternative views of other religions might relate to the dual perspectives on truth—instrumental and ontological. I believe this is a fruitful approach, but would caution against applying it in too simple a manner. It is not only that when truth is viewed instrumentally it reveals a more positive view of other religions, while the ontological perspective leads to a harsher critique or rejection of those faiths. It could work that way, but one could also consider *all* religions as caught within the dynamics of truth, its ultimate inaccessibility and instrumental applications. If no religion has full access from its external expressions, then all share in the same dynamic.

This tension is not the only angle from which we might apply Ross's work to Rav Kook's view of religions. Ross leads her argument to the following conclusion: 'Although every explanation of the ultimate reality misses the mark, all sincere explanations and formulations are valid components of its infinite character, and should be graded hierarchically in terms of their instrumental value . . . According to R. Kook's metaphysical assumptions, any effort to embark upon the attempt to grasp the truth already evinces a reliance upon the upward spiritual pull which leads in the direction of the infinite and absolute reality.' If we only consider this formulation, then we may have a framework from within which to regard other religions as participating equally in the upward process. If intention is the criterion, then the sincerity of the life of believers (it may be too much to apply sincerity to a unit as large as religion) is the ultimate guarantee for their participation in the upward movement. Religions are thereby validated both in light of the intentions of believers and on the basis of the metaphysical recognition that any attempt to grasp the truth already involves one in a partaking of the truth, as it is in principle grounded in the ever-present divine being.

Alongside such validation, we also encounter a sense of hierarchy. A graded hierarchy, drawn from kabbalistic sources, is integrated into a panentheistic world-view. This serves as protection from relativism, and in our case from religious relativism between faiths.

Looking at the question from another angle, to the extent that Rav Kook presents religious truth as instrumental, such instrumentality could, in theory, also benefit from the teachings of other religions. However, as Ross shows us, behind non-realism and instrumentality there is a foundational ontological view. The ontological status of Judaism, or rather, of Israel, is such that it precludes religious relativism. Moreover, Rav Kook would likely argue that the ways of Judaism are more effective as instruments for reaching the higher consciousness. Whether this statement would be made only in relation to Jews or in a more absolute way, in relation to other religions, is part of what a future study should treat.

The critique of other faiths gives expression to a polemical approach that makes moral concerns primary. Rav Kook lived in an age when polemic played a more important role than dialogue. Polemic serves the interests of identity construction and upholding the vision of the religious community. If truth is pitched in an instrumentalist mode, then deviation from a higher metaphysical perspective and the adoption of a moral or theological critique of another religion may simply be one expression of an instrumentalist view of truth. The same freedom that Rav Kook has in adapting positions to circumstances and in letting go of various beliefs could apply to his willingness to view other religions in less than their full metaphysical and panentheist promise.

I offer a concluding reflection in light of the prominent place that truth and the exceptional cognitive attainments of the mystic have occupied in our discussion. Rav Kook certainly qualifies as one such individual. When he considers other religions—do figures like him define those religions? Even more to the point—Rav Kook does not seem to have had formative relationships with members of other faiths, certainly not with individuals who reflected the high points of the spiritual life that he himself had attained. One wonders what impact such encounters might have had on the tension between the different notes sounded in his teachings.

A Brief Synthesis

Having travelled with our authors all this way, I am tempted to revisit the opening anecdote, now from the perspective of a 61-year-old, rather than a 16-year-old. If I had the same talk with David Hartman today (though I doubt I would express myself in terms of truth), how would I articulate what I mean in using the term 'truth' in relation to my commitment to Judaism? There are several insights that I draw from our essays that would make my task easier.

A. Truth is more than a position to be taken on a particular matter, or the sum total of positions taken. It may also be that, but it is a lot more than that.

B. In referring to truth, one refers to an integrated and total way of being. The different strands of the life of faith, of truth, interact with and enhance each other to form a composite whole. Speaking of truth, then, one relates to a totality.

C. Truth finds expression in the flowering of a full life, lived in God's presence, in which the various goals of religion are realized to a significant extent. Truth, then, invokes true and realized living. One realizes truth by truly living out the key virtues of the tradition, its goals, and the ways in which it seeks to shape the person and the community.

D. Because truth is composite, it is not lived in isolation from other core values. It impacts and is impacted by such key traits as faith, humility, and peace. Truth is expressed in the totality of a life, the totality of the person.

E. Crowning this totality is the awareness of, and close association to the point of union or communion with, God. Truth is the realization of divine consciousness, or some meaningful degree of it, or perhaps even an ongoing quest for it, at least partially realized. Truth, by this understanding, is a way of being that partakes of the divine being.

I think I can now articulate much better what it was that the 16-year-old boy was trying to convey. It had to do with wholeness, totality, and a quest for perfection in God. It is only a narrow definition that would exclude these from the purview of truth. Our authors have allowed me to affirm an understanding of truth that is broader and more comprehensive. For this, too, I thank them.

CHAPTER ONE

Old-Fashioned Truth, Telic Truth, and Interreligious Understanding

JEROME YEHUDA GELLMAN

WHEN WRITING about religions other than my Judaism and engaging in interreligious dialogue, I have retained an old-fashioned correspondence theory of religious truth, despite a pronounced tendency away from that view in the field. In addition, I think in terms of what I call 'telic truth' in a religion. In what follows, I present my approach to religious truth and to telic truth and explain how my approach functions for me in interreligious understanding.[1] Then I turn to defending my approach in the face of three widely held objections to my position. These are: the expressionist objection, the nativity objection, and the postmodernist objection. I will conclude that these do not merit my changing my correspondence attitude to the truth of my core Jewish belief. So far, then, I remain content with my convictions.

Here, I can present my core Jewish belief in only a very rough, schematic way. A detailed, careful presentation would require, at the least, a chapter all of its own, and possibly an entire book. With that limitation, my core Jewish belief is as follows:

1. God exists.

2. God has a distinctive, loving relationship to the Jewish people.

3. The Jewish religion has a divine sanction.

4. A Jew ought to adhere to the Jewish religion.

5. Every other religion has at least one false core belief or lacks a crucial religious truth present in the Jewish religion.

---

[1] I borrow the term 'telic truth' from Samuel Fleischacker, who uses it in a somewhat different way than do I. See Fleischacker, *Divine Teaching and the Way of the World* (Oxford: Oxford University Press, 2011), and *The Good and the Good Book* (Oxford: Oxford University Press, 2015).

My references here to 'a religion' include subdivisions within a religion's tradition, or even one person's version of that religion. Thus, this would include not only Buddhism, but also, for example, Theravada Buddhism, Pure Land Buddhism, and Zen Buddhism. And it would include not only Christianity, but also Protestantism and Aquinas's Christianity. My (2) does not imply that God loves the Jews more than others. Rather, in my thinking, God's love of all humans is equal to God's love for the Jews. However, God's relationship to the Jews as a nation serves as a means of revealing God's love of, and to, all human beings.[2]

In asserting the truth of my core Jewish belief, I mean to assert that to each statement in it there corresponds a state of affairs that exists objectively and independently of the ways we might think about it or describe it. God is real. God's relationship to the Jewish people is real. God's sanctioning of the Jewish religion is real. And (4) corresponds to an obligation fact, which is true independently of anyone asserting it.[3] The falsity of a core belief of another religion means that to that belief there corresponds no objective, independent state of affairs. Hence, a correspondence view of religious truth. To assert the truth of God's existence, for example, is to assert the same truth as in the statement that I am now sitting at my computer. In both cases, the truth is due to their faithfully recording something about real reality. Of course, in the two cases the nature of the real state of affairs is very different—God versus a computer—but the nature of the truth is the same, namely: correspondence-truth.

A weaker claim for my core Jewish belief would be that it is much closer to the truth than any of its competitors. To explain just what this comes to, we need to distinguish between belief and acceptance. Belief is involuntary. One, as it were, finds oneself with a given belief. One can choose to try to induce a belief in oneself, but one cannot choose to have a belief. Acceptance, in contrast, involves a choice. With acceptance, one is not sufficiently moved by the truth of a religious core proposition for belief to have emerged. Yet one is sufficiently impressed by its truth to decide to make it one's own. You decide to think in terms of it. You refer to it as your standard by which to judge. You use it in premises in relevant reasoning, and so on. In doing so, you assume its

---

[2] For a full explication of this view of Jewish chosenness, see Jerome Gellman, *God's Kindness Has Overwhelmed Us* (Boston: Academic Studies Press, 2013).

[3] This reflects my belief in moral facts and obligation facts as independent truths. If you do not agree, just omit (4) from the coming discussion.

truth, because it has truth credentials for you beyond any alternative. And so it is worth accepting, worth making your own.[4]

Given the distinction between belief and acceptance, a person might accept a religion because, while it might have problems that bother the person, its propositional truths strike him or her as the most important in the religion, while the falsehoods seem less central, or because it has more such truths than any alternative available. Then the religion will be true enough for that person to want to accept it and follow it.

It is an open question with an individual religious devotee whether and when, or to what extent, he or she believes in, or rather accepts, his or her religious orientation. This distinction between belief and acceptance, with the contrast between voluntary and involuntary, pertains very clearly to the question of what demands a religion can make on a person's intellectual life. That being said, for the sake of simplicity, I will stick, in what follows, to the stronger state of belief.

Now to telic truth. An aim of a religious practice has telic truth to the degree to which that aim is laudatory and to the degree to which that practice has what it takes to advance that aim, and ultimately to fulfil that aim. A religion can have several different practices and a plurality of aims, so I think more of telic truth *in* a religion than of the telic truth, per se, *of* a religion.

Recognizing telic truth is not solely a matter of judging an aim by its correlative teachings. It is, significantly, a matter of witnessing the lives of exemplars who personify the success of that telic thinking. They can give us a better understanding of that telic truth than do writings or sermons. The way these exemplars live, the way they move and speak, the way they react to situations and to the failures of those around them, and more, all give us insights into what the telic teaching means and what it is after in results. The great Christian mystic Thomas Merton once met the great Zen master, Thich Nhat Hanh. Merton wrote that immediately he observed the saintliness of Thich Nhat Hanh, just by the way the Zen master entered the room and closed the door. You could not *see* that in Thich Nhat Hanh's many teachings. The beauty and goodness of exemplars embodies telic truth.[5]

My core Jewish belief acts as a prima facie filter to what I take to be laudable aims of a religious practice in another religion. That does not mean that a telic truth of another religion must be identical to one of my telic truths.

---

[4] For more on belief and acceptance, see Jerome Gellman, 'Beyond Belief: On the Uses of Creedal Confession', *Faith and Philosophy*, 23/3 (2007), 299–313.

[5] For more on the beauty of exemplars see Ian James Kidd, 'Beauty, Virtue, and Religious Exemplars', *Religious Studies*, 53 (2017), 171–81.

Their telic truth may depart from the ultimate aims of my religion, and help me to better understand my own religious aims. And it might cause me to make adjustments to my own telic truths in considering it. In theory, if it came to it, I imagine I could undergo a religious Copernican revolution. Until that unlikely event, given my relatively liberal filter, I am perfectly open to another religion having within it telic truth, and have discovered that to be true of some religious orientations other than mine.

To ignore or reject telic truth in other religions is to miss what is true and not deniable. Consider, for example, the aim of Islam to worship a purely monotheistic God, and Islamic Sufi practices to advance that goal. Such practices possess an impressive degree of telic truth for me. The fact that I believe that it is false, as a fact about reality, that Muhammad was a prophet, and that this belief plays an integral role in Sufism, does not detract from the telic truth of such practices. Or, consider the Christian aim of transforming a person from having pride to having humility, and consider the various practices, including the tradition of contemplative prayer in Christianity, that foster that aim. These practices have high telic truth for me, with a little adjustment, perhaps, to bring them closer to my religious beliefs. This regardless of their being intertwined with the divinity of Jesus, in which I do not believe. So, religions other than mine do, at times, possess high levels of telic truth, while I do not embrace their core beliefs.

It is very important here to accept that having a correspondence-false belief is consistent with a religious practice having telic truth, even to a high degree. I am reminded of Maimonides' category of 'necessary beliefs', which need not be correspondence-true but which do contribute to the aims of the religion by orienting devotees in a fruitful direction.[6]

I enter interreligious understanding with a firm correspondence-belief in my core Jewish belief. And I enter interreligious understanding on the alert for discovering, and having discovered, telic truth in other religions. The effort has enriched my understanding of others and understanding of myself and my spiritual aspirations.

In interreligious dialogue, we should duly study our respective correspondence-truth claims, discussion of similarities and contrasts being instructive and adding to mutual understanding. But that should not exhaust interreligious understanding. At some point, correspondence-truth can be left behind to engage in exploration of each other's telic truths. We should

---

[6] See Maimonides, *Guide of the Perplexed*, trans. M. Friedländer (New York: E. P. Dutton, 1904), iii. 28.

expect to find similarities between some of our telic truths and disparities in others.

◆

My way in interreligious dialogue is guided by what I call epistemological framework conservatism. This holds that if one already has a belief that is embedded within a structure or framework of intertwined beliefs, then one is justified in continuing to hold that belief until one has a strong reason to stop believing in it. A person should not have to relinquish a belief he or she holds unless there is good reason to give it up. The fact that one already holds a belief is itself justification for continuing to hold it in the manner one does.[7]

Epistemological framework conservatism accounts for

a common intuition that when the need to revise our beliefs occurs we should try to revise our set of beliefs piece by piece instead of in totality. So, when we attempt to eliminate inconsistencies that arise in our set of beliefs as we come to form new beliefs, we try to hold on to as many of our original beliefs as possible . . . We are hesitant to do away with our beliefs because intuitively we think that holding a belief, while it does not count as evidence/reason in favor of the belief, merits our retaining the belief until we have reasons to abandon it.[8]

The greater the ingress of the belief inward, towards the most central beliefs of the structure, the stronger a critique will have to be to dislodge it. In other words, the more other beliefs in the structure that you would have to give up because of giving up one belief, the more you are justified in maintaining

---

[7] For decades philosophers have been fighting like mad about what should happen when you realize that others, as smart, well informed, and seemingly honest as you think you are, have religious belief frameworks inconsistent with yours. On the one side, there are the philosophers who argue that this counts as a good reason to suspend your religious framework of belief or at least to keep it only tentatively, while others deny this is a good reason for making such changes in your beliefs. I belong to the latter group and have defended the position in a number of publications. I will not repeat my reasoning here. See Jerome Gellman, 'Religious Diversity and the Epistemic Justification of Religious Belief', *Faith and Philosophy*, 10/3 (1993), 345–64, repr. in Michael Murray and Eleonore Stump (eds.), *Philosophy of Religion: The Big Questions* (Oxford: Blackwell, 1999), 441–53; id., 'Epistemic Peer Conflict and Religious Belief', *Faith and Philosophy*, 15/2 (1998), 229–35; id., 'In Defense of a Contented Exclusivist', *Religious Studies*, 36 (2000), 401–17; id., 'Jewish Chosenness and Religious Diversity—A Contemporary Approach', in Robert McKim (ed.), *Religious Perspectives on Religious Diversity* (Leiden: Brill, 2016), 21–36.

[8] Kevin McCain, 'The Virtues of Epistemic Conservatism', *Synthese*, 164 (2008), 187–8. McCain does not put his view in the same terms as I do here, as epistemological framework conservatism. Nevertheless, his reference to 'sets of beliefs', and his later appeal to the 'coherence' of one's beliefs, come close to the view I am proposing.

that one belief. Beliefs at the edges of a structure of beliefs are more easily discarded.

No doubt my adherence to epistemological framework conservatism carries serious dangers for me. It invites dogmatism, ensuring that nothing from another religion could ever enhance or refine my core belief, or become so convincing that it would challenge my core belief. Adherence to epistemological framework conservatism could well encourage strained protective strategies, invented solely for keeping the outside at arm's length or out of sight entirely.

That is why it is so important to adopt a consciously vulnerable apologetics in interreligious dialogue, one which is open from the very start to the real possibility that elements of one's religious belief might be refined, or weakened. My vulnerable apologetics begins from Jewish tradition yet finds occasion to recast the tradition anew by rejecting or suspending some of its elements, or, if it ever were to come to that, which I genuinely trust will never come to be, to reject or suspend the tradition as a whole. So, in my books I have found it necessary to create a new conception of the Jews as the Chosen People, because I found that the arguments were too strong against extant conceptions. I have proposed also to accept the widely held scholarly view that the Torah can no longer be thought to report, at least in its details, actual historical events. And so I have proposed a theology of Torah and history that accounts for that fact while retaining as much else as possible of the tradition.

Therefore, although my Judaism serves as my religious standard, in time I have learned to refine and enhance my core Jewish beliefs by becoming familiar with other religions. And I have learned of elements within my religion after first finding them elsewhere and then tracking them down in Judaism. And I have had to make some adjustments to my Judaism from elsewhere.

I should point out, though, that engaging in a protective strategy is no sin. In fact, doing so is justified by epistemological framework conservatism, since the latter aims to conserve belief, given the belief structure already in place. Protective strategies are not to be dismissed simply because they are protective strategies, but are to be judged by how reasonable or unreasonable they are for the purpose at hand. I agree that such judgements are hard to make because so many factors enter them. If one is unsympathetic to start with, one will tend to find a given protective strategy rather readily to be unreasonable or irrational. If one is sympathetic from the start, then one might be eager to validate a given protective strategy that really stretches beyond the breaking point. Some equilibrium of judgement must be found, whether on the sympathetic or unsympathetic side, and even then the possibilities of disagreement are great. Here is a reason why one should expose one's admittedly protective religious strategies to the public, inviting reactions that help one see oneself from the point of view of others, and so get help in deciding what is reasonable and what is not. Exposure of one's views benefits the aim of coming closer to the truth.

Protective strategies are fine, per se, and are the stuff of philosophy, the sciences, and everyday life. An academic philosophy journal will display protective strategies in favour of one's favourite philosopher, philosophical position, or philosophical critique. It is no sin, on epistemological framework conservatism, to protect broad ideas you already believe in. What is to be judged is the reasonableness of each protective strategy, given the rather amorphous nature of that idea. The conversation, including on the nature of reasonableness, will only advance us in our endeavours. Developing and trying to defend competing protective strategies help us progress towards the aim of truth more than any alternative. That is because each strategist will, given his or her personal commitment, give their standpoint its best chance, and from the competition truth will be advanced. This is especially true for standpoints of people at the periphery, which includes not only women, and especially women of colour, but all those disregarded in mainstream epistemologies. This should include traditional Jews, whose religious views are hardly paradigms of beliefs that epistemological theories are eager to accommodate.

I have further ground for protective strategies, besides the endorsement of epistemological framework conservatism. This ground is not one of impersonal epistemology, but of a personal relationship with God. At times, I see myself as standing in a personal relationship to God. I pray to God, and sometimes feel God's presence in my life, for example when studying edifying traditional Jewish texts or when feeling spiritual inner progress, or at special moments of life. It would be a serious violation of my relationship with God to forfeit so easily the context in which this relationship is embedded. I owe it to my relationship to God to be extra cautious, to demonstrate what is called in Hebrew *temimut*. This is a word which is hard to translate into English. It has all the following components: being simple, uncomplicated, innocent, trusting, faithful, loyal, being whole, perfect without blemish, being devoted. The concept of *temimut* relates to one's personal relationship with God, as in Deuteronomy 18: 13, 'You shall be *tamim* with the Lord your God' (*tamim* being the adjectival form of *temimut*). Augustine wrote of this stance when he said, 'I will rather not be inquisitive than be separated from God.'

Consider this analogy: the police present a mother with evidence that her son has committed a serious crime. She is certain he did not do it. She displays *temimut* regarding her son's innocence. In some cases, she will be perfectly rational to believe that her son did not commit the crime, despite the contrary evidence. These will be cases where her loving relationship with her son gives her an epistemic advantage over others in knowing deeply what he is like, and knowing, therefore, that it is extremely unlikely that he could ever find the power within him to do such a heinous act. Her sensitivity to his soul might give her a privileged understanding of what her son could and could not do. This, of course, will not always be the case, but it can be the case sometimes. In such cases, the mother's *temimut* can grant her an epistemic advantage over others. My point is that *temimut* can be an epistemic virtue when it affords an insight into the truth of the matter, unavailable to those devoid of *temimut*.

Granted this, any theological task should be undertaken by a theistic believer in a prayerful mode, much as Anselm of Canterbury prayed to God for guidance when setting out to prove the existence of a being than which none greater could be conceived. I am not alone, away from my God and from what God expects of me, in interreligious dialogue. I enter interreligious dialogue in a prayerful mode, praying that God guide me.

◆

Now, there will no doubt be readers who will jump in upon hearing me talk about epistemological conservatism, protective strategies, and competing viewpoints to protest that I have no right to my views about these matters. In this section I want to take up what I find to be the three major influential objections in the literature. I believe that they do not succeed in overcoming my position. These three are the expressionist, nativity, and postmodernist objections, respectively.

The Expressionist Objection

The expressionist objects to the very idea that in endorsing religious beliefs one is making factual claims. R. B. Braithwaite gave a classic statement of this position,[9] based on a general philosophical view (the 'verification principle') which almost all philosophers have since abandoned. That need not

---

[9] 'An Empiricist's View of the Nature of Religious Belief', in Basil Mitchell (ed.), *The Philosophy of Religion* (Oxford: Oxford University Press, 1971), 72–89.

interest us here, though, since I am more interested in the viability of expressionism itself than I am in its historical roots. Here are sample quotations from Braithwaite:

1. '[A] religious assertion is used to express an attitude ... It is not used to assert the proposition that [one] has the attitude; it is used to show forth or evince [an] attitude.'[10]

2. '[Religious assertions are] primarily declarations of adherence to a policy of action, declarations of commitment to a way of life.'[11]

3. 'I myself take the typical meaning of the body of Christian assertions as being given by their proclaiming intentions to follow an agapeistic way of life.'[12]

4. 'There must be some more important difference between an agapeistically policied[13] Christian and an agapeistically policied Jew than that the former attends a church and the latter a synagogue ... The really important difference, I think, is to be found in the fact that the intentions to pursue the behaviour policies, which may be the same for different religions, are associated with thinking of different stories (or sets of stories).'[14]

5. 'It is not necessary, on my view, for the asserter of a religious assertion to believe in the truth of the story involved in the assertions.'[15]

According to Braithwaite, then, to say that 'God exists' or that 'God sanctions the Jewish religion' would not be to assert 'a truth', but to express a positive attitude towards a way of life associated with those sentences, or to express a commitment to an associated way of life. And, what distinguishes a religious Jew from a Christian are the dissimilar stories they tell in their respective ways of life, even were they to otherwise describe their two ways of life in roughly similar ways. If Braithwaite were right, then my assertion of my core Jewish belief has nothing to do with truth, and it is only a symptom of my liking a specific brand of religion. To utter the words 'God exists', then, is more like my saying 'Wow!' about a delicious ice cream than like my saying that I am sitting at my computer.

From my own experience with my co-religionists (and at times also with myself), I suspect that Braithwaite's expressionist view might be correct for some of them. That is, I suspect, though it is difficult to really know, that

[10] Ibid. 78. [11] Ibid. 80. [12] Ibid. 81.
[13] That means having a policy to aim for acting in pure, unconditional love.
[14] Ibid. 84. [15] Ibid. 85–6.

statements such as 'God chose the Jews' and 'God sanctioned the Jewish religion' function for them as no more than expressing their intention to follow the Jewish religious practice, using that language simply as part of what traditional Jews say. Traditional Jews observe the sabbath, eat kosher, and utter sentences such as 'God chose the Jews' and 'God sanctioned the Jewish religion'. In their language practice, such people (and sometimes I) are not making truth claims, any more than they do in the act of eating a kosher meal.

However, from that we ought not to reach the conclusion that this is all there is to such statements, as a general claim about all devotees. Even if it were true that all devotees did use such sentences to express an attitude or a commitment, it simply would not follow that they were not also making truth claims. Using a sentence expressively is consistent with at the same time making a truth claim with the same utterance. Making a truth claim might even be essential for the success of the expressive function. Suppose it is raining hard outside and I see you open the door and are about to leave the house, without taking your umbrella from the umbrella holder next to the door. I call out to you in alarm, 'It's raining hard outside!!!' Now, clearly, I am using that sentence to express a warning, to alert you that you had better not leave the house without an umbrella. A warning by itself (think of 'Be careful!') is appropriate or inappropriate, but neither true nor false. Yet when I say 'It's raining hard outside!', not only am I issuing a warning, I am also making a truth claim that it is raining hard outside, and that truth claim is essential to the achievement of the expressive function of the utterance. There is every reason to think that statements such as 'God exists' often do express an attitude to a way of life *because*, among other things, of the truth claim being made in saying that God exists. It is, among other things, because one believes that God exists that one commits oneself to, or continues with, a theistic religious practice. In my better moments, I intend such sentences to be correspondence truth claims, as do many of my friends. Braithwaite's expressionism gives no reason to think otherwise.

The Nativity Objection

This objection goes back at least to John Stuart Mill, and banks on the fact that where and when a person is born is an accidental fact about that person. Had that person been born in different circumstances, he or she would have had a very different set of beliefs. Here is how Mill put it:

The world, to each individual, means the part of it with which he comes in contact; his party, his sect, his church, his class of society . . . [I]t never troubles him that mere accident has decided which of these numerous worlds is the object of his reliance, and that the same causes which make him a Churchman in London, would have made him a Buddhist or a Confucian in Pekin.[16]

And John Hick states it this way:

It is evident that in some ninety-nine percent of cases the religion which an individual professes and to which he or she adheres depends upon the accidents of birth. Someone born to Buddhist parents in Thailand is very likely to be a Buddhist, someone born to Muslim parents in Saudi Arabia to be a Muslim, someone born to Christian parents in Mexico to be a Christian, and so on.[17]

And Philip Kitcher:

Most Christians have adopted their doctrines much as polytheists and the ancestor-worshipers have acquired theirs: through early teaching and socialization. Had the Christians been born among the aboriginal Australians, they would believe, in just the same ways, on just the same bases, and with just the same convictions, doctrines about Dreamtime instead of about the Resurrection. The symmetry is complete ... Given that they are all on a par, we should trust none of them.[18]

The objector would reach the conclusion, in my case, that there is something defective about my believing my core Jewish belief to be true in the correspondence sense. The argument seems to go like this:

You, Gellman, believe in your core Jewish belief only because you were born Jewish and were raised and educated in a religious Jewish milieu. However, it was a pure accident that you were so born and so educated. You could have been born, instead and for example, a hundred and fifty years ago, in India, and would have turned out to be a Hindu, or a Muslim. Hence, your belief in your core Jewish belief is dependent purely on an accident of your history. So, your belief in your core Jewish belief is epistemically defective. You should disown it, or think of it differently than as involving correspondence truth claims.

The argument might seem especially acute since I have already agreed to there being telic truth in religions other than mine, and even high telic truth. If that is the case then, the objection would continue, I should acknowledge

---

[16] John Stuart Mill, *On Liberty* (London: Longmans, Green, 1913), 10–11.
[17] John Hick, *An Interpretation of Religion: Human Responses to the Transcendent* (London: Palgrave Macmillan, 1989), 2.
[18] Philip Kitcher, 'Challenges for Secularism', in George Levine (ed.), *The Joy of Secularism: 11 Essays for How We Live Now* (Princeton, NJ: Princeton University Press, 2011), 26.

that, had I been acculturated into a religious perspective other than mine—and the fact that I have not been is purely accidental—I could easily have been influenced to confer the highest telic truth to what *then* would have been my home religion. And I would undoubtedly have thought of Judaism as having a lower degree of telic truth. So I should be very hesitant to rely on my present calibrations of telic truth.

There are several problems with the present objection. One is that I do not accept the idea that it is purely accidental that I was born Jewish. Every morning, I thank God for having made me a Jew. That is, I believe that my being born a Jew was due to God's intention, and was no accident. It could not have been otherwise, since God's intentions are not accidental. Yes, had I been born in long-ago Tibet, instead of being born a Jew, I would not have my present religious beliefs. But I could *not* have been born then in Tibet instead of when and where I was born. To claim that my being born Jewish and receiving a traditional education was purely accidental is simply to reject my religious belief from the very start. Why should I pay attention?

Now, the objector might reply that, had I not been born Jewish, I would not have believed that God made me a Jew in the first place. And it was only accidental that I was born a Jew. So, my belief that God has made me a Jew is similarly epistemically defective. Here we meet an impasse. For my reply would be, as before, that I thank God for having brought me to understand that God made me a Jew. The upshot is that the nativity argument might convince the objector, but slides off my back as depending on a false premise.

But even the objector should not be convinced by the present objection. The argument casts too wide a net, snaring the objector within it. Probably the objector believes in democracy, in equality for all humans, and in civil rights in general, or believes in some other contemporary values. But had the objector been born 500 years ago on the River Rhine, and the fact that that wasn't the case is purely accidental, none of these ideas would have been current in society. Upon hearing and understanding these, the objector most surely would have dismissed them as deranged ravings. Nor would the objector have ever thought that the circumstances of his or her birth then were a reason not to believe in Christianity. I assume that the objector is not willing to give up his or her convictions because of that hypothetical possibility, as I am not prepared to give up mine. So, the objector must admit that something is wrong with the argument.

I conclude that, like the expressivist objection, the nativity objection does not prevent me from thinking of my core Jewish belief as stating correspondence truth claims.

Postmodernism

Postmodernism challenges my penchant for making truth claims. Postmodernism enjoys some popularity among academics, especially in the humanities, and their followers. But of course, popularity does not add up to a reason for embracing a philosophical position, any more than unpopularity is a reason for rejection. (Needing to follow the crowd to get tenure is another matter.) So, the question is: Should I embrace postmodernism?

To discuss the problems with postmodernism, first I introduce the concept of a pragmatic contradiction. A plain contradiction states something and what is inconsistent with it, such as: 'It is raining and it is not raining.' A pragmatic contradiction does not state a contradiction, as its content is not internally inconsistent. Instead, the contradiction arises between the content of the statement and the act of making the statement. Consider this statement: 'It is raining and I do not believe that it is raining.' There is no internal contradiction in this statement. We can easily imagine circumstances where it is true. It is raining outside and I do not notice that it is raining. Therefore, I do not have a belief that it is raining. At that moment, it is raining but I do not have a belief that it is. No problem. A problem comes when it is I who is declaring both that it is raining and that I believe that it is not raining. That is because my act of declaring that it is raining undoubtedly means that I believe it is raining. But this contradicts the second part of what I say, that I believe that it is not raining. My declaration involves a pragmatic contradiction.

Another example would be if I were to speak the sentence about myself, 'I cannot speak.' There is no inconsistent content to this statement. You can well imagine me, along with others, not being able to speak. But there is a pragmatic contradiction here, since it is not possible for both the sentence to be true and for me to speak it. When I utter the sentence, I contradict its content. No internal contradiction, but a pragmatic one. The idea of a pragmatic contradiction plays a part in the critique of postmodernism, to which I now turn.

Alvin Goldman, a leading, northern hemisphere, Western, white, male epistemologist, has convinced me that postmodernism has some serious problems not sufficiently dealt with. Goldman has credible arguments against several different positions that go under the name 'postmodernism'. For the full discussion, I refer you to his ample critique.[19] Here I present arguments against three central positions of postmodernism that he

---

[19] Alvin I. Goldman, *Knowledge in a Social World* (Oxford: Clarendon Press, 1999).

addresses, supplemented by some of my thinking, with my labels: constructivism, repressionism, and biasism.

Constructivism

There is no such thing as transcendent truth. What we call true is simply what we agree with. So-called truths or facts are merely negotiated beliefs, the products of social construction and fabrication, not objective or external features of the world.

Goldman asks, 'Wherein consists the truth that there is a consensual belief in a statement?' In other words, what warrants our asserting that 'we' are in agreement about a given statement? Goldman replies that, according to what constructivism itself says, the warrant for believing that there is agreement about a given statement must come from yet another level of our agreement, namely, a consensual belief in a second statement, which says that we have a consensual belief about the first statement. But then, once again, the warrant for the second statement, which declares the existence of an agreed-upon belief in the first statement, must depend on a third statement, which says that we have an agreed-upon belief that there is an agreed-upon belief that there is an agreed-upon belief about the original statement. In this way, an infinite regress is generated of levels of consensual belief. But, since no such infinite regress of consensual beliefs exists, or could possibly exist, constructivism cannot coherently be asserted. The same argument applies to constructivism itself, when it is the given statement. By its own dictates, it is acceptable only if 'we' agree on it. But then the same, impossible, infinite regress will ensue. The impossible regress does not come from the very content of constructivism, but from a person's asserting it as warranted. So it is the confirmation of constructivism that gets us into trouble, and that trouble is a pragmatic contradiction.

Now constructivists might want to maintain that 'consensus beliefs' about statements are themselves exempt from further consensus (and this would apply as well to a consensus belief about constructivism). These sorts of things, they might insist, are exceptions to the principle. The fact that we have an agreed-upon belief does not need further consensus to be warranted. Such statements are simply acceptable as facts. And so, no infinite regress follows.

But why should anyone want to accept such a position? Why should social and psychological statements reporting our agreements not require further agreement to validate them, while everything else depends on our agreement to be validated? This is grossly ad hoc as a metaphysical or epistemological position. Why should a traditional Jew who believes in a real world and a real God, with or without a consensus, be allured to agree with this postmodernist doctrine? I see no good reason to do so, and so I revert to the conclusion that the constructionist version of postmodernism generates an impossible infinite regress.

Another way of raising the problem is to look at the status of stating that 'There is no such thing as transcendent truth.' If true to his own assertion, the person who says this must admit that this assertion itself is also not possessed of transcendental truth. Otherwise, he is involved in performing a pragmatic contradiction. He would be making a transcendental claim that there was no transcendental truth. So this statement must simply be part of his, and his friends', 'narrative', divorced from truth. In that case, though, I counter his statement simply by making the rejection of it a part of my own narrative. Any narrative is as good as any other if there is no truth, so his narrative has no more normative force than mine. On any of the alternatives, constructivism fails to convince.

Repressionism

Appeals to truth are merely instruments of domination or repression, and should be replaced by practices with progressive social value.

Now, unless we are to take this as dogma, which a person like me might choose to ignore, we need to have a reason for accepting repressionism. And such a reason surely must be because of known facts about the way appeals to truth in the real world are wielded as instruments of domination and repression. Foucault, for example, when arguing this about the sciences, did not mean to make up a fictional story.[20] He meant to advance a true report, true facts about the real world. He meant to provide real evidence about the connection between power and claims to knowledge. He did not intend to dominate or repress anyone.

Hence, to assert repressionism as warranted is to produce a pragmatic contradiction. The contradiction is between stating repressionism as warranted, against its negation, and repressionism's content. For when one asserts repressionism as a warranted truth, one implicitly tells us that this appeal to truth is an attempt neither at domination, nor at repression.

If Foucault, and those like him, did not mean to tell us anything true, but were just telling us their 'narrative', well, I have a right then to my own alternative narrative, which might see things differently. And if they did mean

---

[20] See Michel Foucault, *The Archaeology of Knowledge*, trans. Alan Sheridan (New York: Pantheon Books, 1972), esp. 178–98.

to tell us something true, without themselves having any thoughts of repression or domination in doing so, then we have reason to reject repressionism, which tells us that appeals to truth are attempts at domination and repression. So we have no reason to accept repressionism.

On the other hand, repressionism might signal in some postmodernists a sense of moral superiority. For this position to be at all worthwhile for consideration, postmodernists who put it forward must believe that in doing so they are free from desires for domination and repression. And they must also believe that everyone else is motivated by sinister desires to repress, dominate, crush, and enslave. But if the postmodernist can achieve freedom from such sinister desires, why cannot others? Why should postmodernists be the only saintly ones in the world and everyone else power-driven? Does the fact that they uncover repression where others do not see it make them automatically morally superior human beings to all others? Does this make them free of their desires for power and domination, both conscious and unconscious? This is hardly convincing either in theory or in practice. (Think of some academic departments where postmodernism is wielded as a bludgeon to keep junior faculty in line.) I conclude that repressionism does not have enough to it to make it attractive.

Biasism

The last item from Goldman's list on which I will spend time here is biasism: truth cannot be attained because all putatively truth-oriented practices are corrupted and biased by politics or self-serving interests. Biasism implies that biases drive all belief, and that there is always a conflict between biases and the pursuit of truth. The implication being that, since the pursuit of truth is greatly defective, it should be abandoned. With the abandonment of truth comes the desertion of a Grand Narrative, giving way to more modest, competing narratives. Goldman argues extensively against the view that all belief is driven by biases and corruption, and argues against thinking that biases always interfere with the pursuit of truth. I wish to take a different tack here, though. And that is that, if truth practices are contaminated, why not hold that biases and corruption will contaminate whatever takes the place of truth? Corruption comes from people, not from truth. So why should we expect people who are oriented to something other than truth suddenly to be free of corruption? In both cases, the biases are the same: that is, the biases involved in trying to convince oneself and others that one is entitled to what one asserts. Since that is the case, biasism might be simply another statement infected by politics and self-interest.

Lest a postmodernist fan of this view take the high ground and claim to be above human biases in putting biasism forward, I see no reason to grant that person this status of moral and epistemic superiority as against the rest of humanity. Surely, whether consciously or not, your everyday postmodernist is susceptible to any number of collective and personal biases. The fact that a person is well trained to sniff out biases where others don't notice them gives very little reason to think that that person is well aware of, and entirely disowning of, his or her own biases. Postmodernism is not the same as sainttraining.

To reply to biasism head-on, we must distinguish between kosher 'biases' and non-kosher biases. The kosher 'biases' are those with which one starts when spinning out protective strategies for what one already believes. They are kosher under the strict supervision of epistemological framework conservatism. It is good and healthy for competing protective strategies, including postmodernism, to be developed in the presence of one another, so that the truth, or whatever comes in its place, can be advanced in serious intellectual engagement. Thus, these are 'biases', not biases, as far as that term is a disapproving one. Simply put, not all 'biases' are reasons to give up on truth.

The non-kosher biases can pop up as unreasonable or irrational positions, either in the process of articulating a protective strategy or in unwarranted responses to other protective strategies. But here, as I have claimed above, it is not all that easy to make such determinations. But with good will, a healthy sense of self-vulnerability, and respect for others with whom one disagrees, I believe we can creep forward towards meaningful progress. That is my methodological philosophy, with as little desire of repression and domination, and with as little bias, as I am capable of.

I conclude that so far I have no good reason to budge from my commitment to real truth. And so I will continue to engage in interreligious dialogue with both correspondence and telic truth in hand.

CHAPTER TWO

History and Truth in Religion

STANISLAW KRAJEWSKI

IN JUDAISM, as well as in Christianity and some other religions, historical events in the form of canonized stories provide essential points of reference. A fundamental question arises: Is the historical accuracy of these stories really important for religion? Or rather, to make it personally relevant rather than an issue of erudition, is it important for my own religiosity? An additional question is: Is there anything in religion that is constant; that, while belonging to the human, historically conditioned realm, remains outside history, does not change with time? Again, is it important for *me* to perceive an unchangeable essence in my religion?

The problem with answering these two questions emerges from the development and achievements of the critical and scientific approach to history. According to it, everything is subject to evolution, and change is also inevitable in the way we as human beings perceive past events. Therefore, there is no perennial essence of any religion, nor is our picture of past events that engendered the religious tradition accurate. It can't be. The issue is general, and philosophical. As philosopher Bernard Williams puts it, 'accounts which have been offered as telling the truth about the past often turn out to be biased, ideological, or self-serving. But attempts to replace these distortions with "the truth" may once more encounter the same kind of objection, and then the question arises whether any historical account can aim to be, simply, true.'[1] How can one as a religious and modern person address this situation?

Let us deal first with the issue of the (unchangeable) essence, and then with the probably more unsettling problem of the accuracy of historical accounts.

---

[1] Bernard Williams, *Truth and Truthfulness* (Princeton, NJ: Princeton University Press, 2004), 1.

Our Belief in Eternal Essence

Historically speaking, everything is subject to change, birth, growth, decline, and death, including cultures and civilizations, peoples and religions. After all, according to modern science, even nature and its seemingly most stable phenomena undergo evolution: species arise and pass, stars, including our Sun, sooner or later burn out, and the cosmos itself is expanding or perhaps pulsating. From the scientific perspective, Judaism and Jews must have changed, and no aspect of Jewish religion may be claimed to be completely stable. And indeed, if we look at any specific issue, we can point out the change of views concerning even the most fundamental tenets of faith. Let us consider a specific example of an issue in Judaism that seems to have been obviously constant for millennia.

The incorporeality of God has been taken for granted for a long time, but a thousand years ago or more it was less than obvious for Jewish thinkers, who could easily mention many Torah verses that refer, for instance, to God's arm or hand. To be sure, the passages can be interpreted in a way that is compatible with the tenet of strict incorporeability, since we all follow Maimonides and know that *ein lo demut haguf ve'eino guf* ('He has no semblance of a body, nor is He corporeal'). Yet this was not the only way. Thus Natan Slifkin writes, 'the huge number of manuscripts available to us today reveals that in medieval Europe, and especially in Rashi's homeland of France, it was by no means unthinkable to believe that God possesses form. The Tosafist R. Moshe Taku asserts that God sometimes takes on human form, and considers it heretical to deny—as Rambam does—His ability to do so.'[2] To be sure, the issue of the exact content of opinions expressed by medieval rabbis has been debated by experts, but it seems safe to state that the views on this fundamental question, held by the most Torah-true rabbis, were diverging. If this seemingly simple matter exhibits the presence of evolution and change, then is everything in our religious outlook subject to change? Has everything changed?

Well, it seems imperative to state that, whatever scientists and historians can say, we do feel that not everything is subject to change. We have this feeling independently of what historians have found or will discover. I am saying

---

[2] Natan Slifkin, 'Was Rashi a Corporealist?', *Ḥakirah: The Flatbush Journal of Jewish Law and Thought*, 7 (2009), 81–105. Slifkin's piece can also be found on his website, <zootorah.com>. For more claims about ancient Jewish concepts of incarnated deity see Alon Goshen-Gottstein, 'The Body as Image of God in Rabbinic Literature', *Harvard Theological Review*, 87/2 (1994), 171–95, as well as Daniel Boyarin, *The Jewish Gospels: The Story of the Jewish Christ* (New York: The New Press, 2012), and other books by him.

this without the intention to slight historians' achievements. They are valuable and form a basic framework in which we can operate. However, at the same time, their approach is not sufficient for a living faith. This is so important that it mustn't be minimized. As the outstanding German Jewish philosopher Franz Rosenzweig wrote about a hundred years ago, when we Jews say 'we', we hear 'we are eternal'.[3] This is not a historical description; clearly, even according to the biblical account, during the time of Noah there were no Jews. This statement is also not a prediction; clearly, we can imagine the earth without Jews. Yet Rosenzweig's dictum aptly expresses something fundamental to Judaism. We feel that we do touch something beyond and above history, something that historians have no way to grasp as historians. We also assume that the essence of the relation between the Creator and Jews has not changed. That is why my faithfulness, or attempted faithfulness, to the tradition of Judaism reaches beyond historical contingencies. This is more than just a feeling opposite to the picture presented by science. It says something essential about the Jewish tradition.

It is possible to see the contradiction between tradition and science in an even more direct way. Not only is it easy to imagine the future when there will be no more Jews. Actually, we can imagine the future with no human beings, for example after a major cosmic or natural catastrophe. For the Jew who treats the tradition seriously, the question arises immediately: How does this relate to the Torah's statement that God will never send another flood (Gen. 9: 11)? While one can look for consolation in the hope that such a catastrophe will never happen, it is hard to find an answer other than just an expression of this hope, namely, sheer faith. A less extreme situation can be considered. To propose a thought experiment, let us imagine a catastrophe that leaves alive only a group of people on a spaceship. Most of the existing civilizational divisions and group identifications would then lose sense. However, if there were some committed Jews among the survivors, they would probably try to recreate the Jewish 'people' in relation to the tradition. (The same applies to committed Christians, who would try to recreate the Church.) This thought experiment seems to offer an 'empirical' illustration of the thesis about the perennial nature of the Jews. Rosenzweig's statement is thereby confirmed, which does not mean that there exists some guarantee of Jewish perpetuity.

How is it then possible to combine the thesis about the absolute rule of

---

[3] Franz Rosenzweig, *The Star of Redemption*, trans. Barbara Galli (Madison: University of Wisconsin Press, 2005), 317, where this is seen as a property of 'the community of blood', and then for example p. 322, where it is stated: 'the eternal people purchases its eternity at the price of temporal life'.

history, the ubiquitous character of change, with the view that there is something unchangeable, something that reaches beyond the rule of history? I believe that no easy solution is possible. We must remain modest but firm. The situation reminds us of the problem with proofs of the existence of God. Philosophers generally have come to the conclusion that no proof is possible. Every argument assumes at some point the very thesis one attempts to demonstrate. At the same time, I would add, some arguments do sound convincing in the ears of some people. This means that the properly worded assumption seems true to *them*. They believe. Similarly with the supra-historical point of reference. This cannot be objectively demonstrated; historians, sociologists, and other scientists will reject that concept if they are true to their profession. We—and also they, for that matter, when they transcend their professional capacity—can express our belief that we reach, or at least point to, something beyond history. We would also claim an even more comprehensive belief: human beings, in order to see a meaning in the world, must reach beyond the world, towards the realm of transcendence.

Can the belief in something beyond history help deal with the problem posed—in the presence of historical sciences—by the belief in the historical veracity of the stories that make up our religious tradition? Or rather, can this approach help us deal with the apparent necessity to abandon the traditional naive trust in the literal truth of those stories? This is the fundamental question, mentioned at the very beginning.

The Story of Job and the Stories in the Torah

Before proceeding to an analysis of the problem of the truth of biblical stories, let us notice that there exists a general problem of language, that is, of the unavoidable relativity of language. This can be applied to the thesis about the belief in a stable essence beyond history. Namely, assuming the presence of some unchanging supra-historical 'point', we do not need to assume that there exists a perpetual linguistic description of it. Every method of talking about it is relative, proper to its historical period. In the course of history, the understanding of any given description can change. The description can become impossible to understand. In the realm of language, of the means of expression, there is no unchangeability. History reigns supreme. No formulation of an article of faith is ultimate. Only the reality pointed to by an expressly formulated article of faith can, perhaps, be perennial, never its formulation. The form of expression can change; the essence remains. Each formulation is tentative. This picture of the situation is well attested to in the tradition of Judaism. Only a wide enough fragment or even the totality of the tradition can express the truth; never can an isolated statement be sufficient independently of the context. 'Torah speaks in the language of man', as is repeatedly stated in the tradition.[4]

The thesis that dogmatic formulations are impermanent may seem to contradict the Jewish need to preserve the letter, not just the spirit, of holy texts. The stress on the smallest details of the text seems to mean that the literal meaning of the text is given. The contradiction is not really there, however, as each verse, being indeed stable, needs interpretation, or rather a variety of interpretations.

To some extent this disregard for the literal truth of some otherwise highly significant stories is present in the Jewish tradition. Maimonides summarizes the attitudes with respect to the existence of Job:

Some of our Sages clearly stated Job has never existed, and has never been created, and that he is a poetic fiction. Those who assume that he has existed, and that the book is historical, are unable to determine when and where Job lived. Some of our Sages say that he lived in the days of the Patriarchs; others hold that he was a contemporary of Moses; others place him in the days of David; and again others believe that he was one of those who returned from the Babylonian exile. This difference of opinion supports the assumption that he has never existed in reality.[5]

And yet we should treat the problems raised in the book with utmost seriousness:

But whether he has existed or not, that which is related of him is an experience of frequent occurrence [and] a source of perplexity to all thinkers. . . . This perplexity is caused by the account that a simple and perfect person, who is upright in his actions and very anxious to abstain from sin, is afflicted by successive misfortunes, namely, by loss of property, by the death of his children, and by bodily disease, though he has not committed any sin.

What is more, some key parts of the story of Job are seen by Maimonides as literary fiction:

According to both theories, viz., the theory that Job did exist, and the theory that he

---

[4] *Sifrei*, Num. 112. It is an important motif, stressed by Rabbi Ishmael against Rabbi Akiva, in the exposition of rabbinic theology by Abraham Joshua Heschel in *Heavenly Torah, as Refracted Through the Generations*, ed. and trans. Gordon Tucker (New York: Continuum, 2006).

[5] *Guide of the Perplexed*, iii. 22, trans. M. Friedländer (New York: E. P. Dutton, 1904), 296 ff. The next two quotes are also from there.

did not exist, the introduction to the book is certainly a fiction; I mean the portion which relates to the words of the adversary, the words of God to the former, and the handing over of Job to him. This fiction, however, is in so far different from other fictions that it includes profound ideas and great mysteries, removes great doubts, and reveals the most important truths.

Can the treatment of the book of Job be applied to the Torah? Commentators who stand outside the tradition of Judaism have no problem with such applications. For those who locate themselves inside the tradition, the situation looks different. To a pre-modern-style traditionalist, the traditional belief in the truth of the Torah is not to be questioned. To those who combine tradition with modernity, the problem is acute. The approach to the Torah must not be the same as to the book of Job. The story of Job teaches us something important by referring to something we all know from experience—the suffering of innocents. The accounts in the Torah teach us by referring to the reported events as facts. It is not possible just to ignore this if one wants to remain within Judaism. And historians generally deny the truth of those accounts. To give just one example, archaeologists say that no evidence has been unearthed about the presence of walls in Jericho during the period believed to be the time of Joshua, and, more generally, 'the archaeological findings blatantly contradict the Scriptural picture: the Canaanite cities were not "great", were not fortified, and did not have "walls sky-high".'[6] Referring to this, to the improbability of having the crowd numbering 600,000 adult males depart from Egypt and wander through Sinai without leaving any trace detectable to us, and to many other examples of discrepancy between historical findings and the account of the Torah, one cannot but conclude that 'as far as we can judge from the factual evidence, the Israelite conquest of Canaan as described in the Scripture never took place, nor did the Exodus from Egypt'.[7]

Faced with these challenges, a believer may of course ignore historians and dismiss their findings. However, this is not an acceptable move for those among us who treat science seriously. One can choose the approach that Maimonides took with respect to the book of Job. Even fictional stories can be highly significant. However, contrary to the story of Job, the stories about the patriarchs, the Exodus, and much of the rest have the character of historical accounts, and are treated as such in the tradition. It seems impossible to ignore the question of their veracity. And the two extreme answers—the

---

[6] Z. Herzog, 'The Bible—No Evidence on the Ground' (Heb.), *Haaretz*, 3 Nov. 1999, quoted in Naftali Zeligman, 'Letter to My Rabbi' (2005) on the <talkreason.org> website.

[7] Zeligman, 'Letter to My Rabbi'.

History and Truth in Religion 53

picture of their full accuracy and the view of them as literary fictions—seem too simplistic. Is there a way out?

Persistence of a Minimum of Historical Facts

In order to see how a middle way between literal historical truth and literary fiction can be taken, let us consider one of the best-known Torah stories, *akedat yitshak*, the binding of Isaac. It is so well known that it needs no repetition. It is important, however, to stress the fact that new renderings and novel interpretations of the story keep appearing. One recent interpretation is worth mentioning. According to Rabbi Jonathan Sacks,

> In the ancient world, up to and including the Roman empire, children were considered the legal property of their parents. They had no rights. . . . Torah seeks to establish, in the case of children, what it establishes in the case of the universe as a whole, the land of Israel, and the people of Israel. We do not own our children. G-d does. We are merely their guardians on G-d's behalf. Only the most dramatic event could establish an idea so revolutionary and unprecedented—even unintelligible—in the ancient world. That is what the story of the binding of Isaac is about. Isaac belongs to neither Abraham nor Sarah. Isaac belongs to G-d. All children belong to G-d. Parents do not own their children. The relationship of parent to child is one of guardianship only. G-d does not want Abraham to sacrifice his child. G-d wants him to renounce ownership in his child. . . . G-d creates legal space between parent and child, because only when that space exists do children have the room to grow as independent individuals.[8]

Whatever interpretations have been given and will be made, the story of the Akedah remains unexhausted. It is undeniable that, from the perspective of Judaism, this story constitutes an inexhaustible well of meaning. It has become a fundamental point of reference, a durable pillar of tradition, or rather of several traditions. This has been the case despite the fact that there exist no extra-biblical data confirming the reality of the events described in the Akedah story. What is more, in some sense, even for non-religious people, the story functions as a description of reality. Indeed, it is a reality that is always available, more real than most of the events we have witnessed. And, even more important, it really constitutes a point of reference, a source of interpretations important for our lives, much more than most events we experience. We can say that, independently of everything else, that story has

---

[8] Jonathan Sacks, 'The Binding of Isaac: A New Interpretation' (commentary on 'Vayera', 2010 [5771]), Covenant and Conversation website.

become a touchstone, a fundamental truth, and a pillar of Bible-based civilizations as a result of its presence, its interpretations, and even the recurring opposition to the disturbing scene of the offering of the beloved son.

And yet one cannot escape the simple question: Is this pillar really true? No amount of relativizing to a narrative can obliterate the naive question: Did it really happen?

It is important to realize that most modern people, that is to say, people living according to modern values, among which the acceptance of scientific history is so important, will refrain from any defence of the literal meaning of the story. I think that, while nobody can exclude the possibility that it happened in the way it is presented, the certainty that it so happened is completely unjustified by today's standards and expresses a textual fundamentalism. On what grounds may we think it is more than literature?

Even assuming a critical attitude, we see that the story happens in a setting that we treat as real, even though the assessment of the veracity of particular elements can vary. If asked what the angel who stopped Abraham looked like, we can say that it is inessential. The only essential aspect of that motif is that Abraham heard the voice. The voice was 'heavenly', but how it would have been recorded by a microphone is beside the point. Perhaps it could have been heard only by Abraham himself. The ram, however, is described as real, so we can ask how it looked, how it would have been recorded by a camera. Presumably it looked normal, but, as we know from our tradition, *eilo shel avraham avinu* (Abraham's ram) was one of the few things created at dusk on the sixth day of Creation (*Avot* 5: 9). The vision behind this statement is beautiful, and expresses an important insight about miracles, but it is very far from science, a scientific description of events. I think that it should be treated as a metaphor. If so, does it mean that the whole story of the Akedah is a metaphor?

Many modern readers would say that the story is metaphorical and there is nothing more to it than literature. In the pre-modern era, for centuries virtually everyone believed that the story was quite literally true. Even though the approach used by Maimonides to handle the story of Job was available, Torah was considered to be simply true. Today, the approach 'fiction but highly significant' is easily used, for example by saying that 'we believe that, whether the story of Pharaoh, the Exodus, and the Wilderness "actually happened" or not, our present situation calls upon us to relearn and rethink the story. It calls upon us to learn in order to act.'[9] The two extremes are easily

---

[9] Arthur Waskow and Phyllis Berman, 'Relearning and Rethinking the Passover Saga', Jewish Telegraphic Agency website.

definable. If there is nothing in between, one can either be modern and against the traditional religious approach, or anti-modern and traditionally religious. If, however, a middle course is possible, one can be critical and believe in the fundamental veracity of the story. How is this possible?

It should come as no surprise that some elements of any given story can be less than accurate. This happens often in accounts of events, even by eyewitnesses. Additional explanations and details are meant to make the story easier to grasp for the listener. If this is done with good will, with no intention to lie or to manipulate, the story remains true in an important and significant sense, even if, when taken with all its details, it is not true in the literal sense. What is even more important, though, is that something did really happen. This 'something' may constitute only a fragment of the story, or may even be present only in an indirect way. However, to this 'something' the standard correspondence theory of truth applies, that is, the literal truth. I claim that, however large the amount of the content of the story that is outside historical testability, there remains a residue that is subject to the 'usual' truth and testability. Of course, I mean a theoretical testability. No practical test is thinkable at this moment with respect to the Akedah story. The extent of our belief in the historical facts behind the story may be difficult to realize. Yet it is its very presence that is unavoidable if we want to remain believers along the traditional lines.

The Second Step: Treat the Whole Story as if It Were True

I have proposed we assume that *some* historical truth remains to be believed; we cannot explain away everything. The line between literally true and not literally true but significant depends on what other sources of authority one adopts, in addition to one's religious tradition. For example, I accept the findings of natural and historical sciences, with no reservation other than the general claim that they are hypothetical, and, however well confirmed, are always subject to revision.

Let us see some more examples of how historical criticism can be combined with belief in the truth behind the story. Jews and Christians (unlike many Muslims) treat as literally true the fact of the existence of the Jerusalem Temples. This does not mean that all details of the stories connected to them must be literally true—for example, the destruction (*ḥurban*) of both on the same day, 9 Av. To some this was simply the case; to other Jews this can mean that a degree of rabbinic creativity can be detected. One can doubt the claim that the two cases of *ḥurban*, and, in addition, some major disasters in later times, such as the capture of Bethar (135 CE) and the ploughing up of Jerusalem, occurred on that same day, as is stated in the tradition (*Ta'an.* 4: 6). To use the phrase of David Roskies, perhaps the rabbis cut down history 'to manageable size'.[10]

We do not need to agree on every detail. We may put the border between the literally true and the not literally true at various points. My only point is that the border must be set somewhere. The non-literal truth can be called metaphorical, or better, truth relative to a narrative. The residue of the literal truth can be much smaller for us, moderns, than it was in pre-modern eras. It does not need to contain all traditionally conceived truths. The extent of literal truths about history seen in the Torah can change. Something must remain historically accurate, but what exactly is not predetermined.

The above view differs drastically from the traditional approach that assumes as literally true the totality of the Torah. It makes possible a combination of some traditionally conceived religiosity with modernity. What is more, contrary to the initial impression, it does not require the abandoning of the traditional reverence for the received text. We can assume only a limited part of the account to be historically accurate, and still treat the text as if it were literally true. That is, I believe that we are supposed to take two steps. First, as explained above, some truths are relativized to the narrative, and only the remaining residue is taken as simply true. Second, the traditional story is affirmed in its entirety, and it remains an essential ingredient of the religious infrastructure. Let us see how this works.

Let us take, for example, the account of Mosheh Rabenu. We know a lot about him from the Torah. Some historians say that there is no independent proof of his existence, so there is no reason to believe he was a historical figure. The lack of evidence is hardly a disproof, but even if some hints in the direction of disproving his existence were found by historians (nothing more than possible hints seems imaginable), I would not feel threatened. Whatever aspects of the description of Moses are relegated to the realm of unhistorical, metaphorical truth—and there may be many of them—some historical core remains. It may be much smaller than the tradition has it, but there must be something literally true beneath the story. I may be unable to identify that core, but I can still assume its existence. Moreover, and here comes the second step, I have no other choice than to accept the whole biblical story. Some past events—I believe, unique events, without precedent and never repeated—crystallized as the story of Moses in the Torah. To relate to them I must

---

[10] See David Roskies, 'Memory', in Arthur A. Cohen and Paul Mendes-Flohr (eds.), *Contemporary Jewish Religious Thought* (New York: The Free Press, 1987), 582.

refer to the whole story, including the person of Moses and the events in which he took part. As long as I believe that there are *some* unique truths in the Jewish traditions about Mosheh Rabenu, I have to treat the received story of him as if it were literally true. No amount of historical findings can change that.

If we agree to use the term 'myth' in its noble sense, we can say, with Protestant theologian Paul Tillich, that by affirming a story in a non-naive way, we arrive at a 'broken' myth—understood as a myth, but not removed or replaced.[11] Actually, it is not very different from what Maimonides told us about Job. He was ready to see Job's story as fiction. Let us extend this to other stories. I propose to underline an aspect that is usually at most implicit in the modern reappropriations of the biblical stories, namely the persistence of some propositions, relegated to the background and hard to identify, that can be seen as simply true.

The Consequences for Interfaith Relations

It is perfectly possible that the realm of direct historical truth is delineated differently by various believers belonging to the same denomination. This should not be seen as problematic. It is unavoidable, since we can differ in so many respects, including the level of trust in historical findings and hypotheses.

The differences can be much bigger if, for two different religions, the same initial event constitutes an important point of reference. Or, to put it better, if the same initial story constitutes a common point of departure. Sometimes, even in the case of different religions, there may be no significant differences. Probably Jews and Christians can have much the same attitudes to the Akedah story. The interpretations offered by Jews are usually acceptable to Christians. I have no doubt that the above-mentioned new interpretation by Rabbi Sacks sounds interesting and illuminating to Christians, and quite possibly to virtually everyone. Many Christian interpretations can be of interest to Jews, I mean Jews *as* Jews; only the strictly Christological ones would constitute exceptions. Actually, in the rabbinic period, which coincided with the first several centuries of Christian theology, there existed mutual inspirations and influences. Edward Kessler has called them 'exegetical encounters'.[12] In that era the Akedah story was seen as simply true. Nowadays we can still

---

[11] See Paul Tillich, *Dynamics of Faith* (New York: Harper and Row, 1957), 49.
[12] See Edward Kessler, *Bound by the Bible: Jews, Christians and the Sacrifice of Isaac* (Cambridge: Cambridge University Press, 2004).

exchange interpretations. Can we agree about the extent of the literal truth in the story? It seems to me that we can, that the Jewish and Christian attitudes to its veracity can be the same.

This convergence of Jewish and Christian attitudes is in sharp contrast with the contradiction between the Akedah story and the similar one in the Islamic tradition, where it is Ishmael who was about to be sacrificed by Abraham. I am sure I am not alone in feeling very significant difficulties in any attempt to treat the story about Ishmael with the same seriousness as I treat the standard (for Jews, and Christians) story of the binding of Isaac. And I suspect that a vast majority of Jews (and Christians), also those who do not care about religious belief, would share the feeling. It seems also sure that many completely non-religious and anti-religious people from Jewish and Christian families would say the same: the 'real' story is about Isaac. If this guess is correct, this reaction reveals a highly interesting truth about the Jewish and Christian world: at least some of the fundamental stories are seen as true in some unclear but deeply rooted way. Perhaps it is easy to offer some explanation. Many people would probably say that the Akedah story is much older, so it must have been the source for *sura* 37, where a similar story is told—without, however, identifying the name of the son who was ready for sacrifice. This explanation amounts to the simple fact that the Torah is much older than the Quran and the Islamic tradition. Yet it seems that, for almost everyone, the knowledge of the historical facts regarding the dates of the appearance of holy books of various religions comes much later than some familiarity with the Jewish Akedah story. The more important reason for considering it more 'true', in some sense, than the Islamic story would then be one's family education or one's cultural environment, in which it was only the Torah or the Bible that was seen as revealed or at least deserving a special place. Thus, even if no claim about the literal truth of the Akedah story is made, this story is considered not as just one of many possible fictions, but as a special story, treated as if it were a true historical description. And, to repeat, it seems that a large majority of Westerners would be inclined to think that way. Obviously, it is just the opposite with Muslims. Is there a way to overcome the potential for conflict?

In order to see whether it is possible to avoid the conflict over the identity of the son who was about to be offered, let us use the idea of the residuum of literal truth in a significant story as distinct from the rest of the story, which can be only metaphorically true, or rather, true relative to a narrative. The residual literal truth is very hard to pin down. Whatever it is, it can be assumed to belong to both the Jewish and the Islamic stories. Now, let us assume it is the rest of the story that really counts, which means that there are two stories that are true only within their own narratives. If so, the divergence of the accounts is not threatening. After all, the Jewish story is about Abraham and Isaac, and the Islamic story is about Ibrahim and Ismail. They are different, so the contradictions are only apparent; the conflict is not inevitable. At the same time, they are not just fictions; they have grown, we can assume, out of real events, and to the extent they refer to those events, they are factually true.

The Islamic account of the sacrifice attempted by Ibrahim is the basis of the festival Eid al-Adha, also known among Polish Muslims as Kurban Bajram. I must avow that I have no problem whatsoever with Muslims celebrating this festival. The interpretation I have just given provides a good reason: let them celebrate, we can support the celebration; after all, the festival is about Ismail rather than Ishmael. It refers to their story, and it is not really essential what is its relation to our story. The two stories may share a hidden core that is simply true, but it is the way each one functions within its own tradition that is practically important.

The above method of handling the potential conflict is not necessarily applicable in all cases. If, for a religious tradition, a specific story provides a definition of its own fundament, then opposing narratives about the same person or the same event constitute a major source of discord. This can be illustrated by the Christian account of the life and death of Jesus. It is known to Christians and to the wide world from Christian sources. No independent account from that era is known. There exist also later, but ancient, Jewish 'anti-Gospel' accounts of Jesus, such as those gathered in the *Toledot yeshu*. They present an image completely different from the stories known from Christian holy books. To say, as we did before with regard to the Akedah, that a common factual core, even a small one, persists in both accounts seems highly inadequate. The stories that are most fundamental for Christians are ridiculed by the clearly polemical Jewish account. If it is treated as true, even metaphorically true, it has a high potential to engender conflict. Let us remember, however, that those stories about Yeshu are by themselves absolutely marginal to Judaism. The way to avoid the Jesus–Yeshu clash would be to ignore those accounts precisely because of their marginality. Nothing essential for Judaism changes if we ignore them—as has been indeed done in practice by most Jews for a long time.

To put the strategy in more general terms, if an event lives in two traditions, that is, in two contradictory narratives, each fundamental for the life of its tradition, then conflict is unavoidable. That is why emerging sects, the beginnings of new religions within established ones, are necessarily controversial and easily engender antagonism, and also violence. If, however, the event lives in one tradition only, and the account of it in the other tradition performs no vital role, the other account can be rather easily ignored. This strategy can hopefully help avoid a good part of the conflicts generated by religions and perpetuated around us. What is more, it provides hope for ending some conflicts that are at the moment unavoidable because the conflicting narratives continue to play important roles in two traditions. Probably in the future only one tradition will retain the narrative as central, while the other will develop in a way that marginalizes the counter-narrative.

CHAPTER THREE

The Cosmic Eye and Its Pupil
Divine Perfection and the Mediation of Universal and Particular Truth in Rabbinic Theology

CASS FISHER

Introduction

In 1783, under the duress of a public attack demanding he defend his commitment to Judaism, Moses Mendelssohn published *Jerusalem; or, On Religious Power and Judaism*. Perhaps his most surprising and provocative claim in that work is his assertion that Judaism possesses no revealed truths necessary for salvation.[1] While one can readily accept that Jewish theology has forms and functions that distinguish it from Christian theology, is it really the case that there is no cognitive content in Judaism that has any soteriological benefit? Hasn't God revealed to us that God is unique; that God is the creator and sustainer of the universe; and that God has redeemed us in the past and will do so again in the future? Could Mendelssohn really be saying that what Judaism has to tell us about these matters is irrelevant? What could have led him to hold such a view? He explains his position in the following passage:

I therefore do not believe that the powers of human reason are insufficient to persuade men of the eternal truths which are indispensable to human felicity, and that God had to reveal them in a supernatural manner. Those who hold this view detract from the omnipotence or the goodness of God, on the one hand, what they believe they are adding to his goodness on the other. He was, in their opinion, good enough to reveal to men those truths on which their felicity depends, but not omnipotent or not good enough to grant them the powers to discover these truths themselves.[2]

Mendelssohn argues that it impugns God's perfection—both God's benevolence and his power—to suggest that God created humans in a manner that

---

[1] Moses Mendelssohn, *Jerusalem; or, On Religious Power and Judaism*, trans. Allan Arkush (Hanover, NH: Brandeis University Press, 1983), 89 ff.   [2] Ibid. 94.

deprived them of the knowledge and ability to achieve their ultimate good. His argument continues in a more pointed tone:

> Moreover, by this assertion one makes the necessity of a supernatural revelation more universal than revelation itself. If, therefore, mankind must be corrupt and miserable without revelation, why has the far greater part of mankind lived without *true revelation* from time immemorial? Why must the two Indies wait until it pleases the Europeans to send them a few comforters to bring them a message without which they can, according to this opinion, live neither virtuously nor happily? To bring them a message which, in their circumstances and state of knowledge, they can neither rightly comprehend nor properly utilize?[3]

For Mendelssohn, it is self-evident that a perfect God must necessarily be the God of all people, and as such it is inconceivable that human well-being would be contingent upon revelation, an encounter with the Divine that is particularistic. One might think that Mendelssohn's position testifies more to the exuberance of the Enlightenment and its affirmation of human reason than it does to a genuine theological problem internal to Judaism. While he is surely guided by his Enlightenment concerns, the theological dynamic he addresses in these passages is endemic to the idea of monotheism: if God is singular and perfect, then God is, by necessity, the God of all.

It is worth pointing out that nearly a century and a half later, by which time the Enlightenment had lost some of its lustre, Franz Rosenzweig articulated a view that shares some of Mendelssohn's concerns. In 1925, Rosenzweig wrote the essay 'The New Thinking' to help his readers understand the main arguments of his magnum opus, *The Star of Redemption*. In the essay, he states: 'When the actual [ancient] Greek prayed, he was certainly not heard by Zeus or Apollo but rather, of course, by God; nor did he live in the cosmos, but rather in the created world, whose sun, our sun, shone for Homer, too.'[4] To be sure, there is much that distinguishes Mendelssohn's and Rosenzweig's wider concerns; Mendelssohn is advocating for the power of human reason and Rosenzweig is making a point about worship and the Divine–human relationship. Where they stand on common ground is in their belief that God's perfection requires that we take seriously the idea that God is the God of all.[5] On both thinkers' views, divine perfection shapes our under-

---

[3] Mendelssohn, *Jerusalem*, 94.

[4] Franz Rosenzweig, 'Das neue Denken', in *Der Mensch und sein Werk: Gesammelte Schriften*, 4 vols. (The Hague: Martinus Nijhoff, 1976), iii. 146; Eng. trans. 'The New Thinking', in *Philosophical and Theological Writings*, trans. and ed. Paul W. Franks and Michael L. Morgan (Indianapolis: Hackett, 2000), 119.

[5] On Rosenzweig's use of divine perfection see Cass Fisher, 'Divine Perfections at the

standing of God's agency and providence, and conditions our relationship to God.[6] Rosenzweig makes this point even more explicitly further on in 'The New Thinking', where he writes:

> There is no temple built that would be so near to Him that man might take comfort from that proximity, nor is there one so distant from Him that His arm could not easily reach even there. There is no direction from which He could not come and none from which He had to come; there is no block of wood in which He may not once take up his dwelling, and no psalm of David that always reaches His ear.[7]

The belief that divine perfection shapes our universal and particularistic conceptions of truth is not of modern provenance; it is not just a ploy to help Judaism situate itself more comfortably within the contemporary world. To diminish God's providence is to simultaneously diminish God's perfection, and this is a fact the Sages knew well. If we fail to see that the rabbis wrestled with the same problems, we miss important contours to rabbinic theology and deprive contemporary Jewish theology of resources for addressing the perennial issue of how to balance universal truths grounded in divine perfection with particular truths that are unique to Jewish religious life and practice. To be sure, the topic of universal and particular truth is not a problem with a single solution; rather, it is a tension between opposing forces that must constantly be renegotiated. Nonetheless, examining how the rabbis engaged with this topic, both in the solutions they proffered and in the persistence they demonstrated in addressing the issue, can tell us much about the ongoing task of theological reflection in Judaism.

Center of the *Star*: Reassessing Rosenzweig's Theological Language', *Modern Judaism*, 31/2 (2011), 188–212; id., 'Speaking Metaphysically of a Metaphysical God: Rosenzweig, Schelling, and the Metaphysical Divide', in Martina Urban and Christian Wiese (eds.), *German-Jewish Thought Between Religion and Politics: Festschrift in Honor of Paul Mendes-Flohr on the Occasion of His Seventieth Birthday* (Berlin: De Gruyter, 2012), 151–66.

[6] For more extensive discussions of these issues see Cass Fisher, *Contemplative Nation: A Philosophical Account of Jewish Theological Language* (Stanford: Stanford University Press, 2012); id., 'Reading for Divine Perfection: Theological Reflection and Religious Practice in the Exodus Commentary of *Mekhilta de-Rabbi Ishmael*', in Lucie Doležalová and Tamás Visi (eds.), *Retelling the Bible: Literary, Historical, and Social Contexts* (Frankfurt am Main: Peter Lang, 2011), 139–57; id., 'Beyond the Homiletical: Rabbinic Theology as Discursive and Reflective Practice', *Journal of Religion*, 90/2 (2010), 199–236.

[7] Rosenzweig, 'Das neue Denken', iii. 154; 'The New Thinking', 130.

A Few Methodological Issues

Before proceeding, three issues require attention: my principle of selection in choosing rabbinic texts; the notion of divine perfection in rabbinic theology; and the relationship between universalistic claims based on divine perfection, theological universalism, and natural theology. Two interests guide my principle of selection. First, I hope to convey that the rabbis' reflections on the relationship between universal and particular truths were more than a tangential concern; on the contrary, these problems are deeply embedded in the monotheistic idea, and the rabbis did not shirk from confronting them. Limitations of space prohibit a comprehensive overview of the matter, so the best way to make the point is to show that this concern arises repeatedly within a formative but limited body of literature. To that end, I will focus on the halakhic *midrashim* and in particular on the *Mekhilta of Rabbi Ishmael*. A second interest also informs my principle of selection. There is a notable continuity in the language and symbols the rabbis deploy in their reflections on universal and particular truth. In a few instances, I will reach beyond the halakhic *midrashim* in order to observe the development of these theological motifs. As we now live in a time when theology is on the defensive and constructive thought faces a variety of challenges, it behoves us to pay close attention to how the rabbis advanced their own theological reflections.

My argument rests on the presupposition that rabbinic theology shows considerable interest in divine perfection. One might think that, after the work of scholars such as Arthur Marmorstein and Ephraim Urbach, this idea would be unproblematic.[8] For a variety of reasons that is not the case. The term 'divine perfection' suggests a systematic and dogmatic approach to theology that is at odds with much of the Jewish theological tradition. One can also imagine that attributing reflection on divine perfection to the rabbis means that they wrestled with the logical conundrums addressed by Christian philosophical theology, such as God's foreknowledge of future contingents. While the rabbis may be more interested in some of these questions than we typically recognize, they certainly do not engage with these puzzles with the concern or rigour of Christian theologians and philosophers. Furthermore, while some rabbinic theology clearly reflects interest in God's perfection, the rabbis also depict God in terms that appear antithetical to common understandings of divine perfection. As we well know, they envision God as weeping, being bested by humans in scriptural interpretation,

---

[8] Arthur Marmorstein, *The Old Rabbinic Doctrine of God* (Oxford: Oxford University Press, 1927); Ephraim Urbach, *The Sages: Their Concepts and Beliefs*, trans. Israel Abrahams (Cambridge, Mass.: Harvard University Press, 1975).

and much else that would seem to undermine the claim that God is a perfect being. Despite everything that counts against it, it is still the case that an important element within rabbinic theology is to proclaim and defend God's greatness. The rabbis are incessant in their claims that God possesses maximal power and knowledge and that God's justice is unimpeachable.⁹ Part of what makes studying rabbinic theology both challenging and rewarding is that assertions about God's perfection are juxtaposed to theological views that depict the Divine–human relationship in terms that are so dynamic that one can only conclude that God and the Jewish people are mutually dependent upon one another. So, while we cannot avoid talking about divine perfection in rabbinic theology, we also cannot suppose that this topic encapsulates everything the rabbis want to say about God. What I take to be of crucial importance in many of the passages that follow is the cognitive arc of the rabbis' reflections on divine perfection: attempts to understand and articulate God's perfection lead to claims of universal truth. When human reason is directed towards divine ultimacy, monotheism is propelled towards the universal truth that God is the God of all. The task for the rabbis and those who follow in their wake is to balance the universal truths inherent in monotheism with the particular truths that emerge from the Jewish people's relation to God.

The idea that reflection on divine perfection produces universalistic truth claims needs to be distinguished from two related issues, theological universalism and natural theology. In recent years, scholars have identified and analysed rabbinic expressions of universalism, the basic idea of which is that the nations have a share in truth.¹⁰ Marc Hirshman, for instance, has devoted a monograph to exploring the idea that the Torah was given to all of humanity. He argues persuasively that this motif arose from the school of Rabbi Ishmael and that it was closely connected to his priestly heritage. While many

---

⁹ In a presentation of early Judaism that in general gives a rather diminished role to belief, Shaye D. Cohen says: 'That God is the omnipotent, omniscient creator of the universe, exalted above all his creatures, ruling in majestic splendor, and ultimately beyond human ken, is a common motif in the literature of the Second Temple and rabbinic periods' (*From the Maccabees to the Mishnah*, 2nd edn. (Louisville: Westminster John Knox, 2006), 77). On the concern for God's justice see David Flusser, 'A New Sensitivity in Judaism and the Christian Message', *Harvard Theological Review*, 61/2 (1968), 107–27.

¹⁰ See Marc Hirshman, 'Rabbinic Universalism in the Second and Third Centuries', *Harvard Theological Review*, 93/2 (2000); id., *Torah for All the World's People* [Torah lekhol ba'ei ha'olam: zerem universali besifrut hatana'im veyaḥaso leḥokhmat ha'amim] (Tel Aviv: Hakibuts Hame'uhad, 1999); Alan F. Segal, 'Universalism in Judaism and Christianity', in Troels Engberg-Pedersen (ed.), *Paul in His Hellenistic Context* (Minneapolis: Fortress Press, 1995).

of the passages I discuss below also come from the school of Rabbi Ishmael, my concerns move in a different direction. In speaking of universalistic versus particularistic truths, I do not intend to chart the economy of truth between Israel and the nations. Rather, I am interested in the rabbis' internal negotiation between conceiving of God as a perfect and ultimate being who creates and sustains all and the particularistic conceptions of God as intimately related to Israel. Why not, then, frame the discussion in terms of natural theology versus revealed theology? James Barr's Gifford Lectures, published as *Biblical Faith and Natural Theology*, are instructive on this point.[11] While Barr demonstrates that the Hebrew Bible and the New Testament contain natural theology, and argues convincingly that biblical scholars have a methodological obligation to acknowledge this material within the two canons, his argument problematizes the distinction between natural and revealed theology.[12] Commenting on Psalm 19, Barr notes that 'God makes himself known in two complementary ways, first through the great works of creation which control the world, and secondly through his special communication exemplified here by his law.'[13] For Barr, natural and revealed theology are equally biblical. The Hebrew Bible testifies to both the God who enters into relation with Israel through revelation and the God known through reason and experience. In his view, the two conceptions of God cannot be sundered. As he states:

Why can we not reject the entire theistic impulse and confine ourselves to the personal, active, biblical God? The problem is that the theistic impulses appear to have

---

[11] James Barr, *Biblical Faith and Natural Theology* (Oxford: Clarendon Press, 1993). Although I will not be pursuing this matter here, one point of contact between Barr's study of natural theology and Hirshman's universalism is Barr's identification of natural theology with cultural interaction and 'transreligiosity' (ibid. 92, 187).

[12] Barr's comments about the obligation of biblical scholars to acknowledge the presence of natural theology are incisive and bear repeating: 'We thus come to something close to the diametrical opposite of what it has been the fashion to think. The biblical theologian has to take account of processes of natural theology. Even if he or she personally dislikes natural theology, if it is there in the material it has to be taken into account. It forms part of the essential linkage between one part of the Bible and another, and these linkages, which hold the Bible together, are just the matter with which biblical theology is supposed to be concerned. There may, on the other hand, be philosophical or dogmatic reasons, or reasons arising from the modern situation, why natural theology should be ruled out. If that is so, then the dogmatic theologian has to explain why this aspect of biblical thought should be rejected and what effect such a rejection will have on the idea of the authority of the Bible. To most people, however, it would seem odd if natural theology was accepted as part of the working machinery of the Bible and yet was condemned as anti-Christian by dogmatic theology' (ibid. 203). [13] Ibid. 87.

a place within the Bible itself. We cannot be sure that the Bible succeeded in keeping pure the ideal of the personally active biblical God as distinct from the God of theistic universalism. It did not. These tendencies which we have, very inexactly, labeled as 'theistic' are already present in the Bible. They are part of the inner-biblical interpretative process. As far as I can see, they do not belong to any one stratum of the literature but are scattered over all of it . . . From quite early times the interpretative process included some perception of the need for consistency, some sense of a universal perspective which might need to be respected, some sense of the difficulties of simple anthropomorphism, some sense of the difficulty involved with a God who takes part in some earthly events but ignores other events or stands aloof from them.[14]

Reversing the terms of discussion that revelation is primary and natural theology is secondary, if it exists at all within the biblical corpus, Barr goes on to argue that

there is no absolute distinction between revelation and natural theology. In particular, revelation is not a completely separate body of information or channel of material, totally different in substance from what is publicly known or publicly accessible knowledge. Revelation, if we must still use the word, is not a completely separate entity but is a mode in which things already known are seen in a quite new way, and also a mode in which things previously unknown are added to things already known, making a different pattern but including many elements that were the object of anterior knowledge.[15]

There is much to say about this, but where I think it necessary to follow Barr in my discussion is the view that it establishes an artificial distinction to pit natural theology and revealed theology against each other. For that reason, in what follows, I focus on the rabbis' reflections on divine perfection without positing that this is a separate source of theological knowledge, independent from revelation.[16]

---

[14] Ibid. 141.

[15] Ibid. 195. In claiming that natural theology and revelation go hand in hand, Barr does not see himself as offering an innovative position. See ibid. 126.

[16] I do not mean to suggest that the category of natural theology is out of place in the study of rabbinic Judaism. My point is that, in the current discussion, I do not want to separate the two forms of theological language. Barr, I believe, is correct to argue that natural theology is integral to scriptural hermeneutics. He writes: 'Not only does the Bible have to be interpreted, but interpretation goes on within the Bible itself. Much of the Bible, perhaps all of the Bible, is the product of interpretation. But the consequence of this has not always been noticed: the more we stress the importance of interpretation, the more we render probable the influence of something like natural theology . . . But it would really be very strange if there [were] interpretation [that] used no categories whatever that were external to the

Divine Perfection and the Problem of Universal and Particular Truth

For the rabbis, God's perfection is a topic that could be endlessly ramified. To take just a few examples from the *Mekhilta of Rabbi Ishmael*: at the Sea of Reeds, God divides not only the sea but all the water in the world;[17] also at the Sea of Reeds, God provides a perfectly just punishment for each Egyptian (and his horse!) according to his sin.[18] Prior to these events, when God goes out to kill the firstborn of the Egyptians, God does so precisely at midnight, a feat only God can accomplish as no one but the creator of time could know it with such exactitude.[19] Claims such as these permeate rabbinic literature. Clearly, many rabbis read Torah with an eye to embellishing Scripture as a way of asserting God's maximal greatness. If we can hold off the philosophical associations of these terms, we could rightly say that much rabbinic theology sees God as omnipotent, omniscient, perfectly just, and omnipresent. That some rabbis are invested in articulating these points is not an accident. Expressing God's greatness is an act of giving divine praise; the two go hand in hand. Praise requires content and, arguably, the fullest and most reliable source for such material comes from reflecting on God's perfection.

Perhaps the best starting point for a discussion about divine perfection and the tension between universal and particular truths is to look at God's perfect goodness or omnibenevolence. Jews have been too quick to surrender the idea of God as loving and merciful to Christians. Our liturgy instructs us otherwise. In the morning prayer service, before we are commanded to love God in the Shema, the antecedent blessing, 'Ahavah rabah', tells us: 'With great love have you loved us, Lord our God'.[20] Later, at the conclusion of the

material being interpreted. From the material itself, new categories grew, and these called for expression in terms [that] the original material had not contained. But as soon as we admit that such categories may have been used, we face the likelihood that operations of natural theology took place' (ibid. 150). In my own work, I argue that changing notions of divine perfection motivate a significant amount of rabbinic hermeneutics. See Fisher, *Contemplative Nation*, 117–39.

[17] In the following, I quote and translate from the Horovitz and Rabin edition of the *Mekhilta* unless otherwise stated, but I also provide page numbers to the newly reprinted edition by Jacob Lauterbach. *Mechilta d'Rabbi Ismael cum variis lectionibus et adnotationibus*, ed. H. S. Horovitz and I. A. Rabin (Frankfurt: J. Kaufmann, 1931), henceforth HR. Jacob Lauterbach, *Mekhilta de-Rabbi Ishmael*, 2 vols. (Philadelphia: Jewish Publication Society, 2004). The example I cite here is found in 'Masekhta devayehi beshalaḥ', 5 (HR, 104; Lauterbach, i. 153).

[18] 'Masekhta deshirata', 2 (HR, 125; Lauterbach, i. 182).

[19] 'Masekhta depisha', 13 (HR, 42; Lauterbach, i. 67).

[20] *Daily Prayer Book: Ha-Siddur Ha-Shalem*, trans. Philip Birnbaum (New York: Hebrew Publishing Company, 1997), 74.

Amidah, the siddur designates God as 'the Good' on the basis of the fact that God's mercy never ceases.[21] The following passage from the *Mekhilta of Rabbi Ishmael* is ostensibly about the nature of honour and service, but in fact it sets forth a powerful account of God's providential care for the world in its entirety, an act of ultimate and universal beneficence. The text is a reading of Exodus 18: 12, which states, 'And Jethro, Moses' father-in-law, took a burnt offering and sacrifices for God; and Aaron and all the elders of Israel came to eat bread with Moses' father-in-law before God.' The *midrash* addresses the fact that the second part of the verse appears to suggest that Moses did not participate in the meal:

'Aaron and all the elders of Israel came to eat bread with Moses' father-in-law before God' [Exod. 18: 12]. And where did Moses go? Did he not from the start go out to him, as it is said, 'And Moses went out to his father-in-law' [Exod. 18: 7]? But now, where has he gone? This teaches that he was standing and serving them. From where did he learn this? From Abraham our father. Rabbi Isaac expounded on this matter and said: Once Rabban Gamaliel arranged a feast for the Sages. All of the Sages of Israel were reclining in his midst. Rabban Gamaliel stood and served them. The Sages said, 'We are not worthy that he should serve us.' Rabbi Joshua said to them, 'Leave him alone that he may serve, since we find that one greater than Rabban Gamaliel served humans [*beriyot*].' They said to him, 'Who is this?' And he said to them, 'Abraham our father, the great one of the world, who served ministering angels even though he thought they were human [*benei adam*]—Arabs who worship idols. All the more so should Rabban Gamaliel serve Sages who study Torah.' Rabbi Tsadok said to them, 'Leave him alone that he may serve. We find one greater than Rabban Gamaliel and Abraham who served humans [*beriyot*].' They said to him, 'Who is this?' He said to them, 'The Shekhinah, who in every moment supplies food to all who come into the world sufficient for their need, and who satisfies the desire of every living being. And not only for people who are worthy and righteous alone [does the Shekhinah do this] but also for the wicked, who are worshippers of idols. How much more so should Rabban Gamaliel serve Sages and sons of Torah!'[22]

As is often the case with rabbinic literature, ethical and theological discussions are woven into a literary narrative that can overshadow the profundity of the theological and ethical issues at stake. On the side of ethics, Abraham demonstrates that all humans are worthy of our complete and alacritous care. This motif echoes throughout the text with the repeated reference to humans as *beriyot* and *benei adam*. From the theological perspective, Rabbi Tsadok argues that the Shekhinah is the ultimate model of providential care, as God

[21] Ibid. 91. [22] 'Masekhta de'amalek [Yitro]', 3 (HR, 195; Lauterbach, ii. 280).

attends to the needs of all with no regard for their religious merit or lack thereof. The parallel to this text in *Sifrei Deuteronomy* utilizes equally strong language. There it speaks of God as 'the One Who spoke and the world came into being, Who causes winds to blow, clouds to ascend, rain to come down, and plants to grow, and thus prepares a table for each and every person'.[23] While I think it would be a mistake to conflate Mendelssohn and Rosenzweig with each other or with the rabbis, one crucial point of continuity is that they are all compelled to wrestle with the overlapping logics of monotheism and divine perfection that necessitate the universal truth that God sustains all of creation. Of course, the texts in both the *Mekhilta of Rabbi Ishmael* and *Sifrei Deuteronomy* come back to the matter of the Sages and the Torah and privilege both a fortiori. That Torah is the central value for the rabbis should come as no surprise. What is important to see is that the primacy of Torah does not negate God's status as the one who creates and sustains all; this fundamental universal truth is fully compatible with the truths particular to the Torah.

One might admit that the rabbis conceive of God as the creator of the world, whose providence extends to all its inhabitants, but remain sceptical that the rabbis were particularly concerned to negotiate the matter of universal and particular truths. A formulaic expression that repeats throughout the *Mekhilta of Rabbi Ishmael* suggests otherwise.

The Holy One, blessed be He, He is the healer of all who come into the world.[24]

You are the one who helps and supports all who come into the world, but for me especially.[25]

You are the salvation for all who come into the world but for me especially.[26]

For He hears the cry of all who come into the world.[27]

For He feeds and sustains all who come into the world.[28]

You, Your goodness, Your great kindness, and Your mercy are upon us but Your right hand is stretched out to all who come into the world.[29]

I am God to all who come into the world, but despite that I have conferred my name only upon my people Israel.[30]

---

[23] *Sifre on Deuteronomy*, ed. Louis Finkelstein (New York: Jewish Theological Seminary, 1969), *piska* 38, 74.
[24] 'Masekhta devayehi beshalaḥ', 5 (HR, 107); 6 (Lauterbach, i. 158).
[25] 'Massekta deshirata', 3 (HR, 126; Lauterbach, i. 183).
[26] Ibid. (HR, 126; Lauterbach, i. 184). [27] Ibid. 4 (HR, 131; Lauterbach, i. 190). [28] Ibid.
[29] Ibid. 5 (HR, 133; Lauterbach, i. 193). Urbach sees this phrase as indicative of the 'universal character of repentance': *The Sages*, 466.
[30] 'Masekhta dekaspa', 20 (HR, 334); 4 (Lauterbach, ii. 484). Regarding this passage

Taken together, these comments reveal a universalist tendency in rabbinic thought, which has recently drawn the attention of scholars.[31] For my purposes, what is noteworthy about these phrases is the way in which they emphasize God's greatness from two distinct poles. From one perspective, God is truly the ruler of the world insofar as God heals, sustains, and cares for all. At the same time, God is also intimately bound to the particular as represented by both the individual and the community. That God's absolute sovereignty is compatible with a personal relationship with the Divine allows several of these phrases to shift from theological assertion to direct address to God. Read together, these comments capture the dynamic nature of rabbinic theology and the seamless way in which it shifts between speaking of, to, and even for God.

Divine praise, as I noted above, is testimony to God's perfection. A comment in the *Mekhilta* that shares the linguistic features of the above formula suggests that God's greatness is universally acknowledged: 'All the nations of the world speak the praises of the Holy One, blessed be He, but mine are more pleasing and fitting than theirs.'[32] The connection between divine praise and divine perfection is crucial because it secures the place of theological reflection within the religious lives of the rabbis while at the same time extending these concerns into contemporary Jewish thought and practice. One does not have to look far into the siddur to find passages that reflect these motifs. For instance, the sabbath prayer 'Nishmat' says the following:

The breath of every living being shall bless Your name, O Lord our God. The spirit of all flesh shall constantly praise and exalt Your fame, our King.[33] From eternity unto eternity You are God. Other than You, we have no king, redeemer, or saviour

---

Urbach states: 'Apparently the practical significance attaching to this emphasis on the particular conferment upon Israel of the name of God, who is the God of all flesh, is that it is Israel's function to bring the recognition of the God of Israel to the knowledge of the world' (*The Sages*, 542).

[31] See n. 10 above.

[32] 'Masekhta deshirata', 3 (HR, 126; Lauterbach, i. 184). For the alternative view that the nations do not praise God, see *Pesikta derav kahana*, ed. Bernard Mandelbaum, 2 vols. (New York: Jewish Theological Seminary, 1987), ii. 419, *pesikta* 28. Without making too much of a decontextualized textual fragment, it is interesting to consider the different theologies behind the rabbinic assertion that 'all the nations of the world speak the praises of the Holy One' and Rosenzweig's claim, cited at the beginning of the essay, that God was the true object of worship for the ancient Greek. Where the rabbinic comment suggests that the nations get something right about God, Rosenzweig's position emphasizes that it is God's perfection that makes God the true object of human worship.

[33] I am following Birnbaum here by translating *zekher* as 'fame'.

who frees, saves, sustains, and shows mercy at all times of anguish and affliction. We have no king except for You, God of all creatures, Lord of all generations, the one who is praised with abundant praises, who conducts His world with compassion and all of His creatures with mercy. The Lord does not slumber or sleep, the one who awakens the sleeping, who stirs the exhausted, who causes the dumb to speak, who frees prisoners, who supports the fallen, and who causes those who are doubled over to stand erect. To You alone do we give thanks.[34]

Clearly, the rabbis' efforts to affirm God's perfection and God's providence were not a tangential concern. 'Nishmat', a prayer believed by scholars to be ancient as it is common to all rites, continues to place in Jewish mouths and hearts on every sabbath a theological vision in which God's perfection is known to all and in which God's providence extends to all of creation.

As I understand the material above, the rabbis are teasing out a web of ideas that are simultaneously complementary and in tension with one another. The theological elements that are mutually supportive are the offering of divine praise and reflection on God's perfection, particularly the articulation of God's providential care of the entire world, which attests in the strongest terms that God is ultimate. It is God's particular relationship with the Jewish people that appears to pull in the opposite direction. In what follows, I would like to give close attention to the theological language the rabbis deploy to negotiate the tension between the universal truths that emerge from reflection on God's perfection and the particular truths that mark God's relationship to the Jewish people.

The Cosmic Eye and Its Pupil

A passage in *Sifrei Deuteronomy* introduces some of the theological motifs I would like to address. The text is a commentary on Deuteronomy 11: 12, which reads: 'A land that the Lord your God cares for. The eyes of the Lord your God are always upon it, from the beginning of the year until the end of the year.' *Sifrei Deuteronomy* offers the following commentary:

'A land that the Lord your God cares for' [Deut. 11: 12]: [1] and is it for it alone that He cares? Does He not care for all lands, as it is said: 'to cause it to rain upon a land where there is no person ... to satisfy the waste and desolation' [Job 38: 26–7]? So why does Scripture say, 'a land that the Lord your God cares for'? It is as if it could be said that He cares only for it and it is because He cares for its need that He cares for all of the lands with it. [2] Similar to this you say, 'Behold, the one who guards

[34] *Daily Prayer Book*, 331.

Israel does not slumber or sleep' [Ps. 121: 4]. Is it Israel alone that He guards? Does He not guard everything, as it is said, 'in His hand is the life of every living being and the breath of every human person' [Job 12: 10]? Why does Scripture say, 'who guards Israel'? It is as if it could be said that He only guards Israel, and because of His guarding them, He guards everything with them. [3] Similar to this you say, 'and my eyes and my heart will be there [in the Temple] forever' [1 Kgs 9: 3], and has it not already been said, 'the eyes of the Lord, they go to and fro over the entire earth' [Zech. 4: 10], and it says, 'the eyes of the Lord are in every place, keeping watch upon the wicked and the good' [Prov. 15: 3]? Why does Scripture say, 'my eyes and my heart will be there forever'? It is as if it could be said that I have no eyes or heart except for there.[35]

Although I am principally interested in rabbinic views on God's perfection and how they bear on the topics of universal and particular truth, the above passage makes clear that these themes are not alien to the Bible. One remarkable feature of this text and others like it is the effort to hold together the most extreme universal truths along with equally extreme truths particular to the Jewish people. While reflection on monotheism and divine perfection necessarily leads to the embrace of universalistic truths, there is wide latitude in how those truths are conceptualized. Whereas in the quotes from Mendelssohn with which I began the particular cannot take priority over the universal, the above passage from *Sifrei Deuteronomy* defends the alternative position that the universal is sustained on account of the particular. Leaving aside for the moment the contentious issue of priority, I will argue in my concluding remarks that I think we still have much to learn from the rabbis' expansive vision of a God who must be the God of all while remaining the God of the particular. For the moment, what I would like to direct the reader's attention to is the specific theological motifs that the passage draws together. The verses from Job in section 1 reflect a notion we have already seen—that God's providential care extends to all through God's sustaining of the natural order. The regularity and the universality of the natural order make it a compelling symbol to express God's providential care of all of creation. The claim that God extends divine care to the world on account of Israel does not, again, diminish God's relationship to the rest of the created order. Section 2 utilizes Scripture to argue that God is ever attentive and protecting. Section 3 extends this argument in a direction I would like to explore further. Here, utilizing the claims of Scripture, the text asserts that God has eyes that see all of creation. The text concludes differently than the previous comments. Whereas in the

---

[35] *Sifre on Deuteronomy*, piska 40, 80.

earlier sections God cares for and protects the world because he cares for and protects Israel, in the concluding section it seems that God's eyes and heart are only properly spoken of in the context of the 'there' of 1 Kings 9: 3, which is, of course, Solomon's Temple. How does the anonymous tradent understand the implications of this claim? Does God no longer see, or feel for, the Israelites with the destruction of the Temple? Is a more optimistic reading possible in which the 'there' of 1 Kings 9: 3 is a synecdoche for the land or perhaps for the people who worship in the Temple? In fact, the passage has one additional section that I have held back and which reads:

[4] Similar to this you say, 'The voice of the Lord shakes the wilderness; the voice of the Lord shakes the wilderness of Kadesh' [Ps. 29: 8]. Why does Scripture say this? It means in this case it is particularly so.

This final section serves to soften the previous claim that one can only speak of God's eyes and heart in the context of the Temple. If we accept the suggestion that a similarity links the two midrashic comments, that would imply that God's eyes and heart were particularly focused on the Temple, not that they are restricted to that locale or to whatever it might symbolize. As I will discuss shortly, God's eye remains a central motif in the rabbis' efforts to affirm God's perfection and to negotiate the tension between the universal truths that bear on creation in its entirety and the truth that is particular to the Jewish people.

Before giving fuller consideration to God's eye, I would like to address the rabbis' comments on a natural phenomenon that tie together many of the points I have already covered. At the end of the *Mekhilta of Rabbi Ishmael*, 'Bahodesh', par. 9, there are several comments that seek to reconcile Exodus 20: 18—'you have seen that I have spoken with you from heaven'—and Exodus 19: 20—'And the Lord came down upon Mount Sinai'. The passage offers three solutions from Rabbi Ishmael, Rabbi Akiva, and Rabbi Judah. Rabbi Ishmael and Rabbi Akiva both appeal to a third verse to answer the apparent contradiction. In Rabbi Ishmael's case God's voice is in heaven but God's fire is on the earth (Deut. 4: 36), and Rabbi Akiva suggests that God bent the heavens down to Mount Sinai (Ps. 18: 10). It is Rabbi Judah's solution that bears on the current discussion:

Rabbi [Judah] says: 'And the Lord came down upon Mount Sinai, to the top of the mountain. The Lord called Moses to the top of the mountain and Moses went up' [Exod. 19: 20]. I might understand this according to its ordinary sense; however, you must say that just as one of the many servants [i.e. the sun] enters into its place but is not restricted to its place, how much more so is this true of the glory of the One Who Spoke and the World Was?[36]

Although there is a poetic quality to Rabbi Judah's dictum in his play of words (servant = *shamash* and sun = *shemesh*), his point is clear: just as the sun is mobile (in rabbinic cosmology) and can exert its power from afar, so too must this be the case with God. Rabbi Judah's comment is evidence for the fact that, among the rabbis, there was a genuine interest in the question of divine perfection and that their thoughts on this matter were not limited to what they could derive from Scripture. In this case, the natural order tells us how to think about God. This reading finds support further on in *Mekhilta of Rabbi Ishmael*, 'Nezikin', par. 13. Here, the discussion is halakhic in nature and deals with Exodus 22: 1–2: 'If a thief is found in the midst of breaking in and he is struck and he dies, there is no blood guilt. If the sun has risen upon him, there is blood guilt.' The *Mekhilta* comments:

'If the sun has risen upon him': [Rabbi Ishmael says,] Has the sun risen upon him alone? Is it not the case that it has risen upon the entire world? Rather, what this means is that just as the sun represents peace in the world, so if it is known [that the thief] is peaceful but he killed him [anyway], he is surely guilty.[37]

The parallel to this passage in *Sifrei Deuteronomy* suggests that this is one of the few passages in which Rabbi Ishmael interpreted the Torah parabolically.[38] While there is a figurative element to his comment in that the sun is taken as a symbol for peace, the point I wish to accentuate is that the natural order is a source of theological and halakhic thinking for the rabbis that is closely tied to their ideas of God's perfection and their notion of truth.

These two ideas, that God can exert divine power from afar and that the sun shines on all, come together in a third text, in BT *Sanhedrin* 39a. In a passage that purports to be a dialogue between the Roman emperor and Rabban Gamaliel, we find the following:

The emperor said to Rabban Gamaliel: 'You claim that the Shekhinah dwells in every place where there are ten people. How many Shekhinahs are there?' He summoned his servant and struck him with a ladle [Rashi: on his neck]. He said to him: 'Why does the sun shine in the emperor's house?' He said to him: 'The sun rests upon the entire world.' [Rabban Gamaliel said:] 'Just as the sun, which is one of the countless myriads of servants before the Holy One, blessed be He, rests on

---

[36] 'Masekhta debaḥodesh', 9 (HR, 238; Lauterbach, ii. 343).
[37] 'Masekhta denezikin', 13 (HR, 293; Lauterbach, ii. 426). Cf. Tosefta *San.* 11: 9.
[38] *Sifre on Deuteronomy*, piska 237, 269.

the entire world, how much more so should the Shekhinah of the Holy One, blessed be He?'

The basic assumption of this text is both simple and common: surely God must possess all the perfections that are manifest in God's creation.[39] Like the sun, which shines upon the entire world, so too must God's presence be ubiquitous throughout the world. The text bears within it in surprising ways the tension between universal and particular truths. In the passage, it is the emperor who makes a particularistic claim about Judaism by questioning the view that the divine presence manifests wherever ten people are gathered. One might wonder how particularistic the rabbis actually are if they can imagine the emperor as a good student of their teachings and who is knowledgeable about the conditions for the manifestation of the divine presence (cf. *Avot* 3: 6). Even more remarkable, while the emperor begins from the particularistic claim about God's presence in the *minyan*, the quorum of ten necessary for public prayer, Rabban Gamaliel's reply appeals to the universal truth that God's presence rests on the entire world.

To home in on the relationship between universal and particular truths in rabbinic thought, I would like to shift back to the symbol of God's eye. To be sure, there is a similar phenomenology between the sun, which illuminates the entire world, and God's eye, which sees all. That God sees everything is, of course, an inherently biblical belief.[40] Jeremiah, for instance, says, 'Can a man hide himself in secret places that I will not see him?' (Jer. 23: 24). Roughly four centuries later, Ben Sirah would express the idea thus: 'The works of all are before him, and nothing can be hidden from his eyes. From the beginning to the end of time he can see everything, and nothing is too marvellous for him. No one can say, "What is this?" or "Why is that?"—for

---

[39] Along these lines, James Barr states: 'Nothing is more clear about the classic "natural theology" passages of the Bible than their starting-point in creation. God created the world and its wonderful and beneficent design should have demonstrated the reality of the creator' (*Biblical Faith and Natural Theology*, 147).

[40] According to Josephus, the belief that God oversees all of creation was universally held by ancient Jews. In *Against Apion*, he states that 'Among us alone one will hear no contradictory statements about God, such as is common among others—and not just what is spoken by ordinary people as the emotion grips them individually, but also in what has been boldly pronounced among certain philosophers, some of whom have attempted to do away with the very existence of God by their arguments, while others eliminate his providence on behalf of humankind. Nor will one see any difference in our living-habits; we all share common practices, and all make the same affirmation about God, in harmony with the law, that he watches over everything.' Flavius Josephus, *Against Apion*, trans. John M. G. Barclay, ed. Steve Mason (Leiden: Brill, 2007), 2: 180–1, pp. 271–2.

everything has been created for its own purpose' (Ben Sirah 39: 19–21, NRSV). A similar position is attributed to Rabbi Akiva in *Avot* 3: 16, although he avoids the determinism that threatens Ben Sirah's position: 'Everything is seen and authority is given, and according to the good will the world be judged, and everything is according to the abundance of action.' This is, of course, not all that *Avot* has to say about God's vision. Rabbi Judah's comment in 2: 1 concludes: 'Know what is above you: a seeing eye, a hearing ear, and all your actions written in a book.' The *Mekhilta of Rabbi Ishmael* also makes such claims about God's ability to see all human actions. In one case, Rabbi Yohanan ben Zakai addresses the difference between thieves and robbers. His opprobrium towards the thief is greater, as the thief thinks it sufficient to conceal his actions from other people. He says: 'The thief acts as if the eye above is not able to see and the ear is not able to hear.'[41] As we saw with Mendelssohn and Rosenzweig, divine perfection ineluctably shapes rabbinic conceptions of God and the Divine–human relationship.

Just as the sun is perfect in illuminating the entire world, God's all-seeing eye is a theological motif that expresses God's perfect knowledge of creation. The rabbis, however, do not restrict their reflections on God's eye to the subject of divine perfection and the universal providence that entails. They also utilize the image as a powerful symbol of God's relationality in all of its particularity. In this case, scarcely any exegetical work is required on the rabbis' part as Scripture makes explicit reference to Israel as the apple or pupil of God's eye, for example in Zechariah 2: 12, where it says, 'For the one who strikes against you strikes against the apple of his eye.' In the *Mekhilta of Rabbi Ishmael*, Rabbi Judah says: 'It does not say "against the eye"; rather, "against His eye" is written. As if it were possible, this refers to the One above. However, Scripture modifies the expression.'[42] Rabbi Judah reads Zechariah 2: 12 on the strongest possible terms: to harm Israel is to harm God's eye. What is it about Israel that makes it so precious to God? We have a telling hint from Rabbi Judah when he comments, further on in the *Mekhilta*, on Deuteronomy 32: 10, a verse that also envisions Israel as the pupil of God's eye. Here, however, Rabbi Judah infuses Scripture with an alternative meaning. His comment comes amidst a discussion of the giving of Torah at Mount Sinai.

'And all the people saw the thunder and the lightning' [Exod. 20: 15]. Thunder of

---

[41] 'Masekhta denezikin', 15 (HR, 299; Lauterbach, ii. 436). A similar claim is made about the adulterer in *Numbers Rabbah*, 9: 1.

[42] 'Masekhta deshirata', 6 (HR, 135; Lauterbach, i. 196).

thundering upon thundering, and lightning of lightning upon lightning. And how much thunderings and lightnings were there? Rather, this means that they caused each person to hear according to his ability, as it is said, 'the thunder of the Lord according to strength' [Ps. 29: 4, rendered midrashically]. Rabbi [Judah] says, 'This is to make known the excellence of Israel, for when they all stood before Mount Sinai to receive the Torah, they would hear a word and they would interpret it. This is as it is said, 'he surrounded it, he considered it well; he guarded it like the pupil of his eye' [Deut. 32: 10]. As soon as the word went forth they would interpret it.[43]

While in its biblical context Deuteronomy 32: 10 claims that Israel is the pupil of God's eye, Rabbi Judah radically transforms the meaning of the verse such that it now speaks about the manner in which Israel received the Torah at Mount Sinai. Israel, according to this reading, cherished the Torah and lovingly interpreted each and every word as it proceeded from God's mouth.[44] *Sifrei Deuteronomy* goes further:

'He considered it well' [Deut. 32: 10]: This is with respect to the Ten Commandments. This teaches that as the word was going forth from the mouth of the Holy One, blessed be He, Israel saw it, considered it, and knew how much Midrash is in it, how much halakhah is in it, how many a fortiori arguments are in it, and how many legal analogies are in it.[45]

According to these texts, the Israelites received the Torah at Mount Sinai as if they were all disciples of the Sages. Given the growing consensus among scholars that, for many generations, the rabbinic movement was both small and insular, this is truly a utopian vision.[46] On the above readings, Israel is the pupil of God's eye, and the pupil of Israel's eye is the Torah. The message that lies just beneath the surface is that being a pupil of the Torah makes one the pupil of God's eye. While at the time the rabbis could do little else but fantasize about an Israel fashioned in their own image, the hope that the Jewish people would cherish the Torah is deeply biblical. As Proverbs 7: 12 states, 'Keep my commandments and live, and my Torah as the pupil of your eye.'

---

[43] 'Masekhta debaḥodesh', 9 (HR, 235; Lauterbach, ii. 338). Here I am quoting from Lauterbach's text.

[44] Note that the particularistic claim about Israel's immediate interpretation of the Torah is preceded by a claim about divine perfection in God's ability to speak according to the capacity of each individual Israelite.

[45] *Sifre on Deuteronomy*, piska 313, 355.

[46] For an account of the social formation of the early rabbinic movement, see Catherine Hezser, *The Social Structure of the Rabbinic Movement in Roman Palestine* (Tübingen: Mohr Siebeck, 1997). On the Mishnah as a utopian document see Jacob Neusner's introduction in *The Mishnah: A New Translation* (New Haven: Yale University Press, 1988), pp. xiii–xlii.

All these texts reflect the belief that God has an abiding connection to the Jewish people through their nurturing of the Divine–human relationship via their study of the Torah and observance of the commandments.[47]

In an effort to harmonize the rabbinic interests in universal and particular truths, I would like to juxtapose two additional passages from the *Mekhilta of Rabbi Ishmael*. The first text relates a visit to Rabbi Eliezer as he lay sick.

> It happened that Rabbi Eliezer was ill. Four elders entered to visit him: Rabbi Tarfon, Rabbi Joshua, Rabbi Eleazar ben Azaryah, and Rabbi Akiva. Rabbi Tarfon was called upon and he said: 'My rabbi, you are greater for Israel than the orb of the sun, since the orb of the sun illuminates this world but you have illuminated for us this world and the world to come.'[48]

However helpful God's perfection might be for thinking about God and the Divine–human relationship, the primacy of Torah, both oral and written, remains secure. Furthermore, if Torah is a possession of the Jewish people, it is not one that can be deposited. On the contrary, Torah requires constant engagement, even upon one's sickbed. The text I would like to read alongside this one is a commentary on Exodus 19: 5, which states: 'Now, if you will hearken to my voice and guard my covenant, you shall be for me a treasure among all the peoples, for all the earth is mine.'

> 'And you shall be for me': This means that you will be turned to me and engaged in Torah and you will not be engaged in the words of others. 'The most beloved treasure': Just as a person's treasure is beloved to him, so you will be beloved to me. Rabbi Joshua ben Korha says, 'It is [said] in order to break open the ear. Just as a woman treasures what is from her husband, and a son what is from his father, and a slave what is from his master, and a handmaid what is from her mistress, is it possible that you were given to me as a keepsake by others? Scripture says, "for all the earth is mine"' [Exod. 19: 5].[49]

Rabbi Joshua ben Korha offers a stern warning not to take too seriously the idea that the Jews are God's treasured people. Divine perfection places a necessary limit on what we can say about the status of the Jewish people before God. In the end, the only being worthy of worship is the God who is

---

[47] I speak here of both the Divine–human relationship and the Torah as that which distinguishes the Jewish people because in some passages Abraham is depicted as the pupil of God's eye (*Sifre on Deuteronomy*, piska 313, 355) and as the 'orb of the eye of the world' (*Leviticus Rabbah*, 11: 7).   [48] 'Masekhta debaḥodesh', 10 (HR, 240; Lauterbach, ii. 347).
[49] Ibid. 2 (HR, 208; Lauterbach, ii. 297).

God of all, a position echoed in the comments of Mendelssohn and Rosenzweig. While language such as 'treasured people' might best be understood as figurative, it does, in Rabbi Joshua ben Korha's words, serve 'to break open the ear'. It may not ultimately be true, but it awakens the practitioner's consciousness and orients him or her to God. Even given Rabbi Joshua ben Korha's concern about the limits of our theological language, it is difficult to imagine that he would object to the idea that precedes his comment and according to which dedication to Torah and devotion to God are one and the same. It is that dynamic that I would like to address in my concluding remarks.

Conclusion

Since the inception of Wissenschaft des Judentums in the nineteenth century, it has been a common refrain that the rabbis privileged halakhah over aggadah, and that whatever theology they did produce was intended to edify the laity and not as serious theological enquiry. This view is problematic for many reasons, but its most devastating consequence is that it conceals from us the resources for contemporary theological reflection.[50] Living in the twenty-first century, one can imagine that our world is more diverse and that our faith is more challenged by the surrounding culture than was the case for earlier generations. This, I believe, is a trick of our historical imagination. The scope of our historical vision has a tendency to narrow the further it goes back, and as a result we imagine a past that is more uniform and more secure than is likely the case. The fact is that Jews have never lived in isolation and we have always given serious and thoughtful consideration to what it means that our God is the God of all. Our ancestors would have been poor monotheists had they not been concerned about these issues. Once we acknowledge this fact, we can begin to assess whether the solutions the tradition has bequeathed to us remain viable. While the texts I have laid out are but a fraction of the relevant material within the rabbinic corpus, still I would argue that these positions offer a fruitful way forward. Like Mendelssohn and Rosenzweig, I think we should join the earlier Jewish tradition and use divine perfection as a resource for understanding God and the Divine–human relationship.[51] To forgo reflection on divine perfection because it seems metaphysical (it is), or because it allows positive knowledge of God, would be to

---

[50] See Fisher, *Contemplative Nation*, 1–20; id., 'Beyond the Homiletical', 199–236.

[51] On Rosenzweig's use of divine perfection see Fisher, 'Divine Perfections at the Center of the *Star*'; id., 'Speaking Metaphysically of a Metaphysical God'.

abandon one of our most productive sources for thinking and speaking about God. As I have tried to show, Judaism has a rich and long tradition of thinking about God's perfection. If contemporary Jewish theology must depart from the tradition on this point, the onus is on those who hold such a view to make the case.[52] At every stage of the tradition, one can find the idea of divine perfection doing crucial theological work, sometimes explicitly and sometimes implicitly. Even arguments that seek to curtail theological language by appealing to God's transcendence rely on divine perfection to make their case. Whether one wants to deploy divine perfection positively or negatively, the fundamental idea of God's greatness seems to be here to stay. Although divine perfection commits us to the belief that God is the God of all, that should not deter us from reflecting on our individual and communal relationship to God. As Rosenzweig suggests, we have little alternative:

The truth counts as God's truth for me only when I make it my own in the Truly. What is it then that I can make my own? Only that which was imparted to me in my inner Here and Now. Whether that be the 'whole' truth is of no concern to me. It is enough that it was im-parted to me. It became my part. I can discover that God is truth only in the sense which we have now established, as origin of truth, by discovering that he is 'my part', 'the portion of my cup on the day that I call upon him'.[53]

Rosenzweig holds that the truth in its entirety is strictly God's possession. Our task is to affirm and embrace the portion of truth that has been allotted to us. For Rosenzweig, the limits of human cognition mean that a vision of divine truth is something we can aspire to only after death.[54]

In seeking to draw attention to the place of universal and particular truths in rabbinic theology, I bracketed the question of the nations' access to salvific knowledge. While this is not a gap to be perfunctorily filled in amidst concluding remarks, it is possible to return to Mendelssohn's and Rosenzweig's comments that initiated my discussion in light of the analysis that ensued. As compelling as the theological and philosophical concerns are that motivate Mendelssohn's rejection of revealed truth, I suspect that, among the religiously minded, there are few contemporary proponents of the idea

---

[52] Numerous Jewish philosophers and theologians have argued for a Wittgensteinian approach to religious language that makes no theoretical claims about God—a position that would undermine claims about divine perfection and much else. For my response to these arguments see Cass Fisher, 'The Posthumous Conversion of Ludwig Wittgenstein and the Future of Jewish (Anti-)Theology', *AJS Review*, 39/2 (2015), 333–65.

[53] Rosenzweig, *Der Mensch und sein Werk: Gesammelte Schriften*, ii. 437; id., *The Star of Redemption*, trans. William Hallo (New York: Holt, Rinehart, and Winston, 1970), 393.

[54] *Der Mensch und sein Werk: Gesammelte Schriften*, ii. 462; *The Star of Redemption*, 416.

that reason by itself is a sufficient source for redemptive knowledge. Reason, particularly in its scientific and technological deployments, has been a source of incalculable good in contemporary society, but so far it has demonstrated little facility for spurring the spiritual and ethical perfection of humans. While Rosenzweig shared Mendelssohn's view that a perfect God must be the God of all, he also sought to preserve divine relationality and its expression in personal and communal revelation. How did he manage these conflicting commitments from the perspective of religious pluralism? While he came to a position that was more ecumenical than that of many thinkers who preceded him, his account of the other world religions hardly qualifies him as a pluralist in any meaningful sense. The configuration of Rosenzweig's star of redemption has Judaism at its centre, living a redeemed life outside history in the company of the eternal, and Christianity functioning as the rays of the star preparing the way for the kingdom of God. Not only does Rosenzweig ascribe significantly different roles in redemption to Judaism and Christianity, as any reader of the *Star* quickly discovers, Islam and Eastern religions serve as foils and don't figure in his vision of redemption. Between Mendelssohn's defence of God's perfection and the power of human reason and Rosenzweig's construction of a philosophical system based on Jewish particularity lies a wide range of philosophical and theological alternatives. The direction one moves in along the continuum plotted by these positions will, to a large measure, be determined by how one conceives of divine perfection. Mendelssohn and Rosenzweig were right to call our attention to that fact, and we should assume the responsibility of furthering their efforts.

As Rosenzweig points out, ultimate truth is God's possession and thus something for which we can only hope and wait. In the meantime the rabbis offer a model of striving after an ever more adequate understanding of God's perfection and relationality. We would do well to emulate the recursive nature of their reflections, constantly going back and drawing the line more finely. Similarly, like the *paytanim* (liturgical poets), we should have mouths and hearts filled with the tension between God's perfection in its most universal expressions and the preciousness of our own place before God. In the end, we have little alternative but to follow Rabbi Joshua ben Korha and Rosenzweig, and allow a theological humility tempered by divine perfection to serve as that which forever binds the universal and particular truths that are central to the idea of monotheism and its unfolding in the Jewish tradition.

CHAPTER FOUR

Da'at
Universalizing a Hasidic Value

AVRAHAM YIZHAK (ARTHUR) GREEN

Seeking Universal Truth in Particularist Sources

Each of the three great religions of the Western tradition is based upon a narrative that stands at the centre of its faith. For Judaism, it is the Exodus from Egypt and the receiving of Torah at Mount Sinai; for Christianity, the crucifixion and resurrection of Jesus Christ; for Islam, the *hijra* and the revelation to Muhammad. Each sees its own narrative as standing at the centre of human history as the 'greatest story ever told', and its truth (however that term is conceived) is vital to all the faithful. Each of these faiths also bears a long history of more abstract theological truth claims, involving such issues as the unity (or trinity) of God, providence, divine authority for the rule of law, the importance of good works, and so forth. In these, the traditions may be shown to have much in common with one another, making for interesting conversation across religious lines. But the core narratives seem to stand in eternal competition with one another, and it is in their utter loyalty to them that the faiths and their faithful remain most deeply divided.

Much of contemporary interfaith dialogue takes place around the more commonly shared issues of moral teaching. There the well-intentioned participants often feel they are on safer ground. On these matters, there may be differences in style and formulation, but the essential claims are very close. Questions of theology, especially around the sacred narratives, are much more challenging, and are thus thought best avoided. The problem is that this often leaves these noble attempts at dialogue quite far from the place where the core communities of the faithful pitch their tent. Their faith lies precisely in the narrative core of their respective traditions, and it is from devotion to these events that the spiritual life gains its inspiration.

On the face of things, this is true of the mystics within our traditions as well. Mysticism develops at the very heart of a particular tradition, among devotees who come to know and love God through the particular tales and beliefs which constitute that tradition's core, as well as through the practices embodying them. But, living deep within the tradition, these mystics may feel little need to defend the narratives, which are assumed to be true on the historical plane. They are more interested in penetrating into them, searching for deeper meanings and eternal truths. For them, the narratives are highly spiritualized, and devotion to them is completely intertwined with their reassignment as part of a quest for oneness that transcends all symbols and unites all of being. It is only the scholar of religion, examining the mystics' teachings in ways that would be unfamiliar to them, who seeks to distinguish between what appear through the scholarly lens to be distinct strands of thought: utter devotion to the particular truth of a tradition and an opening to a soaring sense of oneness that reaches infinitely beyond it.

Here I would like to examine the thought of one such mystical figure within Judaism, a spiritual teacher who understands the unity of all being, yet comes to it through the path of hasidism, the very heart of Jewish pietism, which was originally completely exclusivist in its religious claims. It is from this unlikely source that I seek insights that might be helpful in moving our contemporary theological and interreligious conversation towards a deeper level of communion. I say from the outset that the contemporary hasidic faithful, in the unlikely event that they might come upon an essay like this, would be surprised, even dismayed, to see me using 'their own' hasidic writings in a theological setting with which they would be quite unfamiliar. But this does not deter me. I stand in a tradition called neo-hasidism,[1] itself now reaching back more than a century, in which scholars and teachers have drawn freely on the hasidic sources, standing on their foundation and building upon them as we do with all the prior generations of traditional Jewish wisdom. We neo-hasidic scholars are non-literalist when it comes to the wisdom we have gained from the original hasidic masters. That is to say that it is not of vital import to us whether a particular encounter recorded in a hasidic tale happened just as told or not; the import lies in the wisdom learned from it. Once we have learned that our faith can survive such non-literalism regarding the hasidic masters, we are willing to apply it to earlier sources as well.

The key hasidic writings were composed in eastern Europe, beginning in the last quarter of the eighteenth century. Although historians rightly con-

---

[1] On neo-hasidism see Arthur Green and Ariel Evan Mayse (eds.), *A New Hasidism*, 2 vols. (Philadelphia: Jewish Publication Society, 2019).

sider hasidism to belong to the early modern period of Jewish history,[2] the creators of the movement saw themselves as standing completely within the ancient rabbinic tradition, and were entirely faithful to the claims of both halakhah and aggadah. They did assert the right of each generation to interpret the tradition anew, but in doing so they remained highly conservative regarding praxis, while taking much greater risks in theological formulations.[3]

These sources take it for granted that the pursuit of serious spiritual life is something that belongs to Jews alone. While they were composed in a region that was rife with intense Eastern Christian piety, including monasticism, the religious, cultural, and linguistic walls separating Jews from Christians were so high that we have found no evidence of any attempt or ability to peer across them.[4] Eastern European Jewry of this period lived in spiritually splendid—and materially not so splendid—isolation. A neo-hasidic reading of them will necessarily have to expand and universalize their teachings, and that is fully my intent here. But first we will need to examine the sources and try to achieve an understanding of them in their own context.

The particular hasidic work under consideration here is the collection of homilies entitled *Me'or einayim*, 'The Light of the Eyes', authored by R. Menahem Nahum of Chernobyl (1729/30–1797) and first published in Slavuta, Ukraine, in 1798. The author was the paterfamilias of the many hasidic dynasties with the family name Twersky; these dominated much of Ukrainian Jewish life in the nineteenth century and continue to play a major role in

---

[2] A full history of hasidism, long a desideratum of Judaic scholarship, is David Biale (ed.), *Hasidism: A New History* (Princeton, NJ: Princeton University Press, 2018).

[3] See my treatment of this theme in my 'Hasidism and Its Response to Change', *Jewish History*, 27/2–4 (Dec. 2013), 319–36. On halakhah within the hasidic world, see Maoz Kahana and Ariel Evan Mayse, 'Hasidic *Halakhah*: Reappraising the Interface of Spirit and Law', *AJS Review*, 41/2 (Nov. 2017), 375–408. On hasidic 'risk-taking' in the theological realm, see Arthur Green, 'Hasidism: Discovery and Retreat', in Peter Berger (ed.), *The Other Side of God* (New York: Anchor Books, 1981), repr. in Arthur Green, *The Heart of the Matter* (Philadelphia: Jewish Publication Society, 2015). These and other essays of mine are available electronically on my website, <artgreen26.com>.

[4] Several attempts have been made to trace such cross-cultural influence, but they remain quite unspecific in their conclusions. These include T. Ysander's *Studien zum Bestschan Hasidismus* (Uppsala, 1933), Yaffa Eliach's 'The Russian Dissenting Sects and their Influence on R. Israel Ba'al Shem Tov, Founder of Hasidism', *PAAJR*, 36 (1963), 57–83 (roundly denounced by Gershom Scholem), and most recently Igor Tourov, 'Hasidism and Christianity of the Eastern Territory of the Polish–Lithuanian Commonwealth: Possible of [sic] Contacts and Mutual Influences', *Kabbalah*, 10 (2004), 73–105. See also several studies that touch on this matter in Glenn Dynner (ed.), *Holy Dissent: Jewish and Christian Mystics in Eastern Europe* (Detroit: Wayne State University Press, 2011).

the transplanted hasidic communities of today. He is considered a disciple of both the Ba'al Shem Tov (the Besht) and the Magid of Mezhirech (Miedzyrzecz), the key founding figures of hasidism, but several of his theological views and attitudes hew most faithfully to the original teachings and attitudes of the Besht.[5] Like nearly all the early theoretical works of hasidism, the *Me'or einayim* is a collection of homilies on the weekly Torah portions, with various addenda. These were originally oral sermons preached in Yiddish.[6] The Hebrew text is a digest of the homilies, prepared for publication by a disciple, in this case R. Elijah Katz of Yurewicz.

The theology emerging from these hasidic sermons weaves together the highly personalist faith of classical rabbinic Judaism, where God is mostly depicted as Father and King, with a strong thrust of mystical panentheism. The mysterious and transcendent God is present and needs to be discovered everywhere, in each moment and in every deed. Hasidic teaching has about it a sense of devotional adventure, a mission of seeking out sparks of holiness throughout the world. While each soul's spiritual journey is unique, many may be inspired by the teachings and personal example of the righteous, the *tsadikim*, themselves the speakers of these sermons.[7] For our author, as for all the original hasidic masters, this teaching applied exclusively to the deeds of Jews. But I say again, in the neo-hasidic spirit, that our goal is to apply the teaching universally. Our licence to do so, I would claim, lies within the very panentheistic language of the hasidic sources. If God is indeed everywhere, as they constantly insist, God cannot be absent from the consciousness—and even the religious praxis—of most of humanity.

---

[5] I am currently completing an annotated translation of the *Me'or einayim*, forthcoming from Stanford University Press. For a detailed consideration of R. Menahem Nahum's place amid the teachings of his two masters, see the introduction to that volume.

[6] For discussion of the process from Yiddish oral sermon to printed Hebrew text, see my 'The Hasidic Homily: Mystical Performance and Hermeneutical Process', in Bentsi Cohen (ed.), *As a Perennial Spring: A Festschrift Honoring Rabbi Dr. Norman Lamm* (New York: Downhill, 2015), 237–65. Further detailed discussion is found in several works by Ze'ev Gries, including *The Book in Early Hasidism* [Hasefer bereshit haḥasidut] (Tel Aviv: Hakibuts Hame'uhad, 1992).

[7] A fuller account of early hasidic theology is to be found in the introduction to my *Speaking Torah: Teachings from Around the Maggid's Table* (Woodstock, Vt.: Jewish Lights, 2013), 28–59. A book-length study of these themes is Rivka Schatz-Uffenheimer, *Hasidism as Mysticism: Quietistic Elements in Eighteenth-Century Hasidic Thought* (Princeton, NJ: Princeton University Press, 2015).

The Language of Religious Awareness

In the *Me'or einayim*, the key term for describing this quest for God is *da'at*, the word that lies at the heart of our investigation here as well. *Da'at* is a nominal form of the verb stem *y-d-'*, usually translated 'to know', hence, 'knowledge'. Its use in a theological context (and this is true for much of Judaism's religious vocabulary) is rooted in the biblical book of Deuteronomy, the last of the five books that constitute the Torah: 'You have been shown to know' (4: 35); 'Know this day and set it upon your heart that Y-H-V-H is God' (4: 39); 'Y-H-V-H has not given you a heart to know, nor eyes to see, nor ears to hear, until this day' (29: 3). The later, much-quoted 'Know the God of your father and serve Him' (1 Chr. 28: 9) implies that worship requires prior 'knowledge' of God. The biblical usage of *y-d-'* in these contexts connotes a faithful awareness of divine presence and causality. This is not mere intellectual knowledge. It is our witness to the divine hand in the events of history, especially in the lot of Israel, that is the object of such *da'at*. But the verb also carries along with it a sense of intimate knowledge, recalling its use also with regard to carnal knowing: 'Adam knew his wife Eve' (Gen. 4: 1).[8]

Theology, or a self-conscious reflection on what this *da'at elohim* ('knowledge of God') might mean, was not a major preoccupation in the formative centuries of rabbinic Judaism. As is well known, the rabbinic community constituted and defined itself around halakhah, or a path of praxis, rather than around fine points of theological distinction. The theology that did flourish was largely in the narrative and homiletical modes, deepening the power of the Exodus-Sinai narrative, along with certain other key episodes of biblical history—Creation, the patriarchs, the wilderness Tabernacle, Solomon's Temple, destruction, and exile. These became the tropes around which the midrashic imagination was spun. To be sure, the rabbis had robust debates about these narratives, conversations that were filled with theological content. But they treated the diversion of views on them with much latitude, seeing little need to resolve or restrain them.[9]

---

[8] This linkage is made explicit in many passages of the *Me'or einayim*, including 'Devarim', p. 298 (all page references are to *Me'or einayim*, 2 vols., ed. Y. S. Oesterreicher (Jerusalem, 2012). See below. The association of religious awareness with sexual intimacy tempts one to seek in the kabbalistic and hasidic world-view a parallel to kundalini yoga in Indian tradition, but we have no indication that such praxis ever existed among the Jewish mystics. The exclusion of women from the study and knowledge of the esoteric tradition was quite total, meaning that it was essentially fantasy and longing for this perfect union that motivated the male devotees, rather than physical experience.

[9] There is a vast scholarly literature on the theology of the aggadah, opening with Solomon Schechter's *Aspects of Rabbinic Theology: Major Concepts of the Talmud* (London, 1901), and

As Jews became exposed to Graeco-Arabic thought, beginning in the tenth century CE, *da'at elohim* was given new prominence and a new meaning. Was it permitted, the rabbis of that era asked, to engage in theological enquiry, discussing the most intimate of religious matters,[10] according to methods and assumptions put forth by non-Jews? They, after all, had not received revelation as we had; they had no 'chain of tradition' that took them back to an authentic experience of the Deity. What was there to learn from the methods, first of the Muslim Kalam and later of the Neoplatonists and especially of the Aristotelians, who put forth logical arguments that seemed totally cut off from the claims of biblical and rabbinic tradition?

The response of Jewish philosophers (themselves leading rabbis in many cases) over the course of five centuries was quite vigorous.[11] True knowledge of God was required for proper worship.[12] Such knowledge could be best acquired through philosophical reasoning, allowing one a pure and true notion of the Deity, especially one freed of any accretions that might be remnants of a pagan conception. Based upon some key biblical passages that spoke of the Divine as being without image (Isa. 40: 18, 25; 46: 5), and building upon the aniconic tradition embodied in halakhah, they offered reason

including E. E. Urbach's monumental *The Sages: Their Concepts and Beliefs*, trans. Israel Abrahams (Jerusalem: Magnes Press, 1975). Most significant to this reader is Abraham J. Heschel's *Torah min hashamayim*, translated as *Heavenly Torah, as Refracted through the Generations*, trans. and ed. Gordon Tucker (New York: Continuum, 2006), an eye-opening guide to discovering the theological underpinnings of countless debates on seemingly small narrative points within the rabbinic corpus. Although Heschel's attempt to divide all of rabbinic thought into two overarching schools is to be treated with caution, his ability to uncover the theological underpinnings of narrative discussion remains unparalleled.

[10] Metaphysics would inevitably lead one into the realms of *ma'aseh bereshit* and *ma'aseh merkavah*, cosmogony and theosophy, described already in Mishnah Ḥagigah 2: 1 as esoteric subjects to be taught only to the most qualified and trusted of disciples. There is a vast literature on the meaning and later treatment of these terms. See, inter alia, David Halperin, *The Faces of the Chariot: Early Jewish Responses to Ezekiel's Vision* (Tübingen: J. C. B. Mohr, 1988), and the bibliography listed there. On the experiential basis behind the designation of these as esoteric teachings, see Nehemia Polen, 'Why Would Someone Cut Plants in Paradise? "Four Entered Pardes" in Light of 1 Enoch 6–8' (forthcoming).

[11] A classic summary is Shimon Bernfeld's *Da'at elohim* (Warsaw: Ahiasaf, 1922), although it has been superseded by several more recent surveys of medieval Jewish philosophy.

[12] This is the point of Simon Rawidowicz's important essay, 'Philosophy as a Duty', included in his *Studies in Jewish Thought*, ed. Nahum N. Glatzer (Philadelphia: Jewish Publication Society, 1974). See also Herbert A. Davidson, 'Study of Philosophy as a Religious Obligation', in S. D. Goitein (ed.), *Religion in a Religious Age* (Cambridge, Mass.: Association for Jewish Studies, 1974), 53–68.

(itself a divine gift) as a useful tool in clarifying one's own notion of God, allowing for a more refined sense of worship as well. The most influential voice of this philosophical school was Maimonides, who listed knowledge of God as first among the commandments, and who placed the *Sefer hamada*, 'Book of Knowledge' (or perhaps better 'Book of the Mind'),[13] which includes a brief outline of Jewish Aristotelian theology, at the head of his great code of Jewish practice, the *Mishneh torah*.[14]

The kabbalists, whose writings first emerged amid the anti-philosophical reaction of twelfth-century Provence and northern Spain, may nevertheless be characterized as intellectualist mystics. They reasserted the biblical link between *da'at* and two other terms for intellection, *ḥokhmah* and *binah* (or *tevunah*). Several Torah verses describing the erection of the wilderness Tabernacle speak of its construction having been carried out in *ḥokhmah*, *tevunah*, and *da'at*; Bezalel, the overseer of this project, was especially graced by God with a combination of these. (The linking of these three is reconfirmed in 1 Kings 7: 14.) It is not clear that the biblical sources really refer to distinctive functions in using the three terms together; they might simply mean 'with great skill'. But the medieval reader, ever seeking guidance from Scripture, worked to discern between them.[15]

The kabbalists now turned these terms around, seeing them not primarily as human tools with which to know God, but as descriptions of the divine mind itself. *Ḥokhmah*, *binah*, and *da'at* were elements within the mind of God, stages of progressive divine self-manifestation as the Deity emerged from utter mystery and incomprehensibility to form the personified image

---

[13] See Bernard Septimus, 'What Did Maimonides Mean by Madda'?', in Ezra Fleischer et al. (eds.), *Me'ah She'arim: Studies in Medieval Jewish Spiritual Life in Memory of Isadore Twersky* [Me'ah she'arim: iyunim be'olamam haruḥani biymei habeinayim lezekher yitsḥak tverski] (Eng. and Heb.) (Jerusalem: Magnes Press, 2001), 83–110. This very careful study suggests that the primary use of *mada* (a cognate of *da'at*) is 'cognition' (p. 87 n. 19), but that it can also be rendered as 'mind' or 'opinion', depending upon context. Cognition in Maimonides includes both rational and imaginative faculties. *Da'at* itself is less common in his writing. In standard medieval Hebrew (that of the Ibn Tibbon translators) it, or its alternative form *de'ah*, is often used for 'opinion', but Septimus claims that Maimonides generally eschews this usage.

[14] Regarding Maimonides' purpose in this, Septimus (ibid. 110) refers us to the formulation of his teacher Isadore Twersky, who spoke of it as a 'conjoining of talmudic law and philosophical spirituality'.

[15] See Rashi, Ibn Ezra, and others on Exod. 31: 3. The talmudic assertion that 'Bezalel knew the permutations of letters by which heaven and earth had been created' (BT *Ber.* 55a) stood in the background of this. The Sages understood the *ḥokhmah*, *binah*, and *da'at* attributed to him by the biblical text as pointing towards something greater than simply architectural skills.

known in biblical-rabbinic tradition. These stages or *sefirot*, always numbered ten, were the subject of endlessly refined contemplation; their unity became the chief focus of devotional intent in kabbalistic Judaism.[16]

Not all systems of kabbalah counted *da'at* among the ten. This, in fact, was a subject of much dispute among Jewish mystical teachers over many centuries.[17] For those who did, however, it came to function as a principle of linkage, drawing together the more abstract and elusive aspects of the divine self, *ḥokhmah* and *binah*, with the more vividly portrayed 'lower' aspects of divinity, depicted in imagery derived from the realms of time and space, drawn in colours of both emotion and gender. *Da'at* came to be associated with the third letter of the Tetragrammaton, *vav*. But the letter *vav* also serves as 'and' in Hebrew; thus *da'at* came to symbolize linkage or conjunction, especially between the unknowable, transcendent mystery of the Godhead and its manifestation in divine personhood. Numerically, *vav* is six. Sometimes it is taken to be the inclusive principle of the six intermediate *sefirot*, those representing the six 'days' of the cosmic 'week', or the *sefirot* ranging from *ḥesed* to *yesod*. Thus it links the mysterious God, beyond all human knowing (*ḥokhmah* and *binah*, representing divine transcendence), with *malkhut* or *shekhinah*, the 'sabbath' or fulfilment of divinity, God's kingdom as immanent within the created world.

This is the (significantly simplified) kabbalistic legacy as it was understood by the early hasidic masters. They saw themselves as heirs to the entire extended tradition; their homilies regularly drew upon canonical sources from all quarters, not distinguishing between their age or original contexts. Anything within the tradition, including occasionally even philosophical formulations that the kabbalists had opposed, was fair game, to be marshalled forth in the course of hasidic discourse. But the hasidic authors did make one very distinctive move.[18] They applied the kabbalah-enriched legacy chiefly to

---

[16] For an account of the *sefirot* and the symbols associated with them, see Isaiah Tishby and Yeruham Fishel Lachower, *Wisdom of the Zohar* (Oxford: Littman Library, 1989), i. 269–307. See also my briefer discussion in *A Guide to the Zohar* (Stanford: Stanford University Press, 2005), 28–59.

[17] For a brief introduction to this matter, see Tishby's discussion in *Wisdom of the Zohar*, i. 242–6.

[18] This is not to say that all the hasidic authors were alike in their discussions of *da'at*, any more than they were in many other matters. The treatment of *da'at* in the *Me'or einayim* very much reflects the language of the Magid, as attested by many passages in the writings directly attributed to him. In the *Toledot ya'akov yosef*, *da'at* (with the association to Gen. 4: 1) is used to invoke the relationship between the sage or preacher and his flock. He must bind himself to them in that fully immediate sense, not just in hoping that his words will influ-

the human rather than to the divine realm. Their interest was not in metaphysics, but in devotional psychology. *Da'at* was then again what it had been prior to kabbalah, an effort of the human mind. But now it had a very different quality to it than it had for Maimonides or others of the philosophical schools. *Da'at* was an awareness of God that linked one to the upper universe. It had little to do with reason. It was an aspect of the human mind that evoked and aroused the same quality that existed within God, thus becoming a mystical awareness, an opening of the human mind that permitted one to be united in oneness to the universal Self that fills the world.[19]

Reading the *Me'or Einayim*

With this background, we may begin examining a few key texts from our *Me'or einayim*. Bear in mind that we are examining this highly particularistic text seeking to pose such universal questions as 'What is the nature of the religious mind? What role does awareness have in personal liberation and in the linking of the soul to its divine source? How does the quest for *da'at* affect the way I am to live my daily life?' Our attempt here is to find in our author a person who is much concerned with these universal religious questions, despite their heavy garbing in the specifics of Judaic forms. We then might better be able to see him as a distinctive type of creative religious personality, one who might be compared and juxtaposed with parallel figures in other traditions. Let us remember to keep our focus trained on the question of what this author might be teaching us, while circumventing the obstacle of 'But his truth claim is not the same as mine!'

Our consideration of the sources will proceed in the following order. First we shall look at texts that establish the nature and object of *da'at*. Of what do we seek to become aware? Just what do we mean by awareness, and where does it lead? Next we will turn to *da'at* and its relationship to the life of devotion. How does awareness of this deeper truth shape the way we stand in God's presence and serve? Here we will look at *da'at* and its relationship to the emotional life that is so much a part of religion. That will take us onward

ence their future conduct. See Jacob Joseph of Polonnoye, *Toledot ya'akov yosef* (Jerusalem, 2011), 'Shelaḥ', iii. 906–7, and 'Vayelekh', ibid. 1343. This reflects his greater interest (compared to the Magid and R. Menahem Nahum) in the social aspect of hasidic teaching. The influence of the Magid in R. Menahem Nahum's formulation of *da'at* does not conflict with other ways, as indicated, in which he remains closer to the teachings of the Besht.

[19] In the kabbalistic mindset, 'an awakening from below' stimulates a parallel response from within God. Thus an act of human *da'at*, awareness of God, arouses *da'at* within the divine mind as well.

to the realms of joy and pleasure. Does awareness bring one to greater happiness, and how is that expressed? Following these considerations, we will come back to an examination of the *Me'or einayim* through a contemporary theological lens and ask what its author has to teach us.

We begin with one of the author's clearest statements of his mystical cosmology:

Creation took place for the sake of Torah and for the sake of Israel.[20] Its purpose was that Y-H-V-H be revealed to Israel, that we become aware and know [*yedu*, a verbal construct related to *da'at*] of His existence. Even though His true nature lies beyond our grasp, once we recognize [*yedu*] that God exists we will do everything for His sake, fulfilling 'know Him in all your ways' [*da'ehu*; Prov. 3: 6] and becoming united with Him. There is no other and there is nothing without Him! There is no place devoid of Him. 'The whole earth is filled with His glory' [Isa. 6: 3]![21]

God's glory, however, is a designation for His garments.[22] The whole earth is filled with God's garments. This aspect of divinity is called *adonay*, related to the word for 'fittings' by which the Tabernacle was held together.[23] This is God's presence as it comes down into the lower and corporeal rungs.[24] Our task is to unite it with the source from which it came, with Y-H-V-H, Who calls all the worlds into being.[25]

In all our deeds, be they study or prayer, eating or drinking, this union takes place.[26] All the worlds depend on this: the union of God within—*adonay*—with God beyond—Y-H-V-H. When these two names are woven together, the letters of each alternating with one another, the combined name *Y'HDVNHY* is formed, a

---

[20] *Genesis Rabbah*, 1: 7. Here we see the religious exclusivism assumed by sources written long before they were taken up by hasidism.

[21] The clustering of these expressions of divine unity and immanence has about it the ring of an ecstatic outcry. See the discussion of this passage in Green, 'The Hasidic Homily', 254 ff.

[22] *Tikunei zohar*, 22 (65a). The natural world as a cloak for the divine self that lies within it is a classic pantheistic formulation, widespread in Jewish mystical sources. See *Tanya*, 2: 1: 'The words and letters [spoken by God in creation] stand forever within the heavens, garbed by all the firmaments.'

[23] He is playfully deriving the divine name *adonay* not from *adon*, lord, but from *adanim*, the fittings or joints by which the Tabernacle boards were held together. The immanent God is the inner structure of the universe, just as the *adanim* were within the *mishkan* as microcosm.   [24] *Tikunei zohar*, 70 (128a).

[25] Here he returns the Tetragrammaton to its original verbal form: *hamehaveh kol havayah*.

[26] The coupling of 'study or prayer' with 'eating or drinking' is a bold, perhaps even intentionally provocative, statement of hasidic ideology. Physical acts have the same possibility of unifying the Divinity, as do prescribed acts of piety. The uplifting of the corporeal and its transformation into spirit is the very essence of devotion. See the full treatment of this idea, called by modern scholars *avodah begashmiyut*, in Zippi Kaufmann, *In All Your Ways Know Him* [*Bekhol derakheikha da'ehu*] (Ramat Gan: Bar Ilan University Press, 2009).

name that both begins and ends with the letter *yod*.²⁷ 'You have made them all in wisdom' [Ps. 104: 24], and *yod* represents that wisdom or *ḥokhmah*,²⁸ the prime matter from which all the other letters are drawn. God created the world through Torah, meaning the twenty-two letters. *Ḥokhmah* is the primal source of those letters. Just as materials are required for any creative act, which is to say all deeds derive from an original matter, so Creation itself emerges from Wisdom. Hence *ḥokhmah* is called by the Sages *hyle*,²⁹ from the words *hayah li* ('it was with Me'). All things were within Wisdom; from it they emerged from potential into real existence. Even though the *alef* is the first of the letters [and thus one might expect that it should be used to designate the first of all substances], *alef* itself is constructed of two *yods* with a diagonal *vav* between them.³⁰ That first *yod* refers to primal *ḥokhmah*, the prime matter in which all the worlds were included. The *vav* [shaped like an elongated *yod*] represents a drawing forth and descent of *da'at*,³¹ the actualization of that potential. Thus were all the worlds created, finally forming the second *yod*, called the lower *ḥokhmah* or the wisdom of Solomon. This is the aspect of *adonay*, divinity as descended below, garbed in all things, alluded to in 'the whole earth is filled with His glory'.³²

When you do all your deeds for the sake of Y-H-V-H, you draw all things in the lower world—that is, in the lower *ḥokhmah*—near to the font of the upper *ḥokhmah*, the Creator Himself, who calls all the worlds into being. By means of *da'at*, you fulfil 'know Him in all your ways'. This *da'at* is a unitive force;³³ it joins together the lower *yod* and the upper *yod*, the primal point. Then the entire universe forms one single *alef*: *yod* above, *yod* below, and *vav* between them. That is why God is called 'the cosmic *alef*'.³⁴

The passage speaks at once in terms of metaphysics and devotional psychology. Indeed, these are not separable in the classic kabbalistic world-view, where the inner movements of the devotee's soul affect the condition of the

---

²⁷ The combining of these two names as an object of meditation is a widespread practice among Lurianic kabbalists. It is found on meditation charts (*shiviti*) and is reflected in many printings of the prayer book, particularly those in use among the Sephardi communities. A reference to this formula also found its way into the *Shulḥan arukh* ('Oraḥ ḥayim', 5), the classic sixteenth-century legal code of Jewry, greatly increasing its later influence.

²⁸ i.e. the letter *yod* of the Tetragrammaton represents *ḥokhmah*; see *Tikunei zohar*, introduction, 5a.

²⁹ The author has no idea that *hyle* is a Greek word carried over into medieval Hebrew usage, and he seeks to offer a Hebrew etymology for it. Cf. Nahmanides on Gen. 1: 1.

³⁰ Zohar i. 26b. ³¹ Zohar iii. 29b.

³² Note the complete identification of *shekhinah*, or the lower *ḥokhmah*, and the lower, including the material, world.

³³ *Vav* in Hebrew also indicates 'and', the conjunction that joins one object to another. It is thus a natural bridge to bring together the upper and lower forms of *ḥokhmah*.

³⁴ *Me'or einayim*, 'Bereshit', 21 ff.

divine cosmos. The text is playing on the graphic appearance of the letter *alef*, as written in the Torah scroll or in printed Hebrew; it has the appearance (with a bit of imagination) of two *yods* connected by a diagonal *vav*. When you, the worshipper, through your devoted deeds, use your *da'at* ('mind' or 'awareness') as a contemplative *vav* or connector, drawing together the upper *yod* of the abstract and mysterious Y-H-V-H and the lower *yod* of the indwelling divine presence (*shekhinah*), you are bringing about that union on the cosmic plane as well. Human awareness is a cosmic force, one on which the worlds depend.

It is written: 'Be aware of [*da et*] your father's God and serve Him' [1 Chr. 28: 9]. Our Sages derived great matters from every *et* in the Torah.[35] Here too they derived that it is essential that worship take place with complete *da'at*. A child, who has no *da'at*, is also one 'whose sexual climax is not considered ejaculation'.[36] This means [symbolically] that the union and coupling above cannot be completed by him. 'Without *da'at*, the soul is not good' [Prov. 19: 2]. One remains a minor whose actions do not become attached to their unitive root; only a person with complete *da'at* can bring about this union and draw the upper forces together. He too then draws near and becomes attached above, along with the letters.

This is *da et*: bring *da'at* into all the letters, from *alef* to *tav*.[37] *Da'at* means union, as in 'Adam knew [*yada*] his wife Eve' [Gen. 4: 25]. This means attaching the letters to our blessed Creator, who is here called 'your father's God'. 'And serve Him': this is called complete service, that of drawing near the blessed Holy One and His *shekhinah*.[38] The letters are called a palace [*heikhal*], also to be read as *heh kol*, the five openings of the mouth, meaning speech, which 'contain all'.[39] This refers to the blessed Creator, who is called All, since He includes all. God dwells amid the letters when you speak with *da'at*. This is the 'great sign' [or 'large letter'], spoken with expanded awareness. But without such *da'at* it is considered 'small' or 'minor'. Thus said my teacher, the Besht,[40] on the verse 'Ask for a sign [*ot*] from Y-H-V-H

---

[35] BT *Pes.* 22*b*. The particle *et* here indicates the direct object to follow.

[36] BT *San.* 69*b*. He has no *da'at*, which can mean 'knowing'. This can have a sexual as well as an intellectual connotation. Here the link between the unitive power of intellectual awareness and the ability to achieve sexual union is made explicit. Maturity of mind is analogized to sexual maturity. The linkage of these is very common throughout the Jewish mystical tradition.

[37] *Et* in Hebrew is composed of the two letters *alef* and *tav*, the beginning and end of the alphabet.

[38] An understanding of R. Menahem Nahum's reading of this verse provides a good summary statement of his religious message: 'Know the God who is present within all your worldly desires, those existing in everything from *alef* to *tav*, and use that desire to draw the *shekhinah*, the lower world, into union with the blessed Holy One, the single Root of all being.'   [39] This interpretation is based on linguistic traditions rooted in *Sefer yetsirah*.

[40] Attested only here.

your God' [Isa. 7: 11]: You should supplicate the blessed Holy One that He give you a letter [*ot*], [one of the] letters that cleave to 'Y-H-V-H your God', so that you merit to link them to their Root....

We know that Torah is called 'good'; this is the 'goodly gift in My treasure-house'. That is awareness [*da'at*], the secret of Torah that is given on the sabbath. This is 'go and inform them [*hodi'am*]'; let them see to bring *da'at* into themselves [i.e. to heighten their awareness].[41] ...

This is entirely about *da'at*, as in 'with *da'at* chambers are filled' [Prov. 24: 4]. You understand with your mind that there is nothing but God, that 'His glory fills all the earth' [Isa. 6: 3] and there is no place devoid of Him. You do not budge or turn aside from this attachment; our path is that of always being present to Y-H-V-H. But the one who turns aside from Y-H-V-H and towards other gods has consciously taken God out of there [the place where he is], making it empty. Space is indeed void and empty without God's living presence, which fills all the worlds.[42]

Again we see the strong link between the sexual and contemplative meanings of *da'at*. It takes a mature mind to draw together all the letters of the alphabet, representing all of creation. Israel needs to cultivate this quality, 'to bring it into themselves'. The content of *da'at* is what we might call 'cosmic consciousness', the awareness that the world is utterly filled with divinity, and that this abundance is bound to its transcendent and mysterious source. This requires a maturity of mind, a *da'at* that can reach a state of *gadlut* rather than being trapped in *katnut*. This pair of terms plays an important role in the hasidic discussion. *Gadlut* (literally 'bigness', but derived from a usage meaning 'maturity' or 'adulthood') points to an expanded consciousness, an opening of the mind that allows us to see beyond our ordinary state of perception, to penetrate to a deeper and unitive vision of reality. *Katnut* ('smallness' or 'immaturity') is the ordinary state of mind, that in which we conduct our daily lives.[43]

This awareness carries within it a demand for self-transcendence. It is no longer the ego-self who is the significant actor on the stage of life, but rather the flow of divine blessing, which animates one in each moment. Even our devotional offerings should not be seen as gifts that we bring to God, but rather as reflections of the universal divine energy that we allow to be manifest within us.

We need to understand why the truly righteous have it fixed in their minds that they

---

[41] On the sabbath we serve as sons, having been given the ability (*da'at*) to rummage freely amid our Father's treasures.   [42] 'Ki tisa', p. 199 ff.

[43] The best discussion of these states is that of Mordechai Pachter, '*Katnut* and *Gadlut* in Lurianic Kabbalah' (Heb.), *Jerusalem Studies in Jewish Thought*, 10 (1992), 171–210.

may not ask for anything on the basis of their deeds, but only for unearned compassion. We begin with the verse: 'Do not say "It was my own strength and the power of my hand that caused me to attain all this." Remember that it is Y-H-V-H your God who gives you the strength [*ko'aḥ*] to act so powerfully' [Deut. 8: 17–18]. Onkelos renders this into Aramaic to mean: 'It is He who has given you counsel to attain these possessions.' According to this translation, the verse means that every Israelite should have faith that in all matters, physical as well as spiritual, including our livelihoods and worldly affairs, the clever counsel that comes into our minds before we act has been sent to us from the holy place above, to guide us in our path. . . .

All of this comes about only through *da'at*. Be aware that all your strength, including the power to act or to speak any word, comes about through the vitality given you from above. Without this you would not be able to move a single limb. Your speech flows into you from the World of Speech above,[44] contracted into the human mouth, as is said, 'He fixed them in the mouth.'[45] Thus Scripture says: 'O Lord, open my lips' [Ps. 51: 17]. The Ari[46] understood this to mean that it is *adonay*, the World of Speech, that speaks from within the human mouth, as we have explained at length elsewhere. This is God's *shekhinah* dwelling within us. . . .

All this takes place through the arousal from below. Having faith and awareness that the mouth of Y-H-V-H is speaking within you allows you to receive the compassion that is generated and carried forth in this way.[47]

Passages such as this—and there are many like it throughout early hasidic literature—point to a radical totalization of the classical faith in divine providence. God not only looks after us and provides for our needs; God is the real actor behind everything that takes place in the world, including actions that we, at first glance, clearly perceive to be our own. But behind this notion, which may seem to be simply an extension of a theologically orthodox claim, lies a mystically charged alternative notion of self and of the relationship between self and other. If every movement of our limbs and every word we speak is really the working of a divine force that transcends us, acting upon us from within, our own identity as a wholly separate self is deeply called into question. That is exactly as it should be. The mystic is one who does not place ultimate faith in the reality of the human self. Each person is one of the infinite variety of masks behind which the One hides itself and through which it is revealed. In hasidic parlance, our seeming individuality is the result of *tsimtsum*, in effect a divine hiding that takes place so that we will go on living

---

[44] A reference to *malkhut* or *shekhinah*, the tenth *sefirah* and the locus of divine self-articulation. The terms *olam hadibur* and its parallel *olam hamaḥshavah*, to appear below, are widely found in the writings attributed to the Magid himself and in those of his circle.

[45] *Sefer yetsirah*, 2: 3.   [46] The famous kabbalist Rabbi Isaac Luria (1534–72).

[47] 'Va'etḥanan', pp. 321–4 (excerpted).

our human lives and fulfilling our human tasks, including that of worship. But the deeper reality, that towards which true *da'at* always points, is that there is only a single Actor on the cosmic stage.

This view of reality leaves us with many challenges, including the well-known one of moral responsibility. The *locus classicus* for that conversation in hasidic teachings (and in many earlier commentaries) is the tale of Pharaoh's role in the Exodus from Egypt. If God has indeed 'hardened Pharaoh's heart', why is the earthly ruler held responsible for his actions? The same applies to all of us and all our deeds, and there is much discussion of this, with various resolutions offered. No true mysticism can allow a mystical notion of non-selfhood to absolve one of moral responsibility. But this notion also has vast implications in the realm of interpersonal ethics, or what Judaism calls 'commandments between person and person'. It cannot be the ultimate otherness of the person before us that is the source of moral resolution, as in the thought of Emmanuel Levinas, since the final truth is one that reaches beyond the distinction between 'self' and 'other'. Rather, it is the ultimate oneness of being, the faith that the other and I are fellow limbs of the single body of cosmic Adam, that makes my betrayal of him or her a foolish act of violence against my own deeper self.[48]

The Mystical Ethos: Love, Awe, and Delight

This very personal consideration of *da'at* takes us to the realm of what hasidism refers to as *midot*, which means both personal qualities and religious emotions.[49] Here we first have to return to the theosophic model on which the psychological discussion is based. We will recall that there *da'at* is

---

[48] Here the religious exclusivism of kabbalistic tradition becomes impossibly inconsistent, even in its own terms. The clear biblical understanding that all humans are descended from Adam is reinforced by the Talmud's 'Why was the human created singly? So that no person could say to another: "My ancestor was greater than yours"' (Mishnah *San.* 4: 5). Nevertheless, the kabbalistic and hasidic sources regularly refer to all the souls *of Israel* as included within the soul of Adam, linking them to the 613 commandments of Israel's Torah etc. Rather than claiming that non-Israelite souls descend from elsewhere, they mostly seem to simply ignore the question. This incongruity may serve to mask a discomfort with saying openly what has ancient roots in the tradition: that the souls of non-Jews are born of demonic or 'unclean' unions, including possibly that of Adam and Lilith. In that case, while descended from the first human, they would still not be part of his 'true' or 'holy' seed. It is difficult to determine whether this discomfort is due to a moral stance or is simply something one thought was unsafe to write openly in works that underwent censorship.

[49] The essay by Septimus referred to in n. 13 above also discusses the use of the terms *de'ot* and *midot* in medieval Hebrew to refer to moral qualities. *Midot*, literally 'measures', has this linkage already in mishnaic Hebrew, as attested by multiple examples in Mishnah *Avot*.

the final link within the primal triad that may be called 'the mind of God', *ḥokhmah–binah–da'at*. It then serves to join those to the next six *sefirot*, representing the qualities or attributes of the personified God. These include *ḥesed* (compassion), *din* (judgement), *tiferet* (glory), *netsaḥ* (triumph or eternity), *hod* (beauty), and *yesod* (fundament). These six are manifest in the religious personality as love of God, awe, integrity, triumph over evil, gratitude, and (all-inclusive) righteousness. The lower *midot* are all seen as rooted in the first two, love and awe. Their cultivation and proper balance is taken to be the very essence of devotional life. They are called the 'two wings' on which prayer ascends to heaven. The relationship of these two to *da'at* is depicted vertically; they are directly below *da'at* on the sefirotic chart. But that relationship is then charted in both directions. Within the human soul, love and awe derive from *da'at*; they cannot exist without it. But in the striving to reach towards God, they are necessary steps on the rung upwards; one cannot attain *da'at* without the proper balancing of love and awe in one's religious life.

In understanding this [Jacob's dream], we must first remember that the source of Torah and the font of wisdom from which we receive the revealed word is in the thought of God Himself; God's *ḥokhmah* and *binah* are the World of Thought. There the Torah exists in a completely hidden way, not revealed at all. In that place there exists neither speech nor language. In order to be revealed as word, the Torah must pass through *da'at*, that which is to bring it from the World of Thought into the World of Speech. *Da'at* includes both love and fear, both compassion and rigour. It is because Moses represents *da'at* that the Torah so frequently says: 'The Lord spoke unto Moses saying, "Speak unto the children of Israel".' We have shown this elsewhere as well: It is through Moses, who represents *da'at*, that the hidden Torah is drawn forth from the World of Thought to be revealed to the children of Israel in the form of speech. This is the meaning of 'Y-H-V-H spoke to Moses': by means of *da'at*, the revelatory power of speech has become one with the hidden source of wisdom.[50]

For this reason the Zohar tells us that 'any word spoken by a person without

---

[50] A most interesting and noteworthy statement of the author's theology of revelation. God 'speaking' to Moses now comes to mean that Moses, as *da'at*, is the channel that brings language and expression to that which had formerly been beyond speech. A key question here is whether we are speaking of Moses as a symbolic realm within God (an ideal type of 'Moses', parallel to 'Abraham the Elder' as depicted in *Me'or einayim* in *parashat* 'Ḥayei sarah') or as a particular human being. In the latter case, he is also one who is present, as our author frequently says, in every generation. Thus the process of revelation, the bringing of transverbal mystery into speech, continues in the words of the *tsadik*. The ensuing discussion makes it quite clear that the latter is intended. All Torah learning, as sacred verbal activity, is a part of the unceasing stream of revelation. The linkage of both Jacob and Moses with *da'at* is widely found throughout kabbalistic and hasidic sources.

fear and love does not fly upward'.[51] As we have said, *da'at* contains both love and fear; only through it can the revealed word be joined to its sublime and hidden source, that which lies beyond our reach.

This is why a person who studies Torah or prays, pronouncing the letters of Torah with both love and fear, can invoke the presence of *da'at*. This allows for a drawing forth into his mind and speech from the World of Thought, the font of wisdom. *Ḥokhmah* and *binah* flow into him from above. The Torah he speaks becomes one with the Source above. His words go right up to their very root above by means of the *da'at* that he evokes in studying with love and awe. As this [newly] revealed Torah flies upward, it becomes wholly united and completely one with its root. Study lacking this *da'at*, undertaken without love and fear, of course is not the same. Here the words that are being revealed are cut off from their root; there is no one to draw from the wellsprings above into the word that is being revealed. Therefore this word of Torah will also not be able to rise and become one with its Source, so that it might draw down upon itself the flow of fine oil coming from the World of Thought, the root of Torah in the highest world. This is the meaning of 'does not fly upward'.[52]

Here we see the central role played by *da'at* in the full panoply of the hasidic religious imagination. As the lowest link in the divine mind, it is the self-articulation principle of divinity. In *da'at* the abstract thought of Y-H-V-H is turned into language, becoming the revealed Torah. Hence it is identified with Moses, the bearer of that revelation. But we can attain that Torah, in the truest sense, only through love and awe, which will arouse our own *da'at*, causing us to understand that our own words, spoken in the course of Torah study, are part of the divine self-revealing process. The two emotions thus serve as our 'wings', raising up our own speech and uniting us with cosmic Torah, ultimately with the mind of God. *Da'at*, or 'mind', is thus the meeting place, in God as well as in the person, between the deepest secrets of the preconscious intellect and their expression in the life of emotion and deed.

Particularly characteristic of the *Me'or einayim* is the sense that this turning of the heart towards God, in the quest for *da'at*, is a pleasurable activity. As I have shown elsewhere, Menahem Nahum of Chernobyl is the hasidic

---

[51] *Tikunei zohar*, 10 (25*b*), referring to words of Torah. In hasidic sources, especially the *Me'or einayim*, this is casually expanded to embrace all of human speech, if conducted in holiness.

[52] 'Vayetse', pp. 100–1. Learning and teaching Torah is a pneumatic act that totally depends on the emotions aroused in the course of it. Although our author has said elsewhere that one should study even without such intent, clearly this is the goal. We should note here that in pre-modern Yiddish there is no separate verb for teaching; *lernen* means both 'learn' and 'teach'. The same is true of his use of *lomed* here. He seems to be using it to refer to the *tsadik*'s public teaching.

author who remains most faithful to the attitude of the Ba'al Shem Tov regarding asceticism and self-denial.[53] Both of them are open to a rather hearty appreciation of this-worldly blessings. This includes the legitimacy of taking pleasure in one's own spiritual life. This is indicated in the letter of the Besht to his brother-in-law, Gershon of Kuty, one of the few unimpeachable documentary sources for his words.[54] There he compares the ascending union of worlds, souls, and divinity to the union of two human bodies in the physical act of love. 'If the physical is pleasurable, how much more so [the spiritual union]', he says. The *Me'or einayim*, recalling the association of *da'at* with the love-act of Adam and Eve, invokes this sentiment in numerous passages.

We know the secret of Egyptian exile: *da'at* was in a reduced and exilic state. They did not have the fullness of *da'at* to serve Y-H-V-H with pleasure and expanded consciousness [*mohin gedolin*], as in 'Know the God of your father and serve Him' [1 Chr. 28: 9].[55] *Da'at* may refer to [sexual] union and pleasure, as in 'Adam knew [his wife Eve]' [Gen. 4: 1]. But in Egyptian exile, their *da'at* was greatly diminished.[56] This was the narrow strait [Mitsrayim/*metsar yam*]; awareness, flowing from the mind of *hokhmah*, was reduced to a narrow current . . . In coming forth from Egypt they emerged from that narrow strait, and awareness [*da'at*] was increased and broadened. Thus 'And God knew' [Exod. 2: 25]; knowledge of God was exalted.[57] Thus [of Israel in Egypt] Scripture says: 'You matured and grew' [Ezek. 16: 7].[58] It was their mental capacity for great awareness that grew and developed, allowing them to serve our Creator with pure and shining pleasure. This is the joy of commandment and devotion. Therefore 'a handmaiden at the sea saw what [even] Ezekiel did not,[59] for their service was that of growing awareness, coming forth from that reduced state and thus into joy.[60]

---

[53] Arthur Green, 'Buber, Scholem, and the *Me'or 'Eynayim*: Another Perspective on a Great Controversy' (forthcoming).

[54] The letter, including its various recensions, is translated and discussed in Immanuel Etkes, *The Besht: Magician, Mystic, and Leader* (Waltham, Mass.: Brandeis University Press, 2005), 272–81.

[55] See n. 38 above. A similar understanding of the verse is possible here.

[56] *Bekatnut me'od*, i.e. they were like minors, unable to achieve coitus. This may be an attempt to explain the alleged sexual abstinence of the Jews in Egypt, referred to in the Passover Haggadah as *perishut derekh erets*.

[57] Notice this bit of 'predicate theology': God's knowing is subtly translated into human knowledge of God.

[58] This verse is quoted in the Passover Haggadah, where it refers to Israel's state during the Exodus from Egypt.   [59] *Mekhilta*, 'Beshalah', 15: 3.

[60] 'Devarim', p. 298. For a parallel text on the relationship of *da'at* and exile, see Jacob Joseph of Polonnoye, *Toledot ya'akov yosef*, 'Vayakhel', 481–2. On the redemption of *da'at* from exile in Egypt, see also *Magid devarav leya'akov*, no. 5.

The pleasure here is that of becoming aware, of the mind's expansion and opening. But it is also one of intimate union with God, bearing an aura of spiritualized sexuality. One might think of it as the de*light* of en*light*enment. But the pleasure of expanded *da'at* does not remain with the person alone.

Rashi interprets the beginning of the blessing [of Gen. 27: 28] with 'and' to mean that God will give again and again.[61] To understand this, it is known that true service of God is in the mind [*da'at*], as Scripture says: 'Know the God of your father and serve Him' [1 Chr. 28: 9]. Such knowing is pleasurable, for the service of God with an expanded consciousness brings forth pleasure from the World of Pleasure. It is well known, however, that if joy is constant its pleasure is diminished; it has to suffer some interruption.[62] When a person serves God with a true feeling of spiritual pleasure, that feeling rises up to the Creator Himself, and He too takes delight in the one who serves Him so joyously. Pleasure is called forth in the Root of all, just as it has been present in that particular part of the all [i.e. the individual worshipper]; now that part is joined fast to Him. There is no real pleasure without this attachment; [and this attachment] arouses the same pleasure in the Root itself. But in order that the joy not be constant [and thereby ruined], his former consciousness is taken away from him as a higher or more expanded mind is given him in its place. This is called the second expansion.[63]

The spiritual pleasure felt by the individual in the course of opening the mind to this expanded state enters into 'the Root', or the mind of God, as the worshipper is joined to it. Like the sexual pleasure to which it is analogized, it belongs to both parties in the coupling. But here that has to be the case also since individuation itself is partly illusory; the person has been a 'part' of the whole, or a branch of the Root, all along. Mystical attainment is nothing other than a discovery of this ancient and eternal truth. The joy of the devotee thus is the joy of God, and in his very enjoyment he is performing the work of 'giving pleasure to his Creator', as the teachers of many generations have admonished him to do. This linking is posed as a response to those more dour voices within the hasidic camp that railed against 'pleasure-seeking' in the religious life, insisting that such pleasure should be given to God alone.

[61] Rashi on Gen. 27: 28, citing *Bereshit rabah*, 66: 3.
[62] 'Constant pleasure is no pleasure' is a saying attributed to the Ba'al Shem Tov; cf. *Magid devarav leya'akov*, no. 125.
[63] 'Toledot', p. 90. On the origins of the term *gadlut sheni*(!), see Hayim Vital, *Peri ets ḥayim*, 'Ḥag hamatsot', 1. In this way our author explains the irregularity of states of expanded consciousness. They have to be diminished, and thus one needs to go through spiritual falls in order to again make the effort that will allow one to rise yet higher. For a parallel text on the joyous expansion of the divine mind due to human devotion, see *Magid devarav leya'akov*, no. 45.

The *Me'or einayim* understands that no such opposition between divine and human pleasure exists in the mystical perception of reality.

Conclusion: Reading the Hasidic Mystic in a Cross-Traditional Context

Our brief journey through the pages of a hasidic classic has hopefully given the reader a sense of the ways in which a passionate mystical devotion is expressed in the highly intellectualist context of rabbinic Judaism. The mystics of this tradition seldom speak confessionally about their own experiences. Everything they say is a weaving together of earlier sources through an interpretative lens. At the same time, the preacher is calling his readers (and originally 'hearers') to a religious life marked by a constant striving for awareness, an effort of both mind and heart. This path is meant to lead to a life of devoted service, but one that, at the same time, is filled with joy and a sense of intimacy with God. *Da'at* serves as the point of encounter between the transcendent God and the mind of the worshipper, but also between the intellectual effort to conceive of a highly abstract notion of the Deity and the intense emotionality of standing in God's presence.

The remaining question is how we make use of these materials in a contemporary religious (and interreligious) context. There is much talk in today's seekers' circles about the cultivation of awareness, or mindfulness, as an essential task of religion. There is also a quest in our world for a connection between such mindful attention and the ways in which we live, including the moral and ethical dimensions, even the political. We hear a new and ever more urgent call these days for the union of the spiritualist and activist agendas. Perhaps the wisdom of the early hasidic masters, revivers of a spiritual core within a tradition always deeply committed to this-worldly action, will have something to teach us in such an age.

The *Me'or einayim* presents us with a Western religious figure whose primary interest is this cultivation of constant spiritual awareness. For him that means the presence of Y-H-V-H underlying all that is and discoverable in the soul's encounter with each and every moment and object of existence. Our preacher's focus is always on the present, rather than on the past. Yes, of course he believes that the children of Israel were actually in Egypt and were brought forth by the hand of God. But the force of that faith lies in the challenge to the devotee: Have *you* yet come forth from your own inner Egypt, the narrow straits (playing on Mitsrayim/*metsar yam*) that constrict your vision and keep you from discovering that 'the whole earth is filled with His glory'? Surely he is certain that Moses and Israel built a portable tabernacle in the desert that served as their spiritual centre through forty years of wandering. But the question that he raises in sermon after sermon is: Are *you* turning yourself into a *mishkan*, a portable dwelling-place for the divine presence, in every moment of your life?

Emunah, or faith, has a significant place in the *Me'or einayim*, alongside *da'at*. But if we look at its use and context in most cases, it too is focused on the present rather than the past.

> You must have full faith that the glory of God fills all the world, that there is no place devoid of Him and none beside Him. Then, by means of that faith, you will come to a longing and desire to cleave to God. This state is referred to as *naḥal*, a stream or valley, containing also a hidden reference to the verse 'Nafshenu ḥiktah laY-H-V-H' ['Our soul waits for Y-H-V-H'; Ps. 33: 20].[64] In this way you come to your root, the spring at the well of living waters. And this is the meaning of 'the servants of Isaac digging in a valley' [*naḥal*]. They were digging in 'our soul waits for Y-H-V-H'.[65]

It is faith in the constancy of divine presence, including the extended notion of providence described above, that opens the doorway to cultivation of *da'at*. This relationship between faith and awareness is symbolically represented by the association of *emunah* with *malkhut*, the tenth *sefirah* and the gateway into the upper realm.[66] As the journey into God begins with *malkhut*, so does the cultivation of one's own spiritual life begin with faith. *Da'at* is a higher rung, open to those who have first entered through the gateway of faith.

The question then becomes one of method. What tools does the mystic offer for the task of creating and maintaining this awareness? On one level, R. Menahem Nahum would certainly respond that the entirety of Jewish practice, the pathway called halakhah, is precisely such a set of tools. Living all of one's daily life in accord with the Torah is meant to sensitize one to the faith that there is no part of existence or moment within human life from which God is absent. He says this clearly in several passages. Because hasidism was born within the heart of a religious tradition so richly devoted to forms of praxis, it developed rather few unique ritual elements of its own. Instead, it

---

[64] In Hebrew, the three letters that begin the three words of this verse spell out *naḥal*. It is faith in divine immanence, the ever-present flowing stream of Y-H-V-H, that causes one to thirst for even more, to 'wait for Y-H-V-H'. [65] 'Toledot', p. 85.

[66] *Emunah* in the *Me'or einayim* is almost always a human attribute, described in *malkhut*-like language as a gateway and similar. Unlike some others in the Magid's circle, R. Menahem Nahum does not retain the kabbalistic association of *emunah* as *raza demehemnuta*, embracing the entire sefirotic realm.

'stylized' the traditional forms of Judaism in its own unique way. But our author's more specific answer to the question of how to train oneself to awareness would focus on the two verbal practices that live at the heart of his Judaism: *torah utefilah*, or study and prayer.

The sermons are filled with exhortations to study Torah in a proper way, intending always to do so 'for its own sake', which means unifying the divine name. For our author, who exhibits no interest in high-powered talmudic dialectics, study seems to focus on the Torah text itself, along with the ability to read it in ever new and creative ways. It also means concentration on the individual words and letters of the text. These are described as palaces that contain the divine light, following the example of the Ba'al Shem Tov, who was able to see the hidden light of creation within the letters of the Torah.[67] The act of study, including this deconstruction of the text's apparent meaning, is thus transformed into a pneumatic exercise, allowing one to look more deeply into the written word. *Da'at* is developed by means of this deep, and often highly creative, encounter with the text. This sets the tone for the way one is to engage with the created world. Since God is present within every letter of Torah, and it is through Torah that God created the world, intense engagement with Torah is preparation for the ultimate religious task of uplifting and transforming all of reality, bringing it back into harmony with divine oneness.

The same applies to prayer. The letters of prayer are those of Torah, now rearranged in order to reverse direction, 'journeying' from the soul back to their source in God. Those letters are also the sacred speech through which God created all the worlds. The words of prayer are carried upward by their humanly given 'wings', those of love and awe. But these same emotions that bring us to *da'at* also embody it. They are the first roads that lead forth from *da'at* and take the seeker into it. This leads directly to the key claim in the *Me'or einayim*, that God is to be served not only in moments of prayer and study but through every activity of human life, through everything that was created by those same sacred letters. In prayer, as in Torah, engagement with the word, entering into language as a sacred vessel, enables us to do the same with the world that word has wrought.

This reading of the *Me'or einayim* as a universal religious text presents us with multiple challenges. Those of us approaching it from within Judaism need to ask whether this spiritual path remains open to generations who can

---

[67] This ability is central to two stories in *Shivḥei habesht*. See Dan Ben-Amos and Jerome R. Mintz (ed. and trans.), *In Praise of the Baal Shem Tov* (Northvale, NJ: Aronson, 1993), 48–9, 89–90; cf. *Sefer ba'al shem tov al hatorah* (Jerusalem: Nofet Tsofim, 1997), no. 27, pp. 54–5.

no longer maintain a literal faith in its mythical scaffolding. Modernity views the Torah text as belonging to a certain genre and age of literary Hebrew, including within it views of various schools and oral traditions that abounded in ancient Israel. It understands this planet to be some thirteen billion rather than six thousand years old, existing aeons before the Hebrew language emerged from its proto-Semitic roots. The human body is not made up of 613 limbs and sinews, corresponding to the commandments of the Torah. The rubrics around which the faith of the *Me'or einayim* was structured seem entirely swept away. Can the building stand once the scaffolding falls away?

For the reader coming from outside the Jewish religious tradition, a different series of challenges is called forth. Can the author's insights be applied to the practices of another tradition? Could we imagine a Christian, Muslim, Hindu, or Buddhist turning to the *Me'or einayim* as a guide? His essential teachings, that God is present in each moment, that cultivating awareness of this is the key purpose of religious life, and that such awareness leads to profound joy, could all seem to work as cross-traditional truths. The value he places upon inwardness and his wariness of practice without an open heart might also serve as useful reminders to devotees within any ritual-based tradition, all of whom sometimes lose their focus on the true heart of the matter.

The reader of the *Me'or einayim* coming with no body of devotional praxis rather than another one might have a harder time with this work. All the wisdom its author has to teach comes from his struggle with a life of regular daily religious practice, and from living within the context of a sacred calendar that offers a rich menu of diverse sacred moments. Yes, all of these are meant to cast light on the ordinary, on the overlooked human moments, to help one find God's presence in those as well. But the sacred energy applied to them has been transferred from the traditionally sacred to the new expansion of holiness into the everyday. Without an experiential basis in this homeland of the holy, as it were, the transfer and broadening would likely become an empty intellectual enterprise. Nor would it have the font of replenishment offered by religious forms when carried out in a heartfelt way.

Yet still, his call for *da'at* echoes in all of our ears. To be a religious person still demands attention to the awareness that he knew and articulated so well. We feel a deep desire to respond to that call. Can we imagine a religious life based on this call for constant awareness of Y-H-V-H and an open-hearted response of *hineni*, 'Here I am', to the discovery of that presence? Such a spiritual path would draw richly on the symbolic language of these hasidic sources. It would find nurturance in living quite fully within the garb of any given set of traditional religious praxis. But in doing so it would not depend upon literalist or historicist claims. Like the faith of the *Me'or einayim*, it would focus on the present, not the past. Nor would it need to be exclusivist in its claims.

I believe that the transition from critical modernity to postmodern consciousness helps to reopen this door for us. Knowing all that we do about the origins of our canonical texts, we choose to engage with them with a renewed intimacy, lending them, by means of our covenant with them, the power to evoke a response from deep within us. Yes, we understand that it is we who have invited this response, and that it might have been evoked by other texts, by other genres of human and divine creativity, or even without them. We, as Jews, claim this as our sacred canon. The deeds, forms, and gestures it prescribes become sacred to us, as do its moral demands. We give ourselves to it, as the tradition has given itself to us, a legacy placed into our hands. In engaging with it, both in study and in deed, we constantly seek—and even occasionally find—the presence of the One, nestled amid its words and letters, its stories and commandments.

We rejoice in the knowledge that there are other such religious communities, and that they too live with the great richness of devotion to both sacred text and sacred praxis. The teaching offered here, that all of these faith communities need to reach deeply inward, going beyond themselves, to bring awareness of the One into the heart of the devotee, is one we delight in sharing. In doing so, I should hope that I provide a model here that will encourage others to share such wisdom texts from their own traditions, universalizing them if necessary, as I have sought to do here. We of the small but growing neo-hasidic community within Judaism would be open to learning from such sources, and would welcome the dialogue of devotion, reaching across borders of language, symbols, and faith communities, that such exchanges would engender.

Our author's engagement with sacred language—a sacrality that we now acknowledge arises from our voluntary submission to it—takes us from the specificity of each tradition's many words to what our author calls the primal Word, that which was there before Creation, that which contains all of our teachings, revelations, and insights within it. That Word, bursting forth from the primal point of universal wisdom with all the energy of the Big Bang, blows our self-protective modernist 'shells' into tiny, scattered pieces, and permits us to again find broken sparks of divine light within all of being. From there we go back to the work of restoring them—and ourselves—to our single Source.

CHAPTER FIVE

The Truth Beyond and Beyond Truth

Religious Truth in Teachings of the Breslav Tradition and Their Contemporary Interreligious Application

ALON GOSHEN-GOTTSTEIN

A COMMON ATTITUDE of adherents of one religion towards another is competition between conflicting truths. From this perspective, religions are commonly considered deadlocked in a dispute over what are essentially competing truth claims. The challenge posed by a contemporary view of other religions is an internal challenge as well as an external one. In thinking of truth in an interreligious framework, we are in fact called to consider conflicting internal understandings of truth, as well as the very meaning of truth in a religious context. What do we mean by truth and how do we access it? Thinking through what religious truth means in an interreligious context provides an opportunity for revisiting existing discussions within our tradition on the notion of truth, and identifying them as resources for contemporary reflection. A primary means of exploring this question is considering positions developed internally and how they might be broadened to a view of other religions. The advantage of this method is that it does not forsake the notion of truth on account of the interreligious encounter. Rather, it seeks to apply to that encounter classical views of religious truth, as these have been developed internally. Particularly relevant in this context are internal views that relativize truth or our ability to access it. Most discussions of truth and falsehood assume a simple dichotomy between the two. Consequently, religions may be classified as one or the other. Classically, 'we' have truth, or at least 'we' possess it fully, while 'they' have falsehood. A richer understanding of truth yields more nuanced ways of describing relations between religions, while preserving the notion of truth. In order to attain such an understanding, one must identify expressions of the internal relativization of the contents of religion.

One cannot assume that internal mechanisms for reflecting upon truth can always be exported to a religion's views of other religions. Certain perspectives and certain flexibilities may be the prerogative of the internal spiritual discourse. Yet to the extent that spiritual literature conditions our view of our own tradition, we can require of it to extend beyond the boundaries of its normal application. If our theological challenge is how to deal with the consequences of applying the language of truth to our religious discourse, then identifying ways in which this very language has already been transmuted within tradition provides an important resource.[1]

The present essay explores the notion of religious truth from the perspective of one hasidic tradition, Breslav hasidism. It centres on two interrelated texts and seeks to make them talk to the present interreligious situation and to the theoretical challenges of a contemporary Jewish theology of religions. The two texts are by the master and by the disciple; the latter elaborates and expands upon the former's teaching. The master is Rabbi Nahman of Breslav, the disciple is Rabbi Nathan of Breslav or Nemirov. The first text we will study is *Likutei moharan*, Part I, *torah* 52, where R. Nahman presents a nexus of ideas within which the notion of religious truth may be appreciated. This text, along with an important midrashic source, provides the basis for an extensive discussion of truth and its axiological value by R. Nathan in his *Likutei halakhot*, a commentary on the *Shulḥan arukh*, based on the theological and mystical foundations of R. Nahman's teachings.[2] These two texts provide an opportunity to think through our views of truth, peace, and tolerance and how they might apply within the present-day interreligious context. Let us begin, then, by looking at the teaching of R. Nahman, which serves as the point of departure for the present study.

Truth: Returning from the Many to the One

Rabbi Nahman opens his teaching with a discussion of how telling lies is harmful both physically and spiritually. The discussion is launched in a moral context, providing reasons for why untruth is harmful. This practical-

---

[1] The ideas spelled out above have been articulated with various illustrations in my 'Towards a Jewish Theology of World Religions: Framing the Issues', in Alon Goshen-Gottstein and Eugene Korn (eds.), *Jewish Theology and World Religions* (Oxford: Littman Library, 2012), 20–33.

[2] On this work, see my essay 'The Halakhah in Light of the Spiritual Life' (Heb.), in A. Berholz (ed.), *The Quest for Halakhah: Interdisciplinary Perspectives on Jewish Law* [Masa el hahalakhah: iyunim bein-teḥumiyim ba'olam haḥok hayehudi] (Tel Aviv: Yediot Books, 2003), 257–84.

spiritual perspective leads to a broader reflection on truth in the metaphysical sense and how it relates to other core values:

The emergence of falsehood, which is evil, which is impurity, is due to the remove from the One. Because bad/evil[3] is opposition; for example, whatever is against a person's will is bad. And in the One there is no opposition, but all is good. As the rabbis taught [BT *Pes.* 50], 'On that day God will be one and His name one'—all will be for good.[4] Because in the One there is no evil/bad. And therefore in the future will be fulfilled the verse: 'The speech [or tongue] of truth will endure forever' [Prov. 12: 19]. Because then all will be One, all will be good.

For truth is one. For example, if we take a silver dish and say that it is a silver dish, it is the truth. But when we say it is a golden dish, it is a lie. So we see that truth is one, because the only truth one can say is that it is a silver dish, nothing else; but falsehood is manifold, because one could say it is a golden dish, a copper dish, and other names. So the lie is in the aspect of 'they sought many intrigues' [Eccl. 7]. And this is why in the world to come evil will be eliminated, as will contrariety and tears.[5] As it says, 'They will not cause any harm' [Isa. 11]—that is the elimination of evil. And it says, 'The wolf shall dwell with the lamb and the tiger with the goat' [Isa. 11]—this is the elimination of opposition. And it says, 'and God will wipe the tears off every face' [Isa. 25]—this is the elimination of tears, which are an aspect of lying.

For then God will be one and His name one, which is all good, all truth. And this is why in the world to come all impurity will be eliminated, as it says, 'I shall remove the spirit of impurity from the earth' [Zech. 13], because then all will be one, as it says, 'Who will produce the impure from the pure; is it not the move away from the One?' [Job 14].

The key to understanding this passage lies in the notion of unity and of moving from the one to the many. The move from the one to the many is understood through a series of associations. It is also a move from the holy to the impure (purity being a means of restoring lost unity). Further, it is a move from good to evil. All these are borne out by talmudic and midrashic associations. In context, Rabbi Nahman adds to this cluster of associations also the

---

[3] Hebrew uses the same word (*ra*) for both, and the present discourse slips between the two senses.

[4] The talmudic interpretation argues that in the future, even what we perceive as bad will be good. Accordingly, the benediction made in response to events will change. Whereas today we make one benediction upon hearing good news and another upon receiving bad news, in the future all will be *hatov vehametiv*, affirmation of God's goodness. Even bad things will be considered good from the perspective of a future vision. Rabbi Nahman quotes the formula of this benediction as a description of the future state.

[5] A reference to the earlier part of the teaching, where lies and tears were related.

distinction between truth and falsehood. Thus, the move away from the one is a move away from truth. Truth is only one, while untruth is manifold.

The association of truth, good, and unity, and their opposition as untruth, evil, and multiplicity, grounds the notion of truth in a very particular context. Truth is not necessarily cognitive, a statement to affirm or a proposition to which one must assent. Grounded in existence itself, truth is to be considered a metaphysical way of being that has a moral and existential counterpart. Seen thus, truth is a total way of being.[6] It is beyond the content of specific faith doctrines, though no doubt these too are implied by the notion of truth. It is, rather, a state of being that can be variously described as true, holy, one, or good. I am reminded of the Vedantic attempt to speak of the ultimate Brahman by appeal to three primary characteristics, which are the only things that may be affirmed of Brahman—*sat, chit, ananda*: truth-existence, consciousness, bliss. Thus, a compound of core attributes is suggested wherein truth plays an important role. This compound expresses a core state of being. One of the ways of speaking of this state of being is truth.

It is interesting to note that none of the sources quoted by R. Nahman refer to truth. They speak only of good and evil, one and many, holy and impure. Reference to truth is thus imported by R. Nahman to this discussion. The import may be accounted for in light of the focus of this teaching, namely the avoidance of lies and the attempt to ground it in a broader metaphysical structure. It may also reflect his own intuitive understanding of how ultimate reality should be conceived of, not only in moral but also in cognitive terms, hence the reference to truth.

Let us proceed further with the reading of *torah* 52 as we seek to understand what truth means to R. Nahman.

Prior to the creation, when creation was still in potential, so to speak, before He actualized it, all was one, all truth, all goodness, all holiness. Even the designation 'pure' was not applicable. This is because purity applies only when impurity is also possible, as it is written, 'You will be purified of all your impurities' [Ezek. 36: 25]. But when all is one, the aspect of 'many intrigues', which is the essence of

---

[6] It is interesting to consider this insight in light of the biblical use of *emet*. The term typically denotes truth, and various attempts to understand truth in Jewish sources take as their point of departure the use of *emet* in foundational sources. However, if we consider its use in the Bible without the prior understanding that it connotes truth, we discover a much richer semantic field, of which truth is but one component. This semantic field may be taken to represent a way of being wherein truthfulness is one significant element. The sense of truth as a way of being, rather than a position or set of propositions that are held, may thus hark back to biblical foundations.

evil and impurity, as explained above, has no place. For purity is a mean between holiness and impurity, through which impurity is rectified, as in 'you shall be purified of all your impurity'.

This is also the aspect of free choice, which is a mean between two things. And this cannot apply before creation, for then all was one, and in the One there is no choice, choice being an aspect of purity. And when God brought creation forth from potential into actuality, there were two things, the aspect of the One and creation. And then free choice applies, which is the aspect of purity, which is a mean between the One, for it is close to it, and has not yet come to the many intrigues, which are the evil and impurity. Nevertheless, it is an indicator and a sign of devolvement, for it can devolve until it becomes bad and evil . . . and this is why it is possible to purify and to raise impurity to purity, for it devolved from purity, as it says, 'you shall be purified of all your impurity'.

And all this . . . the aspect of purity, the aspect of free choice, from which comes the essential devolvement of impurity, which is evil and contrariety, the aspect of lies, all this comes from the aspect of 'after creation'—after creation came forth from potential to actuality, for then there were, so to speak, two aspects, that is, the One and creation. We see, therefore, that the essential hold of falsehood, which is impurity, is on account of its distance from the One, that is, from the aspect of 'after creation'.

The concept of truth is situated, in this discourse, within a cluster of ideas or values. Significantly, truth is not the starting point of this metaphysical presentation, which is focused on the process of creation. Rather, the entire move from truth to falsehood is grounded in creation, in the act of becoming, and in the move from the one to the many. This move is related to the move from holiness through purity to impurity, and also from the one truth to the many intrigues of falsehood. Truth is thus related to, and grounded in, existence itself in the most fundamental way. Accordingly, if we ask what religious truth is on this view, we would respond that it is being rooted in the divine reality itself, a reality both distinct from, and prior to, creation. Truth and unity are identified with the state of existence prior to creation. With creation comes multiplicity, and with it comes the fall away from the one, true, pure, and good state of being. Thus, attaining truth involves gaining a state of being that transcends the created order. For R. Nahman as a mystic, such attainment seems possible, in that our consciousness can rise above the multiplicity of existence and regain a lost unity of being. Rising above creation to the One at its source allows us to enter a state of goodness and truth that is reserved for God alone. Thus, truth is a sharing in God himself. This is a significant insight, inasmuch as all truth would be grounded in God and would be an expression of having entered the divine life in some conscious way. This formulation would exclude the identification of truth with a path, a teaching, even with Torah itself. These could be considered part of the created order, or at least their lower expressions would be identified with it. Only the higher aspects of Torah and religion, those that are grounded in divine being itself, may be said to be 'truth'.

Such an understanding is, of course, full of potential for interreligious relations. It suggests that religion, my religion, is not to be automatically identified with 'the truth'. Rather, truth is a particular high point of the spiritual life, only attained by those who have reached the depths or heights of the spiritual life, or divine reality itself. While nothing is stated in relation to other religions, grounding truth in God, rather than in religion, does open up the possibility that this structure may be applied not only to Judaism, but also to all religions. All religions could span the duality of God and creation, the choice between pure and impure and good and evil that is fundamental to the spiritual life. As such, in their lower expressions, they too are identified with the process of purification, still removed from truth in its highest state. Only as they make direct access to the higher reality of the One available can they be considered truth. And precisely because all comes from the One, all religions may point to that same One and provide access to it.

Reading on in R. Nahman's teaching, we learn:

And through divine providence, even after the act when God brought forth [creation] from potential to actuality, all things are united with Him. And evil draws its vitality from the residue of providence, that is, from behind his shoulders, as is known,[7] and it is far from the One. And through truthfulness God's providence is upon him [i.e. the truthful person], as it says, 'My eyes are upon the truthful' [Ps. 101: 6]. And through falsehood, which is evil, he removes God's providence from himself, as it says, 'He who speaks falsely will not be sustained before My eyes' [ibid.], and his vitality comes only from behind the shoulders.

We see, therefore, that when a person wants the state of 'after becoming' and activity, when [God] brought potential into actuality, to be all one . . . as it was before, when all was in potential, he must keep himself from falsehood, and thereby God's providence is upon him and then all is one.

The metaphysical description has direct moral consequences. Lying removes one from the unity of being and precludes providence, locking a person into the state of multiplicity associated with the becoming of creation. Telling the truth evokes the primordial, pre-created state, where divine unity is identical

---

[7] Suggesting a backhanded reception of divine bounty as opposed to its direct reception. See Zohar iii. 14a.

with the truth. This primordial unity can be evoked because there is a way of applying or drawing forth the state of unity, associated with God and with the pre-created state, within the order of creation and its multiplicity. This is attained through providence. Providence, expressed through the metaphor of God's eyes, is a means of reconnecting with God. As God is the ground of the One, the Good, and the True, so too, he is the means of realizing them within the created order, through providence. This realization is achieved by bridging the metaphysical and the moral. The Hebrew *emet* expresses both 'truth' and 'truthfulness', the former a metaphysical state, the latter a mode of being, a moral virtue. This linguistic identification allows R. Nahman to make the move to the moral domain, affirming that truthfulness is a means to Truth. By telling the truth, affirming the one message of truth applicable to a given situation, one is recalling the higher spiritual reality of the One, drawing forth providence, and in some way undoing the harmful effects of creation. If creation meant a move away from the One, truth-telling, much like purification, leads one back from the many to the One. To speak truth is thus to rise beyond creation, returning to the Creator, identified with the One, drawing forth his providence, living in him.

As my analysis suggests, the governing notion of the metaphysical discussion is unity and its devolvement into multiplicity. This engenders purity, choice, and the move to falsehood. Truth is thus derivative of unity. Why then does R. Nahman place an accent on truth, especially given that his sources give much greater prominence to notions of evil, impurity, and multiplicity than to the concerns of truth and falsehood? The answer seems to be twofold. In terms of his work as a commentator, R. Nahman is explicating a famous mystical passage that speaks of the harmful consequences of telling lies for the mystical quest. In the famous story of the four who entered paradise, as it is narrated in BT *Ḥagigah* 14*b*, R. Akiva warns the other three Sages not to tell untruths, for the one who speaks falsehood cannot remain in God's presence. The latter-day mystic is thus invited to reflect on the relationship between telling falsehood and 'getting it wrong' in mystical terms. R. Nahman's mysticism is based on the experience or reality of return to the One, beyond evil, multiplicity. To this cluster it is easy to add truth and falsehood and to suggest that the moral dimension of *emet* excludes one from its metaphysical counterpart. Thus, one reason for why R. Nahman's thought may feature truth-telling as central to the mystical process may be hermeneutical—his dependence on a text that ties the two together. If so, his primary concern with 'truth' is less with truth in the abstract, theoretical (and we may add philosophical, dogmatic) sense than with its applied sense. We know what truth is in daily life and are required to practise it. Its benefits are the return to the reality of God, itself understood as Truth. Truth, then, is not some independent value, but simply a way of saying 'God'. Where truth takes on specific contours is in the moral domain, in the act of telling the truth.

There may be another reason why R. Nahman offers us such a moral conceptualization of truth in mystical and metaphysical terms. He may simply wish to illustrate the fruits of proper moral behaviour in the spiritual life. His work as a spiritual teacher indeed spans the range of the greatest spiritual heights and their grounding in everyday moral life. If so, it is all the more the case that what matters most about truth is not its abstract formulation. Rather, truth is to be appreciated in daily life through truthful living. Its metaphysical fruits are in the return to union with God, who is Truth. In both aspects, daily truthfulness and divine unity, truth is not some abstract value one must uphold, a statement, an affirmation, but rather reality itself lived properly. Living in the real world properly by telling truth grounds one in reality itself in the truest sense, in God himself.

All this is, of course, highly relevant to how truth is to be approached in the dialogue, or even competition, between religions. Truth, in this view, is not the primary value; reality is. The value of truth is not to be sought by affirmations, declarations, and formulations. Rather, it is to be tested through living and practising truthfulness, and remaining united with God. Truth is in reality, not in the mind or in the proper formulation. And, while R. Nahman may have never been challenged to articulate things in this way,[8] in fact, this formulation removes truth from the field of discussion between religions. If one practises truth, one dwells in the Truth. This is the message of grounding the metaphysical in the moral. It is as applicable to one religion as to the other, thereby eliminating competition over truth.

R. Nathan of Breslav: The Impossibility of Religious Truth

This teaching of R. Nahman provides the foundation for a lengthy exposition by R. Nathan in *Likutei halakhot*, 'Hilkhot ribit', 5. R. Nahman's *torah* provides

---

[8] R. Nahman is one of the most outspoken authors on matters of universalism and a universalistic mission of Judaism and the spiritual life in relation to non-Jews. The only song he composed, which is printed at the opening of *Likutei moharan* under the title *Shir na'im*, incorporates elements of a Jewish view of other religions. In it he distinguishes clearly between the value of Judaism and of other religions, and from a common perspective he would certainly not regard them as possessing equal value. Nevertheless, the metaphysical perspective from which he relates to absolute truth, as expounded in *torah* 52, makes it possible to consider relativizing all religions, including Judaism, in relation to pre-created reality.

the theoretical framework for a detailed analysis of internal Jewish pluralism, in which R. Nathan explores the relative values of truth and peace and presents us with one philosophical and textual strategy for relativizing religious truth. As I noted in the discussion of R. Nahman's text, his use of truth does not include reference to the content of truth in the form of specific beliefs, positions, dogmas, and so on. He avoids the aspect of truth that is typically the focus of considerations of religious truth. It is R. Nathan who introduces this aspect of 'religious truth' into the discussion. He does so by constructing an entire theoretical edifice on the foundations of *torah* 52, quoted above. In the process he comments not only on R. Nahman's teaching, but also on a foundational midrashic text that allows him to work through the value of religious truth and to relativize it. Therefore, before turning to R. Nathan's discussion, let us first consider the rabbinic commentary on Gen. 1: 26, found in *Bereshit rabah* 8: 5:

R. Simon said: When the Holy One, blessed be He, came to create Adam, the ministering angels formed themselves into groups and parties, some of them saying, 'Let him be created', while others urged, 'Let him not be created.' As it is written, 'Loving-kindness and truth met, justice and peace kissed' [Ps. 85: 11]. Loving-kindness said, 'Let him be created, because he will dispense acts of loving-kindness'; Truth said, 'Let him not be created, because he is full of lies.' Justice said, 'Let him be created, because he will perform acts of justice'; Peace said, 'Let him not be created, because he is full of strife.' What did God do? God held Truth and cast it to the ground, as it is written, 'And truth will be cast to the earth.' The ministering angels said before the Holy One, 'Sovereign of the Universe! Why do You despise Your seal? Let Truth arise from the earth!' Hence it is written, 'Let truth spring up from the earth' [Ps. 85: 12].

This *midrash* expresses the complexity of the human person, reflected through an angelic dispute as to whether man should be created. The angels are consulted by God, a rabbinic strategy for making sense of the plural form 'Let us make Adam' in Gen. 1: 26. The consultation yields conflicting opinions, reflecting various possible views of the human person. In terms of both truth and peace, man is judged as deficient and not worthy of being created. Truth and peace are the two values in which the human person is lacking. The angels are locked in what seems like a tie, with each side citing two qualities to support its view. The tie is broken by a surprising act of God when he moves from a position of taking advice to a position of taking action. God casts truth to the ground, thereby expressing his own preference for the creation of man, even at the cost of sacrificing truth. Lest we think that truth is of little value, the text goes on to affirm that it is God's seal, thereby making God's choice all the more pronounced.

This *midrash* is read by R. Nathan in great detail. In what follows, I present excerpts from his reading, too long to be translated in full, and explore their implications for the notion of religious truth as such, and in particular for a contemporary view of religious truth in an interreligious context.

In analysing this *midrash*, R. Nathan begins by posing the question of how truth could contradict God. Recalling the association of God and truth, as we encountered it in R. Nahman's teaching, makes the question all the more relevant. The core strategy that will serve R. Nathan in making sense of this *midrash*, thereby introducing a Jewish theory of pluralism, is a theory of layered truth, whereby truth is appreciated in or through multiple levels, with clear hierarchy between them. The hierarchy is reflected in the choice of heroes of this *midrash*. The text juxtaposes God and the angels with reference to man. Students of rabbinic thought are familiar with the prominent motif of the superiority of the human person to angels. When God seeks to create man, he is, in fact, creating a being that is not only superior to the angels but whose true value eludes them. Truth, in this *midrash*, is a class of angels. Man may be untruthful, but his value transcends that of the angels, who can only judge from their perspective. God sees things differently, so to speak, beyond truth itself.

To understand what makes the human person more than the angels, we must return to the very foundations of creation. Creation was made so that God may be known. But how is God known? The path of humans to knowledge of God passes through the complexities of choices, engendered by the duality of good and evil. It involves descent into the material world. It involves a strenuous process, the fruits of which are qualitatively different to the knowledge of God that those who do not go through such confrontations, that is the angels, can attain. Therefore, only humans, who experience the choice of good and evil, can know God truly, and therefore humans represent the pinnacle of creation when viewed from its ultimate telos, the knowledge of God.[9]

In developing a layered notion of truth, R. Nathan formulates the distinction between *emet*, truth, and *emet la'amito*, best translated as ultimate truth,

---

[9] The conceptual matrix plays humans and angels against each other, as does our foundational *midrash*. Note, however, that in R. Nathan's discourse 'Israel' substitutes for 'humans'. The universal applicability of this theory of truth to interreligious relations, where it addresses its original conceptual framework and refers to humans rather than to Israel, will be the subject of discussion below.

even though its literal rendering is something akin to 'truth in its truthfulness', or 'truly true'. The very notion of a layered truth would seem to go against the principle that R. Nahman had enunciated, that truth is one. Let us see how R. Nathan works around this tension:

There are several aspects concerning truth, for truth is one . . . but one requires great effort to attain truth in its ultimacy. Even in wisdoms of this world it is hard to attain the truth, as scholars who seek to understand through their wisdom recognize, where no wisdom is really fully known (except for mathematics and algebra), all the more so in the wisdom of the knowledge of God, which cannot be attained through any wisdom and mental attainment, except through efforts and the labours of the true righteous, who withstand temptation and are purified of all earthly desires. Only they attain in truth the knowledge of God, to the degree that their knowledge, in the world to come, will be the source of the angels' knowledge of God. (subsection 16)

Affirmation of the unity of truth is now focused on ultimate truth, which is the only real truth, though relative truth is still recognized as truth, albeit on a lower level. Note how experiential and grounded in life truth is. It must grow from experience, not from speculation or mental formulation. And it is only the experience of free choice and confronting evil that provides access to truth. If, for R. Nahman, free choice was a sign of falling away from the One, for R. Nathan, free choice, associated with the human person, is the only means of attaining the ultimate truth. This is a reversal of the process from metaphysics to spirituality. From the perspective of metaphysics, choice is a descent from ultimate truth. From the perspective of human experience, choice is the only means of purification, through which one attains the ultimate truth.

A closer comparison of the teachings of the master and the reworking of his disciple shows the originality of the latter, who almost stands the thought structure of the teacher on its head. Unlike R. Nahman, for whom truth was part of a cluster that included the values of good, holy, and the like, R. Nathan constructs his discussion exclusively around truth. The move from the one to the many, from God to creation, from truth to untruth, is actually not a move away from the truth but the means of attaining the truth absolute of *emet la'amitah*. What characterizes ultimate truth is that it can only be known through human experience, not angelic. And human experience, by definition, is founded on the move from the one to the many, on entering into life on the earth plane, characterized as it is by conflict, the challenges of impurity, and multiplicity of opinion. What for R. Nahman was a fall away from truth is for R. Nathan the necessary and exclusive means of attaining the higher, divine truth. By going through the trials and tribulations of an earthly life, a higher kind of truth can be discovered, a truth unknown to the angels. Thus, the truth that God desires is a truth that grows out of multiplicity, conflict, contrast, the move away from the One, the Pure, the True.

In this light let us revisit the description of God casting truth to the ground. If, on first examination, this was an expression of rejection of truth's counsel and an indication of God's desire in the creation of the man, R. Nathan's reading suggests a more specific meaning to the act of casting to the ground.

> Ultimate truth can only be attained in this world by passing through trials. And this is why God took truth and threw it to the ground, removing it from Himself. Because God does not choose such a truth, even though its intention is, in truth, well received, yet it has not yet attained the truth of God's knowledge, not having been in this world of free choice and not having been purified and refined in the multiplicity and untruth [through which] truth can be ascertained from multiplicity and untruth. This is why [God] decreed to cast truth to the earth, for this itself is the rectification and working out of truth, by throwing truth to the ground . . . By this very means truth will be worked out and purified, through the truly righteous, and only then clear truth will be revealed, so that one can attain the knowledge of His truth, in a way that it would have never been possible to attain when truth was above in the supernal worlds, where there is no untruth. (subsection 19)

To cast to the ground is thus to point to an alternative truth, a higher truth in fact, one that rises from the ground, tested through plurality of opinions and the multitude of temptations that make up our life.

In the move from the one truth, which represents the state of the world before creation, to truth as it is known here below, one must not seek to replicate truth as one, unique, and exclusive, as indeed it ultimately is. Rather, the move to multiplicity within creation means that truth in its unique sense cannot be known in our common reality. Metaphysical multiplicity translates into ideological pluralism. This does not mean renouncing the uniqueness of ultimate truth, but it does make it far less accessible. Ultimate truth becomes accessible only to those who successfully traverse the multiplicity of reality, with its attendant imperfections and impurities—a very narrow group of individuals, *tsadikim*, spiritual masters who are able to discover the deeper unifying power within that multiplicity.

R. Nathan does not tell us in what such truth consists and how it is different, but there are several keys that allow us to suggest that it is precisely its composite, synthetic nature, grounded in the plurality of opinion, that makes it richer and somehow more authentic than angelic truth.

One of the keys is the view of the messiah as the one who is able to reconcile and harmonize all forms of truth into a greater whole, from which the fullness of divine truth emerges. The messiah comes at the height of multiplicity, when the world has been greatly filled by people.[10]

The core revelation of truth in its fullness will be through our righteous messiah, who will come at the end of these days, when the world has become increasingly populated. And the multiplicity is primarily a multiplicity of opinions, that there is great divergence of opinions . . . and messiah, in the fullness of his righteousness, will attain the absolute truth and reveal the truth in the world, and then redemption will be complete and the purpose of creation will have been fully realized. (subsection 18)

The messiah, so it seems, does not simply affirm one truth over another. Nor is he presented as simply withstanding temptation or the confusion generated by the multiplicity of opinions, affirming one particular world-view. Rather, I would suggest that the messiah has the capacity to integrate and accommodate the plurality of competing views in a synthetic, composite, or otherwise fully realized view of the truth.[11] This understanding is corroborated later in the teaching, when R. Nathan speaks of the changes that occur in the world and how one must discover the truth through these various changes. In this context, he says the following:

Messiah, through whom is the essential revelation of truth in the entire world, will come at the end of days, precisely after time has been extended and gone on for long from the creation of the world till the time messiah will come. And so there will [already] be many people and many opinions and wisdoms, which is the essence of multiplicity and changes, on account of which untruth has taken a hold, leading God to cast truth to the ground . . . it is precisely then that the great rank of

---

[10] In one wording R. Nathan speaks of the numerical increase of Israel (subsection 17). In another he refers to population explosion and its attendant pluralistic explosion of opinions (subsection 18). Even if he does not extend his thought so far, the concept of multiplicity leading to messianic revelation invites broadening to include all peoples and opinions, both in view of the expanse of the human family and in view of the universal mission of the messiah.

[11] Such a view is, of course, the messianic vision of Rav Kook. I believe I am not simply reading Rav Kook into R. Nathan. Rather, R. Nathan's thought structure leads to this point, though he himself never articulates the full meaning of this way of thinking. His concerns are different, contained within a more limited social framework. The fact that he did not spell out the full implications of his thought structure does not take away from their potential. The continuation of the present paragraph lends further support to this reading.

the messiah will be seen, as he reveals the truth then out of so many changes. (subsection 49)

To speak of truth as being revealed out of many changes seems to be more than affirmation of the ability to uphold one truth despite many challenges to it. Rather, the one truth seems to grow out of these changes, transcending them and pointing beyond, to a higher reality. This higher truth integrates, synthesizes, and harmonizes these various changes into a higher perspective.

Another suggestive way of thinking of attaining the truth through the process of struggling in the midst of multiplicity on the earth plane grows directly from the image of truth being cast to the ground and from the proof text in Psalm 85: 12, 'truth will spring up from the earth'. Casting truth to the ground is read by R. Nathan as an analogy to the sowing of a seed in the earth.[12] For a seed to give life, it must first rot, thereby giving life to a higher or fuller form of being. Similarly, the narrower understanding of truth, angelic truth, identified with a particular viewpoint, must give way to the fuller divine truth, ultimate truth. And just as sowing requires human effort, so the attainment of truth requires the efforts of the righteous, who seek to realize truth in its purity. This analogy does not make clear in what way the new truth is different from the truth that had to rot. One way of making sense of it could be that it is precisely the letting go of the narrow confines of one single perspective that enables a new growth, which gives life by its very rootedness in earth and through the fullness and totality that it provides as it sustains all that grows on it.

For R. Nahman, truth belongs to the realm of 'before creation'. The created order, characterized by multiplicity, is the realm of untruth. The two are bridged by truthfulness, a moral virtue that evokes divine providence. What R. Nahman does not address is the status of conceptual truth, the very subject of our discussion of religious truth as conventionally understood. Into this gap steps R. Nathan, who claims that, indeed, one cannot refer to the ordinary sense of religious truth as a series of propositions, views, declarations, or statements within the created order. Any attempt to grasp the one truth within the multiple aspects of reality is doomed to fail, that is, except for those who have gone beyond its multiplicity and impurity and have been successfully tested. But in the conventional sense religious truth is meaningless and impossible to attain. The angels are correct, though not because man is a liar. Rather, it is because untruth is fundamental to the act of creation and, as such, is desired by God for purposes higher than those known to the angels.

---

[12] See subsection 22.

Let us hear R. Nathan on this:

The essence of free choice touches upon the matter of truth and falsehood, as we learn from *torah* [52]. For falsehood is evil. It is impurity that attaches itself to the removal away from the One. For as soon as creation came forth from potential to actuality, there were two things, and choice [became possible]. So we see that the essential hold of untruth is in the aspect of multiplicity through removal from the One. And the greater the removal from the One, the greater is the multiplicity, and untruth becomes more prominent. As we see that as soon as Eve was created and there were two people in the world, they caused harm and ate from the fruit of good and evil and brought about death for generations. . . . And so later, when Cain and Abel were born and people started multiplying, there was conflict between them till Cain killed Abel, and so all that went wrong was a consequence of multiplicity increasing. As it says, 'When human beings began to increase in number on the earth . . . The Lord saw how great the wickedness of the human race had become' [Gen. 6].

However, in truth, the essential value of truth and its perfection is precisely where one seeks out and reveals ultimate truth in the place of multiplicity. And the greater the multiplicity, and the more untruth has its hold there, when one attains the realization and revelation of truth there, that is the very worth of truth and its perfection, and this is the purpose of all of creation, from beginning to end. . . .

And so the *tsadikim* [righteous ones] achieve the purpose of creation by withstanding the trial and being purified, uncovering the ultimate truth from the multiplicity to which untruth becomes attached. (subsection 17)

What all this means is that in the here and now, in the realm of opinions, social relations, and competing world-views, no one, that is except for a very rare and narrow class of individuals, can really access truth.

Because it is hard to attain ultimate truth, controversy is multiplied. And controversy is caused by truth itself, where everyone considers that truth rests with him. [This is] because with regard to truth and falsehood there are many nuances. There is a great liar . . . and there is also the case of someone who is not a liar, but because he is not sufficiently pure in his deeds, his thought is misguided from one error to another till truth is reversed for him, to the point that he calls good evil and evil good, thinking that is the truth . . . And there is someone whose error is refined, and someone whose error is the finest of the fine, as in the case of some great masters who erred in a law or in a certain matter, even though their intention was desired by heaven. And especially with regard to controversy . . . for in this world truth has fallen, so that even great saints and true sages cannot attain ultimate truth. (subsection 16)

Note the reference to intentionality. As part of a thick application of the notion of truth, R. Nathan introduces this further dimension to the concept.[13] Thus one must distinguish between the substance or essence of truth and the intention to attain truth. Religious life involves both intentionality and attainment. True intention proffers validity and meaning to positions that may be faulty in terms of their substance. Such a notion of intention parallels, in some ways, R. Nahman's own reference to speaking truth. Both are ways of realizing truth within the order of multiplicity and the falsehood associated with it. Within the reality of multiplicity, intention provides a way of referring to the truth, even if it is not attained and even if it must be distinguished from ultimate truth.

As R. Nathan states further along:

There are two kinds of truth. There is ultimate truth, when one attains and knows the matter as it is, and there is another truth, where one's intention is truly desirable, though one is mistaken. (subsection 20)

In fact, the angel of truth himself should be considered 'truth' only in that sense. He intended to speak the truth, except that truth was spoken only according to his perspective, distinct from God's higher view of truth.

This is a very rich notion, particularly within an interreligious context. Once it is recognized that all truth escapes us and that really, within the realm of multiplicity, one cannot, with rare exceptions, attain truth, then intention functions as a primary means of validation that provides meaning to one's quest for truth. It is much easier to recognize the honest intentions of members of other faiths than it is to admit the truth of their faith claims. A notion of truth that highlights intentionality is thus one that fills the void created by the affirmation that we cannot access truth. It makes it possible to recognize proper intentionality, and hence some dimension of truth, in another religion.

Truth and Spiritual Virtues: Faith, Humility, Peace, and Compassion

Looking at R. Nathan's conceptual edifice, one realizes that ultimately truth is beyond our reach. In the same way that the angels could not grasp truth, so too no human person (except for outstanding spiritual masters) can access it. What we know is only that we do not know, and the consequence of that is the

---

[13] For a rabbinic precedent for such usage, see Tosefta *Yev.* 1: 3. The intentionality of Beit Shammai and Beit Hillel is the ground for applying to them a verse that describes their positions in terms of truth.

privileging of faith over truth.

> In this world the perfection of truth is in faith, for the principle of truth is to know that one cannot attain the essence of truth, for the essence of truth is God alone, as it says, 'and the truth [of/is] God forever' [Ps. 117: 2]. And this cannot be attained. So the principle of truth is to know that one cannot attain the essence of truth, in the aspect of the proverb stating, 'the goal of knowledge is to realize that we do not know'.[14] Therefore, the essential perfection of truth is in faith. (subsection 21)

The emphasis on faith, rather than truth, is a hallmark of R. Nathan's thought. In my view, if there is one single contribution by means of which we can appreciate R. Nathan in relation to, but also in contrast to, R. Nahman, it is this emphasis on faith. R. Nathan converts large portions of R. Nahman's thought, based as it is on mystical insight and on the centrality of understanding and recognition, into the domain of faith. This move is representative of his position as the disciple who sees himself as secondary to the great master and his direct insights. It is also a position that serves a pedagogical function. It presents a virtue that an entire community can practise, even when they cannot attain the rare heights witnessed in the scriptures that reflect R. Nahman's own experiences. Thus, if R. Nahman's teaching, presented above, assumed that truth was within reach and that one could somehow attain the pre-created state either by mystical experience (implicit in his presentation) or by proper moral conduct and truth-telling (explicit), this emphasis gives way to the recognition that truth, in its higher sense of ultimate truth, is beyond us. All we can hold on to is faith.

Affirmation of faith over and against truth is ultimately founded on a humility that recognizes our moral, spiritual, and epistemological limitations. This humility provides the psychological ground for the practical pluralism advocated by R. Nathan. Because we cannot attain truth, we must adopt a pluralistic approach to the multiplicity of opinions by which we are surrounded. This leads us, then, to R. Nathan's emphasis on tolerance and peace as core virtues that, in practical terms, should prevail over truth. Even if, in a purely theoretical way, truth is recognized as the ultimate virtue, because it is inaccessible, it must be balanced by the moral and social teaching that privileges peace and tolerance.

As R. Nathan formulates it, the greatest obstacle to absolute truth is truth itself.[15] This recognition orients both a psychological approach to oneself and a social approach to the reality of controversy. Psychologically, it provides a guiding principle for someone who is facing challenges to his spiritual path

---

[14] A common Breslav paraphrase of a Maimonidean saying.   [15] Subsection 20.

from others marshalling a concept of truth, something R. Nathan himself suffered from greatly as he was drawn into the hasidic movement, and in particular into the special relationship he had with R. Nahman. The way to deal with opposition is to constantly distinguish between the levels of truth. Seeking the point of truth in one's heart, one must ask in the face of competing truths what the ultimate truth is. Needless to say, R. Nathan assumes one can reach that point, at least with the aid of great spiritual masters.

The tension between truth and ultimate truth has further consequences for personal psychology. Truth can actually be a very destructive force in a person's self-evaluation and an obstacle to progress in the spiritual life. Consider the following: a truthful assessment of oneself would expose one's sinfulness, leading one to despair.

All moving away from the spiritual life and internal despair come from truth, because a person recognizes in himself the truth of what defects and harm he has caused [through his sins]. And even now he is as he is [i.e. imperfect]. And so he says to himself: 'after all, I know the truth concerning myself, how profound the harm I have caused is', and thereby he despairs and moves away from the spiritual life. So his moving away and his fall are all through truth. But in truth one must remove oneself from such truth because this is not really truth. Rather, we must know that we do not really know. And even though we have not yet come to that degree wherein the goal of knowledge is that we know nothing at all, which is a deep and hidden recognition, nevertheless, in the most basic sense, we do not really know how things are. The only thing we really do know is that God is true and His Torah is true, and He has revealed to us, through His true *tsadikim*, the depth of His grace and compassion, which is limitless. And this is the core of truth . . . and His thoughts are deep and He knows how we have been created from dust, and every movement and transformation, no matter how slight, that a person manages to achieve in this world, drawing himself to God in this material world, is very precious to Him . . . as it comes from a distant place. And this is the essential truth, a truth that comes from the earth and that is specifically from the [physical] earth plane. (subsection 24)

Thus self-critical truth is contrasted with ultimate truth with reference to one's personal spiritual standing. A limited sense of truth is judgemental, condemning the person and leading to despair. Divine truth, by contrast, is full of compassion, appreciating that which is positive and honouring every small step taken, precisely as it is taken in a physical environment. The truth of God's compassion is far greater, and more ultimate and absolute, than a self-judging truth. Truth can thus become an obstacle and a source of downfall in the individual spiritual life.

Even more dominant is R. Nathan's application of this core insight to contemporary social relations and the disputes that arise over issues of truth. R. Nathan spends significant attention on the controversy between hasidim and *mitnagedim*. Each group considers that it possesses the truth. It is truth that leads to controversies and disputes that sunder families and the entire society.[16] The angelic counsel against the creation of man remains a driving force of history. It is a judgement, a *kitrug*, that is sounded constantly wherever a truth-based criticism of the other occurs. Such criticism is never false; it is only partial. Yet its partiality makes such truth dangerous and destructive. The practical consequence of this approach to truth is pluralism.

R. Nathan critiques ideological controversy, based as it is on the supposed quest for truth, as a social vice that is of no benefit.

Every person must know this, so that he is spared the pitfalls that come precisely through truth that has not been properly clarified. This [recognition] will save him from the fire of controversy and opposition, which uproots those who engage in dispute from both worlds unnecessarily. For this quality is the worst of all bad qualities in the world. For other qualities and desires are at least somehow necessary, though one must deal with them according to the Torah, even when they are permitted, so as to not engage in them too much. Still, they are needed for human existence, as in the case of eating and drinking and similar activities. But the matter of controversy is completely unneeded for a person. It destroys him and uproots him from both worlds more than all desire . . . and the controversy concerning the service of God, which is the controversy between the hasidim and the learners, or within the different camps of hasidim and learners—this controversy is worse than anything and destroys much and prevents redemption more than all sins of the Torah. And this controversy is simply unnecessary hate,[17] and all this on account of truth, that everyone considers that truth is with him. But in truth, if he looks to the ultimate truth and does not mislead himself, he will certainly avoid controversy. For he will look at himself [and ask whether] maybe he is misleading himself. And even if he is not mistaken, he will recognize that you cannot achieve anything through controversy . . . especially during these generations, when Israel is in a lowly state

---

[16] Note, however, that R. Nathan's work contains a healthy dose of attack against the reformers and Enlightenment forces. He never considers broadening his line of reasoning to include forces that undermine his own understanding of the fundamentals of religion. It is left to us to ask whether a different historical vantage point might justify such application. Even more radical is the application of his principle of tolerance to other religions. Of course, in some way they might be regarded as less threatening than internal forces, by the very fact that they are situated outside, as well as in view of existing precedents that legitimate other religions.

[17] *Sinat ḥinam*, the talmudic expression for the worst kind of hate, said to be the cause of the destruction of the second Temple.

and we have no political power—how can one rectify what requires rectification, especially by means of controversy? Because rectifying the world and drawing the entire world to the service of God can only be attained by means of peace ... and this is why Elijah and the messiah, who are the instruments of the world's fundamental rectification, will engage only in peace-making ... and therefore, if truth incites one to engage in controversy, one must throw such truth away from oneself, casting it to the ground, for God does not desire such truth. (subsection 23)

Truth can guide the individual aspirant towards making the best spiritual choices for him- or herself. But once the truth becomes a social force, it must be controlled. The point of control is where it is associated with controversy. In the axiological confrontation between truth and peace, peace wins hands down.

The relationship between peace and truth is spelled out explicitly by R. Nathan, who revisits the rabbinic *midrash*, posing the following question:

When God cast Truth down to the ground for finding fault in the creation of the human person, why did God not take Peace to task? After all, Peace too found fault in the creation of man ... [The answer is] that Peace found fault in man, who is full of fighting. But in truth all the fights and the controversies are due to truth that is not purified and properly worked out, so everyone considers that truth is with him, thereby increasing fights and controversies in the world. ... Therefore God only took Truth to task, casting it to the ground ... because by casting Truth to the ground the fault-finding of Peace is already addressed, because once Truth is cast to the ground there are no more fights and there is peace ... because all controversies arise from too much truth.

And this is why one is permitted to change the truth for the sake of peace. For the sake of peace one must change and remove truth, for this is the core truth that God desires, to change truth for peace, for this is the aspect of God casting [down] Truth, who found fault in man's creation, teaching us thereby that one must throw and remove such truth from which fault-finding and controversies arise. (subsection 36)

R. Nathan has a wonderful expression here—too much truth. Partial truth is not too little (absolute) truth. Rather, it is too much truth, relative to the measure of truth we really need to live our spiritual lives properly. Truth should guide us, but not lead us to disputes with others. He also appeals to the halakhic precedent allowing one to change the truth.[18] Here the halakhah provides him with a clear axiological hierarchy, where peace is to be preferred to truth. Truth, in this practical halakhic instruction, refers to the dimension of

---

[18] Whether this is really telling untruths or only slightly modifying the truth, a concern of later halakhic discussion, is secondary to my present point.

truth addressed by R. Nahman, telling the truth in situations of daily living. R. Nathan extends this halakhic principle from truth-telling to the theoretical concerns of religious truth. Thus, the quest for peace serves as the overarching value that supports pluralism at the cost of truth.

Compared with R. Nahman's existential-metaphysical view of truth, a state to be attained, R. Nathan provides us with a view that is theoretical, inasmuch as truth is largely renounced in favour of another religious reality —faith, supported by peace and humility. Instead of the possibility of attaining a mystical realization of divine reality prior to creation, expressed as truth, R. Nathan offers us a vision of religious humility that forgoes truth in favour of a humble, peaceful, and accommodating faith. Rather than a virtue grounded in the highest metaphysical view, truth becomes a religious menace, an angelic vice, and a temptation that can distract one from true spiritual life and can lead to violent expressions of narrow, egoistic views. While never completely renouncing the concept of truth, R. Nathan limits its attainment to the kind of great masters who can live the teaching of R. Nahman, thereby redefining what truth is for the common faithful. Ultimately, not only is religious truth beyond our reach; it is more of a vice than a virtue.

Moving Outwards: Religious Truth and Interreligious Relations

What are the implications of R. Nathan's views on religious truth for interreligious relations? R. Nathan himself might have never considered applying these ideas beyond the confines of internal Jewish disputes. His key examples are the conflicts of hasidim and *mitnagedim*. However, the structure of his thought invites, or at least permits, such expansion, and several suggestive readings offered by him lend such an understanding further credence.

Perhaps most importantly, the entire discussion is grounded in the midrashic tale of the creation of man, even if R. Nathan immediately limits it to Israel. From the perspective of the human person, the dynamics of truth, peace, and transcending conflict are universal and are rooted in an understanding of the human person, both as an individual and as a member of society. R. Nathan's argument relies on the realization that the quest for truth takes place in the movement from the many to the one. This dynamic is obviously relevant to the entire realm of phenomenal existence, caught between the one and the many. But it has special relevance to a consideration of multiple religions. These are expressions of the many, while at the same time they also point to the One and provide access to it. If our core attitude is epistemological humility and recognition that divine truth transcends the boundaries of our understanding, should not this view also include the fact that multiple religious traditions point to the one ultimate reality? Our association of exclusive truth with one religion only may be an angelic drive that has to be transcended in favour of a divine view of reality. Finally, if axiological priority is given to peace over truth, is peace between religions not a primary expression of this axiological priority?

There are some specific references within R. Nathan's teaching that provide further insight for a discussion of 'truth and peace' between religions. In a gorgeous hermeneutical moment, he reads the story of the breaking of the Tablets of the Covenant by Moses, following the episode of the golden calf, in light of the dynamics of this teaching.

Moses saw the great destruction brought about by the sin of Israel having transgressed the entire Torah and served idols, so that, according to the law of truth of the Torah, Israel should have been distanced [from God] and destroyed... therefore Moses had the wisdom to throw the Tablets of the Law to the ground, which is the aspect of 'and you have thrown truth to the ground', as God cast truth to the ground after finding fault in the creation of man. So did Moses do, and he attached himself to God, and took the Tablets of the Covenant, which are the aspect of truth, the aspect of the Torah of truth, and cast them to the ground. By so doing he taught that even though they are the Torah of truth, nevertheless, if one considers that on their account one has lost hope and one can no longer pray for Israel, they must be cast to the ground, and [he] removed them from himself and strengthened himself to believe that one cannot attain the depth of the divine mind at all, till he recognized that, despite the sin, God want[ed] [Moses] to pray for them [Israel]. And therefore he prayed much for them, till he achieved through his prayer God's pardon. (subsection 28)

Moses repeats the primordial act of divine casting down of truth, preferring man, or Israel, over truth. It is R. Nathan's genius to identify the common gesture in both stories and to attribute to it the same significance. Now, here what is cast down is not truth as something abstract. Rather, it is the Torah itself—almost at the very moment of its revelation. The Torah is truth, and it must be cast to the ground in favour of a higher principle. The two principles that we have identified are compassion and peace. Divine compassion allows the individual to remain in God's sight and not to lose hope. Peace allows society to remain intact and not to become undone through conflict and controversy. If the Torah itself is sacrificed in the act for the sake of compassion or peace, this suggests that there is something beyond religion itself. It is God. God is beyond religion, which would then correspond to truth and be susceptible to the faults and errors of the angelic perfection, exercised in relation to religion. If one can paraphrase R. Nathan by saying that God transcends religion, and that religion itself, truth, Torah, must be cast to the ground for the sake of peace and God's compassion, does this principle not invite application beyond a specific religion, Judaism and its Torah? Could this not provide guidelines to what should be the attitude of all religions to truth, and therefore to each other? If so, religions should see each other in the eyes of God, through peace and compassion, and cast aside concerns for a truth that is ultimately beyond the reach of almost all believers.

Revisiting the notion of truth that is discovered through plurality could provide us with further indication of the applicability of R. Nathan's teaching beyond the internal Jewish context. As I suggested above, the truth that is attained through the earthbound orientation of multiplicity and plurality should be considered a synthetic truth that encompasses varying perspectives within a broader unitive framework. If so, it is worth noting that R. Nathan's reference to truth emerging from multiplicity extends beyond internal parameters and reaches out to the seventy nations, the archetypical representation of all that is not Jewish. He applies the principles of this teaching to the festival cycle of the month of Tishrei, understood as revealing truth through varying circumstances, even circumstances that are far from what is usually considered the core of truth. Following a reference to Sukkot as an expression of unifying internal diversity, R. Nathan refers to Shemini Atseret as a time of unifying diversity without.

This is the aspect of the four species [taken on Sukkot], which are inclusive of the various classes of Israel, those who learn Torah etc.,[19] so that even the willow is bound with the other species, representing those who are far removed, and who have neither taste nor smell. For through truth it is revealed that also from them God receives pleasure and in them He takes pride, through any true movement that is found in them, by means of which they draw themselves to God.

And this is the aspect of Simhat Torah and Shemini Atseret. Atseret refers to gathering, for it gathers and contains everything, bringing all close to God, even those who are very far removed, through the sukkah of peace in which we sat, for then [i.e. during Sukkot] we offered sacrifices even for the seventy nations,[20] to draw them all close to God, in the aspect of 'then I will restore to the peoples a pure

---

[19] A reference to the *midrash* that draws a correspondence between the four species and adherence or lack thereof to either Torah study or fulfilment of the *mitsvot*. See *Vayikra rabah*, 30: 12.

[20] It is worth noting that in other contexts R. Nathan presents a non-inclusive reading of the meaning of offering sacrifices on behalf of the seventy nations. See e.g. *Likutei halakhot*,

language, so that all of them may call on the name of the Lord and serve Him with one accord' [Zeph. 3: 9]. (subsection 27)

It is noteworthy that the harmonious inclusion of all is a consequence of the peace associated with the sukkah. Thus, peace prevails and it redefines the meaning of truth, so that the seventy nations are included in it and are subsumed under the broader notion of truth. If so, it does not seem like a stretch to include their respective truths as part of the broader quest for truth, reconciled, harmonized, and synthesized in the person of the messiah, who fulfils the purpose of multiplicity by discovering the unity of truth in the greatest diversity of religious opinion.

Both R. Nahman and R. Nathan provide us with approaches that can be translated to the concerns of truth and the interreligious situation. For R. Nahman, truth is grounded in the order beyond creation. As such, it transcends all multiplicity, including the multiplicity of religions. Where through reflection and mystical experience one can rediscover this higher metaphysical ground is where religions can meet. For the rest, concerns for the content of belief captured as religious truth should be cast aside in favour of the concern for truthful living in the everyday world.

R. Nathan offers us another lesson. For him, it is not the quest for the highest truth—the truth beyond—that could provide the formula for interreligious harmony. Rather, it is the recognition that truth cannot be attained and that other values are superior to it—are beyond truth. It is God's will that we live in peace and compassion with one another, and focusing on truth ultimately goes against the very foundations that make it possible for humanity to exist, imperfect as it is. God does not will truth, nor can we attain it. God's highest purpose, the ultimate truth, points to compassion and peace as the guiding values of life, and consequently these should also govern interreligious relations.

While R. Nathan addresses Israel as the subject of his discussion, there is further ground in his teaching to legitimate extending it also to other religions. This may be suggested by closer consideration of who it is that R. Nathan explicitly excludes from the mandate of harmonious validation, in the name of peace and at the expense of truth. Farther along, he examines the laws of idol worshippers, referring specifically to various superstitions that are typical of idolaters. In this discussion he offers us a portrayal of where truth can go wrong and of the limits of recognition.

'Hilkhot rosh hashanah', 4: 8, and many other similar occurrences. In the present context, he offers an inclusive reading, seeing the nations as incorporated in the higher reality, which is characterized by truth.

The essential truth of the majority of people is to know that one cannot attain consciously the essence of truth; therefore, one has to become strong in faith, which is dependent on truth . . . but whoever does not attain ultimate truth, but only misleads himself as though he seeks truth, but his intention is for his own sake, such as honour and other desires, he can be greatly misled through his truth . . . not only can he be misled through his truth to confused ways, he can also come to false beliefs through his confused faith, which is the aspect of all the superstitions of idol worshippers, who are very strong in their faith, and nevertheless all is untruth and falsehood, because their faith is a consequence of their desires and the search for honour . . . and whoever is removed from truth to superstitions, it is very hard to bring him back to truth . . . because someone who is mistaken with regard to truth, even though it is very hard to bring him back to ultimate truth, there is nevertheless hope that he can be brought back, because one can prove to him that truth is not as he considers, even though it requires great effort. But someone who has strayed from the truth till he came through a confused truth to superstitions, it is very hard to bring him back to truth and straight faith, because faith is something that has no reasoning, because when one understands the reason of faith, it is not faith . . . because even if one proves conclusively that the matter is not so, he will say, I forgo my understanding and believe in this with full faith, with no reason, because this is how faith works, and for this reason it is hard to find truth in the world. (subsection 43)

This section seems to suggest that R. Nathan might not go along with us in the application of his teachings to the attitude towards other religions. Are these not mistaken faiths, affirmations that are made regardless of reason, in the name of pure faith? Actually, it seems to me that the passage can be read to the contrary. R. Nathan's view of superstitions growing out of idolatry—and it almost does not matter if he also viewed contemporary Christianity in such terms or not[21]—is that these are founded on impure motivations. Desires and the search for fame and recognition are the motivating factors that corrupt one's thinking, eventually leading the impure believer into a set of capricious beliefs that others cannot successfully engage with. If so, it would be very unfair to approach other religions as we know them today from such a perspective. If purification of desire and purity of motive serve as yardsticks, then there is a moral control to the entire discussion, one that precedes the discussion of substantive faith and the particularities of truths held by different religions. If so, intellectual honesty—our own truth prerequisite—requires us to recognize that the religions we meet in the present encounter with other religions share the premise and prerequisite of seeking to transcend human

---

[21] The halakhic context upon which he is commenting is not contemporary; he addresses the superstitious beliefs of religions of old.

weakness and to live a life in true service of God (or truth). If so, their beliefs cannot be dismissed as irrational nonsense, fortified in the name of faith. Tertullian's famous maxim of belief because something is absurd would be irrelevant to an interreligious exchange. What is reasonable or not reasonable, what is subject to discussion and what is beyond discussion, would be conditioned by a prior investigation of the moral quality of life and the deeper intentions that inform the religious life of members of another religion, certainly of their finest and most sincere practitioners. If so, the same principles that apply to internal differences concerning truth should also apply to competing truth claims between different religions. We recall that one of the dimensions of truth that R. Nathan recognized was intention for truth. In members of other religions we should be able to identify at least that level of sincerity of the quest for truth, supported by a moral life and the intention to reach the Divine, which would allow us to apply to them the same principles that we are asked to apply to internal differences. If so, R. Nathan's great lesson is that one must cast aside all arguments of truth. We must consider the human person, even as God did at the very moment of creation. We should not judge like the angels, but practise a higher level of truth, associated with God himself. This will lead us to prefer peace and compassion, under all circumstances, to the particularities of the beliefs we hold as true. A life of faith, lived humbly in relation to God and bearing the fruits of peace and compassion, is the ultimate proof of the truth of our beliefs. This can be recognized across religions, suggesting a higher harmony and pointing to a future messianic peace.

CHAPTER SIX

The Cognitive Value of Religious Truth Statements
Rabbi A. I. Kook and Postmodernism

TAMAR ROSS

In relation to the highest divine truth, there is no difference between formulated religion and heresy. Both do not yield the truth, because whatever positive assertion one makes is a step removed from the truth of the Divine.[1]

R. KOOK, *Orot ha'emunah*, 23–4

Or how do you MYSTICS, who maintain the absolute incomprehensibility of the Deity, differ from sceptics or atheists, who assert that the first cause of all is unknown and unintelligible?

DAVID HUME, *Dialogues Concerning Natural Religion*,
Pt. IV beginning, attrib. to Cleanthes

The core of faith is [the belief in] the greatness of infinity [Ein Sof], so that anything that enters the heart is only an insignificant spark compared to what ought to be imagined, and what ought to be imagined does not even approach the category of insignificance as against what really is. And if the heart's understanding is torn from its source, then it becomes impoverished and has no value. And there is no remedy that will make it shine forth in a vivid manner, except through connecting with the light of faith, which is the general illumination transcending all particular values, and because of this it is the basis for all particular values. All matters of faith excepting [the belief in] the greatness of infinity [Ein Sof] are merely explanations so that we may arrive by means of these to the core of faith, and the explanations are like the limbs of the king, and some of them are like the garb of the king, and whoever disrespects the garb of the king, he, too, raises his hand [against the king] and is punishable by death, and in any case it is necessary to explain gradually the differences between the core of faith and its explanations, and within the explanations themselves one also must explain the differences in their levels.

R. KOOK, *Orot ha'emunah*, 41–2

---

[1] All translations of R. Kook are my own unless otherwise stated.

THE above three quotations tell the whole story of this essay. The first poses a simple proposition as a paradox. The second sees in this a radical problem. The third offers a solution.

Non-Realism in Theology

That truth consists in some sort of agreement between our thoughts or statements and what is the case is a very ancient and undisputed insight. Some philosophers have construed this 'agreement' on the model of 'copy and original'—hence the so-called 'correspondence' theory of truth. Others have denied the appropriateness of this model, and have suggested different models for construing this insight: the relationship between 'sapling and tree' was appropriated by some exponents of the coherence theory of truth (Brand Blanshard), and 'a preliminary idea leading to further satisfaction' in the pragmatist theory of truth (William James). However, these different philosophical theories concern our statements when they are meant to be descriptive and literally understood. What happens when our statements are meant to be metaphorical and non-literal?

Consider, for example, the story of King David and Uriah the Hittite (2 Sam. 12). David lusts after Uriah's beautiful wife Batsheva, and arranges for Uriah to be sent to the front line of battle. Uriah is duly killed and David marries Batsheva. The prophet Nathan goes to David and tells him the story of two men, one rich and one poor (2 Sam. 12: 2–7):

The rich man had very large flocks and herds, but the poor man had only one little ewe lamb that he had bought. He had tended it and it grew up together with him and with his children; it used to share his morsel of bread, drink from his cup, and nestle in his bosom; it was like a daughter to him. One day, a traveler came to the rich man, but he was loath to take anything from his own flocks or herds to prepare a meal for the guest who had come to him; so he took the poor man's lamb and prepared it for the man who had come to him. And David flew into a rage against the man, and said to Nathan . . . 'The man who did this deserves to die! . . . because he did such a thing and showed no pity.' And Nathan said to David: 'That man is you!'[2]

Here we have a parable. Nathan's story was not meant to be literally true, even though David mistakenly took it to be so. It was, rather, intended to get David to see his own situation in a new light. It pointed out a similarity between David's situation and that of the imaginary rich man of the story. Such parables are the basis of a great many *midrashim* and statements of the rabbis in talmudic literature. In many other non-literal uses of language, as in similes

---

[2] *Tanakh: The Holy Scriptures* (Philadelphia: Jewish Publication Society of America, 1978).

('as industrious as an ant') or metaphors ('the Lord is my shepherd'), it is not so much factual truth that is sought, but rather instruction, illumination, and so on.

But what of religious statements that are made in the context of the biblical references to God—that he is jealous, has a right hand, fingers, nostrils, and the like? Are these intended as literal truths or is the use metaphorical? Since ancient times such descriptions have been treated in the Targumim, in talmudic literature, and especially in medieval Jewish philosophy, as paradigm cases of metaphorical uses of language. The motivation for this has largely been a discomfort at the realization that these involve anthropomorphism, and a feeling that such anthropomorphisms reflect a homely but unjustified predilection for describing God in terms that we find familiar. Since Hellenistic times at least there was also a philosophical motive for stressing the metaphorical character of these statements: the feeling that they involved a material, sensational mode of description where only a purely spiritual, non-sensible sort of description should have been appropriate. There was a growing understanding that God was not only invisible (and thus unlike anything that could be imaged or pictured, as the Bible itself insisted), but also purely spiritual, and thus incapable of being sensed in any other manner as well. Hence, since God could not, in principle, be heard or smelled or tasted or touched, as well as not being capable of being seen, all the verses in the Bible that used such categories had to be, of necessity, interpreted as metaphorical. Nor was there special difficulty in appreciating what their metaphorical meaning was, in most cases. Thus the verse 'Taste, then, and see that the Lord is good' (Ps. 34: 9) must mean something like: 'Consider and you will recognize' (Targum); 'this is "the heart's seeing"' (Ibn Ezra); or 'Taste his word—the Torah' (Rashi).

Taking this difficulty one step further, however, what are we to make of talk of the very existence of God, and how are we to characterize the 'religious facts' he generates, such as creation, the chosenness of the Jewish people and their deliverance from Egypt, the voice of God as it was heard in the revelation at Sinai, and many more? Regarding this last issue, the medieval commentators hesitated between a sound specially created by God and 'hearing the voice' being a metaphor for 'prophetic understanding'. The assumption was that our unguarded and grossly physical talk of God could always be interpreted figuratively, as something that would be appropriate to a purely spiritual being. But concerning the assertion of God's very existence and other anthropomorphic ramifications of his activities—here the medieval philosophers and kabbalists began to be troubled. This was because they were influenced by the Platonic and Neoplatonic conception of the One who was 'above words'. Nevertheless, even in these cases, the non-literalist interpretations of the medieval authorities always assumed that there was some cognitive function to the crucial religious statements speaking of God, his existence, his actions, and so on. The kabbalists understood anthropomorphisms as inadequate but necessary symbolic representations of something even more real on the spiritual level. God does not speak with a voice in the human sense; nevertheless, the human voice partakes, in grosser form, of the same characteristics of divine speech. On the other hand, when the rationalist philosophers were faced with the difficulty of conflicts between the surface meaning of religious truth statements and the spiritual nature of God or the evidence of logic and science, they often opted for reinterpreting biblical passages which appear to be reporting supernatural events in a non-literal fashion, so that they may be understood as visions, optical illusions, abbreviated descriptions, and the like, but such passages were still viewed as saying *something* about the real world. Even a metaphor is a metaphor of something, and as such demands reconciliation of sorts with a rival scientific contention. By contrast, non-traditionalists tend to totally discount the value of religious truth statements as primitive myths of a bygone age because they do not correspond to the way things are and refer to nothing real whatsoever. A total non-cognitivism and non-realism in this regard is a relatively new phenomenon, dating, in the civilization of Christian Europe, from the 1830s. These early non-realists were not really defenders of the established religious tradition, but, at most, sympathetic interpreters. But it is their work that eventually led to the development of a more charitable view of religious truth statements, which, while still denying their literal value as informative propositions regarding the world, God, and history that can be simply verified or falsified empirically, nevertheless regards them favourably as tools for establishing or expressing a set of values uncommitted to any hard and fast metaphysical or ontological claims.

The first well-known interpreters of religious statements and beliefs as non-cognitive in function and non-realist in significance were two figures among the followers of Hegel. David Friedrich Strauss (1808–74) expounded the view that religion, and Christianity in particular, is an expression of the human mind's capacity to generate myths and treat them as truths revealed by God to man.[3] His historical investigations of the life of Jesus convinced him that the principal importance of the Gospels was aesthetic and philo-

---

[3] David Friedrich Strauss, *Das Leben Jesu Kritisch Berbeitet*, 2 vols. (Tübingen, 1835–6); Eng. edn. *The Life of Jesus Critically Examined*, trans. George Eliot (London, 1848).

sophical. Hence, the Gospels represented an unconscious invention, or myth, which attempted to envision the Absolute in terms of images derived from sensible experience. They should be viewed as poetic renderings of man's desire to realize the immanent goal of Spirit in its journey towards the Hegelian Being-in-and-for-itself.

An alternative revision of Hegelianism was offered by Ludwig Andreas Feuerbach (1804–72),[4] who explained the myth-making mechanism that was characteristic of man, and which reflected his superiority over the animals, as a means by which man 'projects his being into objectivity, and then again makes himself an object to this projected image of himself thus converted into a subject; he thinks of himself not as an object to himself but as an object of an object, of another being than himself.' Thus religion is nothing but the consciousness which man has of his own infinite nature. Man is self-transcending, and religion is one of his means of objectifying his own essence in ideal terms, of spinning out visions of what he might be. Christianity reflects the dream of man to become God and the realization that this can be achieved only through a transcendent love of one's fellow man.

Such views of religion, although reductionist in character and widely attacked by reactionary opinion, nevertheless provided a sympathetic interpretation of religious myth-making. In their wake there grew an attempt to give a still more positive interpretation of the myth-making involved in religious talk, which could be accepted by religious believers themselves. Hence the attempts of such theologians and biblical scholars as Rudolf Bultmann (1884–1953) to regard the mythical language and non-historical character of the message of the New Testament as an indirect description of the conditions and possibilities of human existence rather than of the real world. Bultmann interprets the Bible in terms of the existentialist notions of Martin Heidegger regarding the importance of authenticity in living one's life. The 'demythologizing' of the religious texts reveals their character as a philosophy of life guiding man in the task of overcoming his angst. This is a form of existentialist reinterpretation and dwells on the importance of the internal life.

The writings of Ludwig Wittgenstein (1889–1951) also provided the basis for a sympathetic understanding of the importance of religious life. Even though he did not regard himself as a religious believer, some of his followers (in particular R. B. Braithwaite and D. Z. Phillips) who regarded themselves as religious believers have espoused a religious non-realism, in which religious language and myth provide an overall 'picture' which comes to

---

[4] In his *Das Wesen des Christentums* (Leipzig, 1841); Eng. edn. *The Essence of Christianity*, trans. M. Evans [George Eliot] (London, 1854).

encourage and reflect a moral way of life. For Braithwaite, the myths and stories perform this function only partially successfully in that they point to a profounder level of religious experience, 'the mystical', about which we can say no more. For Phillips, the stress is on the function of religious statements as part of the 'language game' in which they function.

What is common to all such non-realist accounts of religious language is that they remove the need for any ontological claims being attached to religious statements. Despite the fact that some of the twentieth-century exponents of this view (Braithwaite, Bultmann, Cupitt, Phillips, etc.) combine the completely non-cognitivist and non-realist interpretation of the religious statements which they use with a declared religious allegiance, it is widely assumed that such theologians and philosophers will be liberal in their attachment to their religious traditions. Particularly within Judaism, one of the criteria generally assumed to this day to be a definitive dividing line between traditional and non-traditional modes of thinking is the ontological grounding attributed by each to religious truth statements. When traditionalists speak, they may be divided regarding the degree of faithfulness to be attached to the literal meaning of these statements, but all generally concur that they do bear some degree of cognitive value.[5] Something informative is being said about the way things are.

To take one example as illustration: a traditionalist will most likely demythologize the famous saying of R. Yohanan that three books are open on Rosh Hashanah, and that the fate of those for whom good and bad deeds are balanced is sealed on Yom Kippur,[6] by understanding that R. Yohanan is not referring to actual book-balancing in the physical sense. But he will still understand this statement as a metaphorical expression of the fact that these dates indeed do bear ominous metaphysical significance in determining our fate in the world to come. The newer type of non-traditionalist, on the other hand, will not discount the value of R. Yohanan's statement altogether, but the degree of demythologizing he will apply to this statement will be far more radical in that it denies not only the concept of God as a divine bookkeeper,

---

[5] See Avi Sagi, 'Tolerance and the Possibility of Pluralism in Judaism' (Heb.), *Iyun*, 44 (Apr. 1995), 195.

[6] BT *RH* 16b. It may interest the reader to learn that this example came up for discussion in one of my classes (on Maimonides' theory of Divine Providence) at Midreshet Lindenbaum in 1995, in the wake of Yitzhak Rabin's assassination. Some of my students asked (out of theological and not political interest): must we not conclude that questions of life and death, unlike other matters of Divine Providence, are definitely determined in advance on the High Holidays, so that Rabin's death must be regarded as the will of God, and cannot be ascribed to chance?

but also the idea that our fates are ever sealed in advance on any particular date. According to this, R. Yohanan's statement will be viewed merely as a way of inculcating in human beings the feeling of awe and responsibility for their deeds.

One of the least noted and appreciated aspects of R. Kook's thought is the originality and audacity of his approach as a traditionalist in precisely this area, in spite of his unswerving loyalty to traditional Jewish thought and practice. This is not to say that R. Kook was a complete non-cognitivist. But in his view, the ontological commitment of most religious truth statements is a relative matter, as is notoriously the case in the view of many mystics, ancient and modern. And especially as a result of his subtle reinterpretation of the kabbalistic tradition, he adopted an extremely bold and hypermodern account of human religious truth claims, which brings some of his opinions regarding faith proclamations very close to a non-realist position.

R. Kook as a Non-Realist Option for Tradition

Given his commitment to Jewish tradition, R. Kook is surprisingly sceptical regarding the ability of any religious formulation to capture the truth finally and completely. His scepticism in this matter stems from much more profound questions regarding the absolute value of truth statements in general. In this sense, R. Kook was definitely a modern, who accepted all the repercussions of what has come to be known in general philosophy as Kant's 'Copernican revolution' in the theory of knowledge.[7] Man necessarily thinks in certain categories, in terms of space, time, causality, and the like, and these categories serve as a kind of structure or sieve through which all our impressions of unadulterated reality are sifted and mediated. However, he did not think that this assessment of truth claims was an innovation of Kant. As he writes in one of his letters:

Even the 'neo-Kantian' revival cannot match even the smallest part of Israel's strength. It is true, and we [Jews] have always known it—and we did not need Kant to reveal this secret to us—that all human cognitions are relative and subjective. This is the Kingdom as a vessel that has no power of its own, and the Synagogue or Moon that receives illumination. All our acts, our emotions, our prayers, our

---

[7] Kant compared the revolution that Copernicus generated in cosmological thinking when teaching that it is really the earth that revolves around the sun to the revolution he initiated in the theory of knowledge by demonstrating that it is not man's mind that travels 'around' reality, but rather, our reality is shaped by the categories and constructs that human thought imposes upon it.

thoughts—everything is dependent on Zot—*bezot ani bote'aḥ*, 'in this will I be confident' [Ps. 27: 3].[8]

In other words, R. Kook seems to be implying that Kant's innovations were superfluous to Judaism because long before him, the kabbalah had already taught us that Malkhut (Kingdom), the lowest of the ten sefirotic manifestations of Ein Sof, the Infinite Godhead, has no inherent essence of its own. As an empty vessel, it merely serves as a receptacle or conduit for all the lights of the higher *sefirot* reflected within it. This is why the kabbalists likened this *sefirah* to the moon, which has no light of its own but reflects the light of the sun, or to the synagogue, which is not intrinsically holy but rather receives its sacredness from the assembly of those who come to pray. The illumination of Malkhut is merely a marker of pathways to the infinite, and is not to be equated with the Absolute itself. Nevertheless Malkhut is also called Zot (This), because it is the only manifestation of the Ein Sof definite and specific enough to be discerned.

This equation on the part of R. Kook of the relationship between the last *sefirah* and those above it in kabbalistic thought to the relationship between the phenomenon and the noumenon in the Kantian terminology is, of course, not entirely accurate.[9] The kabbalah, which still follows the Neoplatonist tradition, accords Malkhut a lower value in the hierarchy of knowledge on grounds that are more ontological than epistemological. In other words, the apprehension of Malkhut is inferior not because it presents the source (Ein Sof) in a mediated, distorted fashion, but because it *is* a secondary, derivative reflection of the original source of light, a weak shadow of the 'real' world. According to Kant, however, the difference between the phenomenon and the noumenal reality is a perceptual one, making no direct commitment at all regarding their respective ontological status. Nevertheless, if there is a basis for comparison between the kabbalah and Kant, it is because both views assert that all our perceptions are somehow limited, based as they are

---

[8] *Igerot hare'ayah* (Jerusalem: Mosad Harav Kook, 1985), i. 47–8.

[9] See the comments of the translator and annotator of the English version of the above passage, who adds: 'Malkhut stands to the upper sefirot as does phenomenon to noumenon in Kantian terminology' (A. Y. Kook, *Selected Letters*, trans. and annotated by Tzvi Feldman (Ma'alei Adumim: Maalot Publications, 1986), 92). It seems to me, however, that if Malkhut corresponds to the phenomenal world, then the proper Kantian parallel to the *sefirot* above it are the categories of human thought, with the Ein Sof corresponding to the noumenon. Another possibility of interpretation is equation of the upper *sefirot* with the divine essence of Ein Sof (as is generally done in Lurianic kabbalah), and of Malkhut (as an empty vessel containing nothing of that essence) with the categories of human thought in filtering the sefirotic reality while relaying it to our world.

on how things appear to us, after having been filtered through the apparatus of human categories (for Kant) or the structure of the *sefirot* (for kabbalah), rather than confronted in raw and unmediated experience.

Although R. Kook is perhaps unique in explicitly making this connection between the Neoplatonic and the Kantian view, he certainly was not the first Jewish traditionalist to have merged the older kabbalistic grounding for the limited understanding of the human point of view in understanding reality with more modern varieties of epistemological modesty. This amalgam already appears in the writings of all the allegorical interpreters of the Lurianic doctrine of *tsimtsum*, who distinguish between God's point of view (or absolute truth) and our human point of view.[10] It is also interesting to note that these ideas erupted in the Jewish world at approximately the same time that Kant (1724–1804) was explicating them to the world at large, and may be taken in part as a religious counterpoint to the Kantian revolution expressed in kabbalistic idiom.

However, for Kant, the categories of thought that mediate between the two realities were understood to be fixed forms of apprehension with which our phenomenal selves operated, whereas R. Kook, as opposed to the previous exponents of the allegorical interpretation to *tsimtsum*, is closer to the neo-Kantians of the late nineteenth century and early twentieth century in the Back to Kant movement, who viewed all the basic categories of our apprehension which we use in order to grasp reality, as well as the more localized concepts to which they give rise, as fluid, tentative instruments subject to revision. Herein, as is well known, lies one of the seams connecting the neo-Kantian tradition with what has come to be called Pragmatism. Certainly this is one of the factors that lend R. Kook's thinking its uniquely modern and non-traditionalist flavour, and lead him to pay greater attention to new issues that stem inevitably from recognition of the relative and non-objective nature of the human perspective. Even when not directly formulated as such, his writing—as opposed to that of his kabbalistic predecessors—provides the raw material for extrapolating answers to such typically contemporary questions as:

---

[10] For an exposition of the Lurianic doctrine of *tsimtsum*, see Gershom Scholem, *Major Trends in Jewish Mysticism* (New York: Schocken Books, 1946), 244–86. For more extensive discussion of the allegorical interpretation of this doctrine, see Louis Jacobs, *Seeker of Unity: The Life and Works of Aaron of Starosselje* (London: Vallentine Mitchell, 1966), 90–110; Tamar Ross, 'Two Interpretations of the Doctrine of *Tsimtsum*: R. Hayim of Volozhin and R. Shneur Zalman of Liadi' (Heb.), *Jerusalem Studies in Jewish Thought*, 2 (1982), 153–69.

- Do subjective and relative truth statements bear any ontological grounding at all, or does so-called truth-seeking activity now have a different, non-cognitive purpose?
- If truth statements are ontologically grounded, what could possibly be the basis for this conviction, and if they are not, what remains as a valid criterion for deciding between rival truth claims when the certainty of objectivity has fallen?

The most that can be gleaned from the traditionalist Jewish non-objectivists preceding R. Kook regarding the first question is either that, since all our perceptions are relative and non-objective, the purpose of any truth-seeking activity must be to try and transcend the illusory veil of reality and merge existentially with the noumenal beyond, or that we must resign ourselves to remaining with the imperfect perception we have now.[11] The latter view comes out of a realistic acknowledgement of the fact that the subjective perception is all we will ever have to work with,[12] or a more affirmative sense that this perception does bear some infinitesimal connection with its more authentic source.[13] But other issues arising out of the second question (such as 'What is the basis for these various convictions?' or 'What should be the criterion for preferring one subjective or relative view over another in the event of rival perceptions?') are virtually ignored, and the positions taken seem to merely reflect the personal existential experience or tradition of the writer concerned. R. Kook, on the other hand, appears in these issues to be voicing new themes, which have their parallels in the post-Kantian tradition.

Admittedly, R. Kook did not develop his ideas in the form of a rigorous, precisely articulated, and full-blown philosophy, and one must be wary of anachronistic attempts to equate his views with more extensively worked-out responses to the Kantian critique that were developed in European philosophy. Nevertheless, it may be possible to extract the bare bones of a coherent position from scattered instances where he implements his views in practice in order to assess the relative validity of rival truth claims. Although not presented systematically as such, some of the ideas he expresses regarding these questions foreshadow stands taken in more modern debates which have arisen in the wake of the difficulties posed by the adoption of historicist

---

[11] See Ross, 'Two Interpretations of the Doctrine of *Tsimtsum*' (Heb.).

[12] Eliyahu Dessler, *Mikhtav me'eliyahu*, ed. Aryeh Carmel and Hayim Friedlander (Benei Berak: Hapo'el Hamizrahi, 1964), iii. 257.

[13] Hayim of Volozhin, *Nefesh haḥayim* (Vilna, 1874), sha'ar 3, perek 7, p. 31a; sha'ar 4, perek 27, p. 47; Ross, 'Two Interpretations of the Doctrine of *Tsimtsum*' (Heb.), 160.

premises for the enterprise of contemporary theology. Thus one may ask, given our newly intensified understanding of the time- and place-bound conditioning of truth claims: Can religious beliefs still be regarded as having absolute validity? One may also ask, once cultural relativism is acknowledged: How is it possible to speak of any truth as absolute in the ultimate sense that religious truth statements have traditionally claimed for themselves? As a result of this new relativist emphasis, discussion among general philosophers of religion now focuses less on substantive questions and more on the issues of meaning, truth, and justification in theological construction; more precisely, part of the debate centres upon what religious language is *about*, or to what it is meant to refer, whether theologians make truth claims at all, and, if so, what theories of truth are operative, and how such claims, when made, can be justified. Various kernels of thought in R. Kook's writings might be regarded as precursors of contemporary non-realist answers to these questions, and they establish an interesting precedent, illustrating how such ideas can be incorporated within a traditionalist world view.

'Necessary Truths' and 'Absolute Truths'

Because of his initial scepticism regarding the transparency of human perception, R. Kook writes in a very Kantian-like vein not only of the impossibility of knowing God, but of ever knowing the essential nature of anything at all:

We cannot know the essence of anything, not of ourselves, and a fortiori not of others. We are constantly skirting the core of knowledge, engaging in surmises and suppositions, basing ourselves on the world of appearances, and only from these making hypotheses regarding their causes.[14]

On the basis of his recognition of the subjective and relative nature of human knowledge, R. Kook arrives at some particularly startling conclusions about religious belief. Thus, for example, when weighing up the most basic issue of faith versus heresy, he asserts:

In relation to the highest divine truth, there is no difference between formulated religion and heresy. Both do not yield the truth, because whatever positive assertion a man makes is a step removed from the truth of the Divine.'[15]

[14] *Orot hakodesh* (Jerusalem: Mosad Harav Kook, 1985), iii. 119.
[15] *Orot ha'emunah*, ed. Mosheh Gurevitz (Brooklyn: Langsam Associates, 1985), 23–4. This passage was copied from the original edition of *Arpelei tohar* (Yaffo, 1914), whose publication was curtailed shortly after its initiation and the book was rendered virtually unavail-

The rationale, of course, for this surprisingly radical statement is the understanding that the moment we attempt to define 'the thing as it is in itself' (to use Kant's terminology), we necessarily distance ourselves from it and distort it with mediating concepts.

The lack of strict attunement between religious truth formulations and the reality they purport to embody is clarified in another passage, where R. Kook distinguishes between levels of belief. In this passage, he borrows terms from Maimonides' *Guide* iii. 28, and refers to 'necessary beliefs' (*emunot mukhraḥot*) as contrasted with 'true beliefs' (*emunot amitiyot*), which are defined as the base which sustains faith in general (*hayesod hamekayem et kelalut ha'emunah*). As R. Kook puts it:

> All beliefs are divided into the two categories that Maimonides already commented upon: true beliefs and necessary beliefs. The true beliefs serve as the basis which sustains faith in general, and the necessary ones are like an outer peel, and protect the fruit commensurate with the value of each nation and each group which rallies under the banner of a particular belief.[16]

It is worth noting that, despite some resemblance in usage, R. Kook's appropriation of the Maimonidean terminology is misleading. In *Guide* iii. 28, Maimonides does discuss the differences between what he terms true beliefs and necessary beliefs. But in his usage, true beliefs are those that do teach, in a literal fashion, some absolute truth about God, such as his existence, unity, eternity, and omnipotence. Their purpose is to enable one to attain intellectual perfection. Necessary beliefs, the basis of which is tradition and not philosophy, are expressed in figurative form and fulfil a political function in that, by instilling obedience to the Torah, they regulate the social relations of human beings. In addition, they enable people to acquire noble qualities.[17] But in R. Kook's usage, the distinction between true and necessary

---

able. The passage reappears in somewhat revised form in a second edition of *Arpelei tohar*, ed. Yitshak Shilat (Jerusalem: Mahon Harav Tsevi Yehudah, 1983), 45, published long after R. Kook's death. This later edition (from which all other references in my essay are taken) features occasional editorial tampering, which serves to mute some radical tones in the original. For a more detailed and updated account of the editing process of R. Kook's spiritual diaries (which are gradually being released in uncensored form) and its motives, see Avinoam Rosenak, 'Hidden Diaries and New Discoveries: The Life and Thought of Rabbi A. I. Kook', *Shofar: An Interdisciplinary Journal of Jewish Studies*, 25/3 (Spring 2007), 111–47.

[16] *Orot ha'emunah*, 48.

[17] As Arthur Hyman phrases it, Maimonides understands necessary beliefs as propositions that are true in some respect though not in another. See Hyman, 'Spinoza's Dogmas of Universal Faith in the Light of their Medieval Jewish Background', in Alexander Altmann (ed.), *Biblical and Other Studies* (Cambridge, Mass.: Harvard University Press, 1963), 189.

beliefs is not between the absolute truth of the philosophers and the political truths required for the masses. The distinction is rather between truths that cannot be formulated at all (neither by the philosophers nor by the masses) and truths that, for all human beings as such, are a means for acquiring the former. Moreover, these secondary truths are necessary not only in the political but even in the conceptual sense. R. Kook's neo-Kantian sensibilities are especially revealed in the last sentence of the above passage, in which he establishes the transitory nature of necessary beliefs. As opposed to *ha'emet ha'elyonah* (the sublime truth), which is constant and universal, necessary beliefs are always relative and liable to be in a state of flux. This is because there is a dialectical relationship between these institutionalized beliefs (which R. Kook elsewhere terms *emunah metsuyeret*) and the unformulated moral urge to which they are giving expression.

The weak ontological status that R. Kook grants to religious truth claims is further elaborated upon in passages where he distinguishes between various levels of religious understanding. At the base of this hierarchy of knowledge is what we refer to when we speak of religion in the raw, or what R. Kook terms sometimes *ikar ha'emunah* or *ikar hayedi'ah*.[18] This raw sensibility can only be characterized as an elemental life force, a feeling of yearning undefined by any more substantive content. At the other end of the scale is the ultimate object of the raw religious urge, which he terms *ha'emet ha'elyonah*[19] or *yedi'ah elyonah*.[20] If *ikar ha'emunah* precedes words, *ha'emet ha'elyonah* is beyond them, and therefore it, too, defies definition, transcends any type of dogmatic labelling, and is absolutely universal. This concept roughly parallels the concept of *emunot amitiyot* of the previous passage. But in between the virgin sensibility that precedes words and that which is beyond them lies an intermediate stage which, in R. Kook's terminology, is often labelled *otsar hayedi'ot* (the storehouse of knowledge),[21] *otsar haruhaniyut* (the storehouse of spirituality),[22] or *ha'emunah hametsuyeret* (formulated belief).[23] This concept corresponds to what he previously termed *emunot mukhrahot*, and signifies the articulated expression of our unformulated convictions. It is on this level that the yearning for perfection may assume many different forms—and not all of them need be professedly religious ones. In this sense both doubt and faith, while each has some validity, are limited ontologically, never fully capturing the object of their depictions. What institutionalized religion (or irreligion) does is to try to give our most elemental feeling some form, some cultivated method of expression.

---

[18] *Arpelei tohar*, 31.   [19] *Orot ha'emunah*, 23–4.   [20] *Arpelei tohar*, 13–14.
[21] *Orot hakodesh*, i. 56.   [22] *Arpelei tohar*, 31.   [23] *Orot ha'emunah*, 23–4; *Arpelei tohar*, 45.

All this does not mean that religious claims in R. Kook's eyes are a total free-for-all. His view of religious truth does not serve as grounds for pure relativism and reduction of exclusivist religious commitments.[24] When dealing with the preverbal, raw sensibility common to all created beings, or the ultimate object of this elemental life force, it would appear that R. Kook regards these as self-evident and in no need of further justification.[25] But when dealing with the middle level of verbalized formulation, not all religious claims are equally valid; some contain only a grain of truth, and others are better because they contain more. But since, in absolute terms, all are equally off the mark, the justification for preferring one alternative over another must now be based on criteria for truths that are not primarily cognitive. Various criteria present themselves in his writings; some of these are still traditional and do not necessarily negate the presumption of agreement with reality. Thus, in a passage which weighs the merits of creation ex nihilo versus emanationist views of the world, one reason offered for preferring the latter is the elegance of its simplicity. Since, as R. Kook puts it, it is perfectly possible to adopt the emanationist view without any obstacles, we should prefer it, as this is the easiest and most obvious explanation of creation.[26] Other passages suggest comprehensiveness (i.e. the ability of one umbrella truth to accommodate more particularistic truths within it)[27] or a type of holistic coherence, or internal consistency as a criterion for establishing the validity of religious truth claims (i.e. the fact that all the various pieces of truth fit together and interact harmoniously in a systematic whole).[28] Even the criterion of popular consensus (the fact that a society willingly adopts these claims as truths), which also features quite prominently in R. Kook's writings,[29] need not necessarily be understood as forgoing the hope of grasping what really is, especially if one attributes (as R. Kook does) to the specific society concerned a special capacity for intuitively apprehending ultimate reality.[30] But the most striking criterion for adoption of religious truths in R. Kook's writings is an instrumental one—the fact that a certain theory is

---

[24] *Orot ha'emunah*, 41–2. [25] *Arpelei tohar*, 13–14; *Orot ha'emunah*, 66.

[26] *Arpelei tohar*, 32–3. See also *Orot hakodesh*, ii. 349. Presumably the emanationist view (which understands creation as something like birth) is simplest because it allows God to fashion the world out of something that is already there (himself) and it is certainly more reasonable than the paradox of creation ex nihilo.

[27] *Orot* (Jerusalem: Mosad Harav Kook, 1969), 130–1.

[28] *Arpelei tohar*, 13–14; *Orot hakodesh*, ii. 538.

[29] *Eder hayakar* (Jerusalem: Mosad Harav Kook, 1982), 39; *Igerot hare'ayah*, i. 193–4.

[30] For passages which accord a special status to the truth-perceptive abilities of Keneset Yisra'el, see *Orot hakodesh*, i. 145; *Orot*, 88–9, 138; *Orot hakodesh*, iii. 67–8.

useful (in a sense to be illustrated in the examples which follow) is what makes it true. In many instances it is for this instrumentalist reason, and not because of theoretical claims to truth, that R. Kook will assert that, although no particular religious model captures the truth in its entirety, which particular model of truth we choose to adopt is not a matter of indifference.

What is the instrumental value of religious truth claims? R. Kook is well aware of the fact that, although the structures we impose upon reality do not capture the way things are exactly, they do have a formative influence upon us. When we live within these models and allow them to become the lens through which we look out on the world, changing our attitudes, and converting our consciousness, they can have a critical influence on the way that we conduct our daily business. But in R. Kook's view, the final objective of the instrumentalist criterion is a moral one. As he puts it:

> The manner in which human depictions relate to reality obviously has a special influence upon the development of man's morality and the rest of his exalted missions as well, each generation in accordance with its depictions, which come and go, in order to render everything compatible to the purpose of the general good and God's eternal bounty.[31]

It is because the religious view has a better influence upon us morally that statements of faith have more ultimate value for us than statements of doubt.

Now the contention that faith necessarily promotes morality is one that some people might regard as a debatable point. But here it is important to note that what R. Kook usually has in mind when he talks about morality is not the willingness to adopt this or that particular set of norms and values. He is not saying that people who profess loyalty to this particular organized religion or that one are, at bottom, morally superior to secularists. Whenever R. Kook speaks about morality, what he is really referring to is that same preverbal sensibility that he regards as the most elemental life force, stemming from the innermost recesses of *all* beings, extending even to the cosmos at large. In other words, morality, in his terminology, is an all-pervasive universal yearning for improvement, creativity, and perfection which religious and secular people share alike. Morality, in this very broad sense, is the impetus lying behind any constructive form of human activity—even the wish for material advancement and the bettering of our physical welfare. And it is this basic striving for perfection, in his eyes, that really is at the heart of any articulated world view, even when it does not consciously see itself as religious.[32]

---

[31] *Eder hayakar*, 38.
[32] For similarities between R. Kook and Henri Bergson's concept of the *élan vital*, see

Although we cannot adequately capture the nature of reality *in se*, some depictions are better for us than others, because they will prove themselves more affirming of life and promote human flourishing. If the religious outlook has the edge on atheism, it is not because this outlook is absolutely true and the agnostic one absolutely false, but because the religious view of reality is more capable of imbuing us with a feeling of optimism and self-worth. It teaches us the importance of our actions, produces in us a sense of significance, and therefore succeeds in expressing and developing the unconscious, preverbal life force within us, rather than allowing it to wither and die. By contrast, metaphors of heresy, which disrupt relationships and foster disharmony with people and with nature, are to be discarded because of their harmful effects. Thus, instead of facticity being the ultimate test for 'truth' in the religious sense, the real measure of such statements is instrumental—that is, the extent to which they lend significance to the moral yearning that they strive to embody and contribute to its flourishing. The religious view is to be preferred only because, from *our* point of view, the religious formulation of reality appears closer to truth, and thus leads to greater morality, than the irreligious model.[33]

Theological Claims as Necessary Truths

In light of the fact that even the debate between religion and irreligion cannot be resolved in terms of absolute veracity, it should not surprise us to discover that, in a whole series of cases of competing truth claims among theologians regarding the correct religious view, R. Kook appears to adopt an extremely pliable and relativist view of the method for determining their solution, which totally disassociates them from any exclusivist claims to truth. In all these instances, where the traditionalist might be expected to decide on the basis of 'objective' considerations, the determining factor for R. Kook seems to be merely the strictly instrumentalist question: what does each view achieve for man? And although in each of these cases he does express a preference for one view rather than another, he also recognizes that this preference need not be applied to all people at all times.

One of the most striking and explicit expositions of this instrumentalist and pliable approach to truth appears in an essay that R. Kook wrote in

Shemuel H. Bergman, 'The Theory of Evolution in the Thought of R. Kook' (Heb.), in id., *Personalities and Paths* [Anashim uderakhim: masot filosofiyot] (Jerusalem: Ha'ahim Green, 1968), 350–8.

[33] *Orot ha'emunah*, 23–4. See n. 15 above.

defence of Maimonides' unconventional views in downplaying the centrality of man in creation.[34] The essay was written in reaction to sharp criticism voiced by the Jewish historian, Zeev Yaavetz. Although recognizing Maimonides' stature as a great halakhist, Yaavetz nevertheless takes him to task for having introduced foreign (i.e. Greek) ideas to Judaism in his philosophical writings. R. Kook begins his defence with the general declaration that if any idea served the faith of a man like Maimonides, who are we to object to it? Everyone has the right to choose the path (that of Maimonides or that of his opponents) suited to him, according to his spiritual state. Later on he relates specifically to the question of the centrality of man in the cosmos and argues that, on the contrary, we should feel gratitude to Maimonides for demonstrating to us how faith can be grounded even in a scientific view that, on the surface, appears less congenial to religious belief (just as he did with the Aristotelian idea of the eternity of matter). If the man of faith can make peace even with this concept, then how much more so can religious tradition dispense with the anthropocentric idea of creation. Moreover, he adds that, in general, one should not adopt an unequivocal stand on such general and abstract issues. The ultimate purpose of all the various positions regarding the place of man in creation is only to clarify in an understandable way (*rak lesaber et ha'ozen leva'er al yadam*) man's exalted moral relationship to his Creator. Sometimes one theory does the job better, and sometimes another. It all depends on the circumstances which theory will be more effective and have a more beneficial effect upon man.

In two other passages,[35] R. Kook attempts to evaluate the creation ex nihilo claim versus the emanationist view of the origins of the world on similar grounds. In both passages he opts for the emanationist theory because of its beauty and the beneficial moral influence it has upon man in highlighting the connection of all existence to God. Once again, there is no attempt to resort to the type of rational, scientific, or philosophical arguments that are customary in discussions of this issue.

A third example is a discussion of the relative validity of the slave–master model in describing the relationship of man to God versus a more liberated

---

[34] 'A Special Article (Against R. Zeev Yaavetz's Method in His Work *The History of the Jews*)' (Heb.), in *Ma'amerei hare'ayah* (Jerusalem: Hakeren al shem Golda Katz, 1980), i. 105–12. This article was written despite the fact that R. Kook's general attitude to Maimonides' world-view was equivocal. See Lawrence J. Kaplan, 'Rav Kook and the Jewish Philosophical Tradition', in Lawrence J. Kaplan and David Shatz (eds.), *Rabbi Abraham Isaac Kook and Jewish Spirituality* (New York: New York University Press, 1995), 41–78.

[35] *Arpelei tohar*, 32–3; *Orot hakodesh*, ii. 349.

conception. Here, too, there is no attempt to assess the rival metaphors in terms of what actually is the literal truth (as if such matters were 'facts' waiting to be described), but rather which model will serve to liberate man from servitude to his evil inclination.[36] In a fourth instance, when attempting to determine which is preferable, monotheism or pantheism, R. Kook first establishes that a monotheistic view is basically a depressing one, because it impresses upon man his relative worthlessness before a perfect Being with which he has no substantive connection.[37] He proceeds to weigh the advantages and disadvantages of pantheism, and to construct an amalgam of the two that will totally fulfil 'all the other conditions of happiness that man harbours in the secret recesses of his heart'. He then sums up with the astounding conclusion: 'The idea that all of existence is divine, and that nothing exists besides God, extremely pleases the heart. The spiritual pleasure that this idea evokes is the proof of the truth that it expresses.'[38] It could be argued that the concept of pleasure, in the mystic view, carries some ontological significance.[39] But nevertheless the more obvious thrust of the argument is that models of God's relationship to creation are ultimately decided on the basis of their value to man in providing a conceptual framework that will encourage his moral productivity and not debilitate his spiritual self-image with feelings of despair. In a fifth example,[40] one of the core ideas in R. Kook's theology (the idea of a perfect God who requires the quality of lack in order to be complete) is introduced as an answer to the classic question: what was God's motive for creation? In the attempt to weigh the various possibilities, R. Kook first takes the wind out of the sails of the very question by pointing out that it is a legitimate question only from *our* point of view, since all questions of purpose and teleology only make sense in a world which includes the perception of lack. In God's perfect world, the value of existence is self-evident and requires no justification. But even when going along with the human need for asking the question, R. Kook accompanies what he regards as the preferred response with the telling phrase: 'we will profit much by' assuming this answer to be the true one. It is as if he is inviting us to his private workshop for the fashion-

---

[36] *Arpelei tohar*, 44.

[37] *Orot hakodesh*, ii. 395–6. See also ibid. 397–8, where R. Kook speaks of the jealousy of God that the monotheistic picture arouses in man.   [38] Ibid. 396.

[39] In the kabbalah, God's pure unity is described as the delight of self-sufficiency, which is dependent upon no 'other' for its gratification. See e.g. R. Kook's commentary in *Olat re'ayah* (Jerusalem: Mosad Harav Kook, 1985), i. 23–4, on the words *leshem yiḥud kudsha berikh hu ushekhinteih*. See also Yosef Ben-Shlomo, *Rabbi Mosheh Cordovero's Teachings on Divinity* [Torat ha'elohut shel r. mosheh cordovero] (Jerusalem: Mosad Bialik, 1965), 60–2.

[40] *Orot hakodesh*, ii. 464–5.

ing of theological systems and frankly laying out his cards on the table, weighing up the various answers to a serious theological issue on no more objective grounds than the very anthropocentric consideration of: Where will this lead up to in terms of profit to man?

Non-Theological Truths

What has been established until now is a fresh and unexpected reluctance on the part of R. Kook to bring questions of truth in the 'objective' sense to bear upon the validity of religious belief statements. But it could be argued that all the instances of truth cited thus far deal with theological and relatively abstract issues, and therefore confrontations between religious claims and hard empirical evidence are more elusive and easily avoided. Although there are some non-realists who do maintain a 'global' subjectivism or anti-realism, arguing that the common-sense view of scientific objectivity is naive all across the board, others distinguish between theology and science. On the basis of important disanalogies and discontinuities between theology and the sciences, they conclude that the notion of objectivity in science is roughly right, and that the objectivity of theology is a special problem.[41] In order to determine R. Kook's exact position regarding the realism of religious truth statements, therefore, it might be more instructive to examine what he does when dealing not with theoretical philosophical arguments, but with claims made in our religious tradition that can be examined in the light of more concrete empirical evidence from the realm of science or history.

Pursuing this track, however, we will discover that, even regarding the conflict with truth claims that have to do with more concrete and observable phenomena in the natural world and in history, R. Kook exhibits a remarkable readiness to disassociate the religious truth from claims that are liable to empirical testing. In an interesting programmatic statement which paraphrases Kant, he writes: 'If modern science will boast that it has been liberated from theology, it must know that over against this, theology has been liberated from science.'[42] True to his word, he elsewhere declares that all the

---

[41] See David Brink, *Moral Realism and the Foundation of Ethics* (Cambridge: Cambridge University Press, 1989), 5–7, where he lists several forms of realism and anti-realism on the basis of a similar distinction between ethics and science.

[42] *Arpelei tohar*, 40, as translated by David Shatz in 'The Integration of Religion and Culture: Its Scope and Limits in the Thought of R. Kook', in Y. Elman and J. S. Gorock (eds.), *Ḥazon Naḥum: Studies in Jewish Law, Thought and History Presented to Dr. Norman Lamm on the Occasion of His Seventieth Birthday* (New York: Yeshiva University Press, 1997), 529–56. For further discussion, see also Shatz's essay, 'Rav Kook and Modern Orthodoxy: The

so-called scientific bases for heresy may be generally regarded as pseudo-arguments.[43] Testimony to this is the fact that religious belief has managed to coexist in peace with all manner of scientific theories (e.g. Ptolemaic, Copernican, and Galilean).

In an oft-quoted letter written to his beloved disciple, Rabbi Mosheh Zeidel,[44] who was obviously troubled by the clash between the biblical account of Adam's expulsion from the Garden of Eden and current evolutionary theory, R. Kook's response is that, although not every suggestion introduced in the name of science is necessarily true, there is no reason to feel threatened by potential clashes between the Torah's purported description and the assertions of science, because the ultimate purpose of the Torah is not to teach us 'facts and historical occurrences', but rather the inner or spiritual significance of these.[45] And in a second letter to the same Rabbi Zeidel,[46] R. Kook appears to go even further in this attitude when he addresses the question of limits: just how far can non-literal interpretations be extended in approaching the text of the Torah? Here too, although the general temper of his stance indicates an obvious inclination to accord a great measure of credibility to tradition, in principle he is prepared to leave the answer to this question to the 'clear sense of the nation', which 'finds its paths not in isolated bits of evidence, but in general impressions'. And even if some details of the biblical account appear to be contradicted by current research, we must assume that inexact data, phrased in accordance with the misconceptions of the time, serve 'some important and holy purpose'.

Another example of R. Kook's relatively indifferent attitude in principle to the historical accuracy of the Torah occurs when he deals with the scepticism of Jewish agnostics in his day.[47] Because, in his opinion, such sceptics

---

Ambiguities of "Openness"', in Moshe Z. Sokol (ed.), *Engaging Modernity: Rabbinic Leaders and the Challenge of the Twentieth Century* (Northvale, NJ: Jason Aronson, 1997), 91–115.

[43] *Eder hayakar*, 36.   [44] *Igerot hare'ayah*, i. 163–4.

[45] In all fairness, it must be noted that R. Kook apologetically adds that he wrote this letter in a hurry and did not manage to explain himself fully. For this reason there may be grounds for claiming that, when he dissociates the literal meaning of the biblical tale of the expulsion of Adam and Eve from the Garden of Eden, it is not to say that he divests the story of *any* informative content. It could be that he would interpret the story as applying not to historical man but to his primordial spiritual forerunner, before the latter's unified soul was split into the multitude of historical souls to be generated from it, and before his ethereal matter became coarsened as a result of his original sin. This would be in consonance with normal kabbalistic interpretations of the Genesis accounts of creation, which view it as applying to the genesis of the higher metaphysical entities rather than of their earthly counterparts.

[46] *Igerot hare'ayah*, ii. 118–19.   [47] *Igerot hare'ayah*, i. 48–9.

cannot deny the current centrality of Jewish influence upon the world, all that remains for them as the basis for their agnosticism is to doubt the veracity of the biblical narrative regarding the past influence of the Hebrews in the early stages of civilization. It is absolutely clear that R. Kook does not credit such doubt in the slightest. Moreover, he is totally convinced that once these doubters of the faith practise their tradition as 'inside members of the household', they will not require external proof of its veracity because such truth will be self-evident. Still, what is significant for our purposes is the fact that he is not averse, in principle, to grounding acceptance of tradition at least temporarily merely on its instrumental value. If the biblical stories could have so beneficial an effect upon the Jewish national image and concur with the finest of the world's moral aspirations, this is sufficient basis for belief in the divine nature of the Torah. Now, it could be argued that what R. Kook is doing here is merely adopting a strategic expedient in the hope that this will be an effective draw card for the religious life. Nevertheless his lack of purism regarding possible historical grounding for belief, which was certainly not the norm among his colleagues, may have been made possible, at least in part, by his ideological readiness to dispense with a reliance upon the informative value of religious truth statements.

In a similar discussion regarding doubters of the principle of Torah from Heaven (i.e. the divinity of the Torah),[48] R. Kook can accept such denials of faith which prefer to attribute the source of the Torah to the greatness of man's spirit, and even see in these heretical protestations a more substantial profession of faith than in rote declarations of belief which are based on weird and nonsensical conceptions of heaven that actually fuel the doubter's fire. Presumably this is because faith in the divinity of the Torah consists, in his mind, not so much in a particular belief as to when and how it was delivered, or even by whom. It consists, rather, in recognizing the sublime and exalted nature of its content, which, in keeping with R. Kook's pantheistic tendencies, bears greater relationship to the religious genius of man than to a very literal-minded and primitive conception of God standing over and above man and forcing his commands upon him from without. Of course man's autonomous spirit is not the full explanation of the Torah's source, leaving out as it does any notion of transcendence. But what R. Kook seems to be implying is that, in modern times, the feeling of human connectedness to biblical content is a more valid religious sensibility than the perception of Torah as a heteronomous imposition, antithetical to human nature, and forced upon man from without by some foreign anthropomorphic source—

[48] *Orot ha'emunah*, 25.

because such a belief has a more beneficial effect upon the contemporary man's moral urge.

A comparable sentiment is expressed more explicitly in another passage,[49] when R. Kook discusses the source of the authority of the Oral Law. Many people, he asserts, mistakenly believe that its obligatory nature is based on the greatness and holy stature of our Sages. Therefore, they think that, in order to throw off the yoke of rabbinic decisions, all that needs to be done is to cast doubt upon their elevated nature. They do not understand that all such effort is futile, because the binding nature of this law (and that of the written Torah as well!) does not depend upon who gave it, but rather upon more internal considerations, such as the consensus of the nation to accept this law upon itself, the divine importance invested in this nation, and its unique nature, which is evident throughout its history. Although in practice R. Kook is by no means ready to detract from the greatness of our Sages (or from the authority of Moses' prophetic ability), he seems here again interested in principle in divorcing questions of theology from considerations of factual circumstance, so that the literary and historical genesis of the Torah and its religious value become two separate issues. The binding nature of the oral and even the written Torah rests ultimately on popular consensus—the fact that the Jewish people voluntarily accepted this Torah upon itself as the ultimate authority. This point recurs in a letter written to Isaac Halevy regarding the basis of halakhic weights and measures (*shiurim*)—do these derive their authority from the Written or the Oral Law?[50] The Babylonian Talmud regards these measures as *halakhah lemosheh misinai* (inviolable law transmitted at Sinai), but the Jerusalem Talmud appears to adopt a more historical approach. R. Kook concludes, despite the fact that he tends to the position of the Babylonian Talmud, that this discussion bears absolutely no practical implications, because the ultimate reason for accepting these measures is not their Mosaic source, but the popular consensus of the nation (*kabalat ha'umah*). This allows him to establish a much more far-reaching hermeneutical principle: that even in the study of Torah, the determining factor in understanding its contents is how it was understood by the nation, and not the conclusions of scientific-historical analysis.

The Constraints of Science

From all this, are we to conclude that religious statements are to be judged exclusively on instrumental grounds, with scientific data exercising no

---

[49] *Eder hayakar*, 39.   [50] *Igerot hare'ayah*, i. 193–4.

control at all on their formulation? Are religious truth statements totally subjective, and therefore immune to falsification? Are they so relative that they make no claims about the real world? If we continue the passage quoted above,[51] which speaks of formulated beliefs as relative to the people and circumstances concerned, this seems to be an obvious overstatement of R. Kook's position. For immediately after this, he adds: 'And to the extent that the basic belief is more exalted, eternal, and true, to that very same extent will the things that accompany it be more bright, strong, clear, and understood, answering to the purest moral demands and the clearest light of science.' In many of his writings, R. Kook indicates that there can and should be significant communication between internal feeling and outside perceptions.

One reason for this is the role that intellect plays in the constitution of our humanity. 'A belief to which the intellect does not assent encourages vexation and cruelty, because the supreme aspect of man, namely the intellect, is impoverished by its impact.'[52] Since man has an inbuilt generic need for rationality, rationality may not always be an ultimate criterion,[53] but it does have at least instrumental value in the promotion of religious beliefs. A religious truth statement that cannot accommodate a scientific statement within it is just not acceptable to most people.[54] More importantly, because the function of religious truth formulations is not merely static (to express the moral urge) but also dynamic (to advance this urge to what it might be), these formulations do not remain at a standstill. They do sometimes get outgrown.

[51] *Orot ha'emunah*, 48.

[52] *Arpelei tohar*, 105. The translation of this passage appears in an essay by Shalom Carmy, 'Dialectic, Doubters, and a Self-Erasing Letter: Rav Kook and the Ethics of Belief', in Lawrence Kaplan and David Shatz (eds.), *Rabbi Abraham Isaac Kook and Jewish Spirituality* (New York: New York University Press, 1995), 205. The original passage also appears in *Orot ha'emunah*, 101–2. See also *Arpelei tohar*, 62.

[53] *Orot hakodesh*, i. 218–19; *Arpelei tohar*, 13–14; *Orot ha'emunah*, 101–2. As David Shatz has pointed out in 'The Integration of Religion and Culture', there is a certain ambiguity in R. Kook's epistemology when he distinguishes between two possible sources of religious knowledge and feeling. Alongside the necessity he sees in developing one's religious knowledge dialectically, via the confrontation with scientific claims, he also allows for the possibility of revealing an innate conviction which transcends rational thought and renders it superfluous. On occasion, this natural, uncultivated, intuitive feeling of certainty is accorded a higher value than the acquired understanding painstakingly arrived at by 'considerations of external reality'. It is interesting to note the remarkable parallels between R. Kook's emphasis on the importance of intuitive feeling and Friedrich Schleiermacher's affirmation of the way of feeling or immediate self-consciousness as the true avenue to the noumenal world.

[54] *Orot ha'emunah*, 101–2. Even the continuation of this passage, in which R. Kook nevertheless accords greater credibility to 'higher faith', which stems from divine revelation,

In a particularly poetic metaphor, R. Kook likens the moral urge to a tiny sapling that begins to grow, and every once in a while needs to be transplanted or its soil renurtured in order to support and cultivate this new development.[55] The need for such transplantations arises whenever a discrepancy is revealed between the size of the plant and the breadth of the soil on which it stands, that is, when our authentic spiritual-moral urge is no longer adequately expressed by our existing religious formulations. Thus it is clear that R. Kook allows room for a significant transformation of religious paradigms whenever reason convinces us that we have outgrown more primitive forms of religiosity and are ready for a new, more refined, stage of belief. The vehicle for this process of disenchantment is science. It is the clash between previous and now inadequate religious formulations and the evidence of science that goads us into discovering a fresh form of spiritual truth that is capable of accommodating the new scientific picture, and thus of enlarging upon previous and now inadequate religious views. R. Kook understands the clash between science and religion, whenever it occurs, as a heaven-sent signal that those troubled by the challenge of science are now ripe for evolving a new perception of reality and of their own selves.

Ostensibly, then, religious truth formulations do have to answer to objective, external criteria. However, when we examine the manner in which R. Kook appeals to scientific evidence in practice, we discover that his attitude to such evidence is not entirely unequivocal. Although he does, on occasion, attempt to confront the challenges raised by the natural sciences of his day regarding several specific issues, such as evolution,[56] the age of the Earth,[57] and the historical accuracy of the Torah in points of factual detail[58] and in several isolated points of biblical criticism,[59] he appears rather vague about how significant or insignificant the contribution of science really is. As has been pointed out by David Shatz,[60] his rereading of problematic texts, where it does take place, has a voluntary, optional character to it that medieval interpretations do not have. In most of the major passages that deal with these issues, he offers not one but several different ways of relating to conflicts between religious and scientific truth claims. These often run a full gamut of possibili-

expresses the conviction that the basic compatibility between rationality and more 'hidden' sources of religious knowledge will eventually become apparent. See previous note.

[55] Ibid. 74–5.   [56] *Orot hakodesh*, ii. 538–42; *Igerot hare'ayah*, ii. 163–4.
[57] *Igerot hare'ayah*, i. 105–7.   [58] *Eder hayakar*, 37–8; *Igerot hare'ayah*, ii. 118–19.
[59] See e.g. *Eder hayakar*, 42–3 regarding parallels to biblical passages found by Assyriologists in the texts of other ancient tribes.
[60] In 'The Integration of Religion and Culture', 536.

ties, ranging all the way from a cognitivist position, which relates seriously to the constraints which scientific discovery places on the truth claims of religion, through a diametrically opposed view which discounts the claims of science as completely unreliable, to a totally non-cognitivist view of religion, which discounts such scientific claims as simply irrelevant to statements of religious belief.

Several suggestions could be offered to explain this anomaly in R. Kook's thought, which allows him, on the one hand, to speak for the importance of integrating religious truth claims with science, and in almost the same breath to entertain the possibility of ignoring or downplaying the conclusions of science in practice. Thus, his ambivalent attitude regarding the answerability of religious truth claims to science, and his disinterest in engaging in a serious and thorough examination of scientific challenges, could be viewed, at least in part, as simply the function of his personal temperament and inclination. By his own testimony,[61] R. Kook was just not the type of analytic scholar who would relish going into the clarity of fine points of detail. Another possibility is, of course, to conclude that his conservative tendency and refusal to accord certainty to contemporary science was his true traditionalism showing, a loss of nerve when faced with the opportunity of implementing radically non-traditionalist theoretical pronouncements in actual practice.[62] One could also add his objection to the dissemination of ideas that the community as a whole is not ready for, even if the individual believer knows them to be true.[63] All of

---

[61] *Arpelei tohar*, 31; *Igerot hare'ayah*, i. 131; *Orot hakodesh*, iii. 259–60.

[62] Benjamin Ish-Shalom sees R. Kook's conservatism in matters of practical implementation as characteristic of a certain type of radical thinker in the attempt to safeguard their attachment to tradition. See his *Rav Avraham Itzhak HaCohen Kook: Between Rationalism and Mysticism*, trans. Ora Wiskind-Elper (Albany: State University of New York Press, 1993), 168–72, 236–7. Michael Nehorai, on the other hand, views R. Kook's conservatism in certain halakhic issues as stemming from his understanding that his generation was entering the messianic age, and therefore it had to stand up to its ideal measures; see his 'Halakhah, Meta-Halakhah, and the Redemption of Israel: Reflections on the Rabbinic Rulings of R. Kook', in Lawrence Kaplan and David Shatz (eds.), *Rabbi Abraham Isaac Kook and Jewish Spirituality* (New York: New York University Press, 1995), 120–56. Nehorai's article is an adaptation of the Hebrew original, which appeared in *Tarbiz*, 59 (1990), 481–505. For a different approach to disparities between R. Kook's broad liberalism in his theoretical statements of principle and his conservatism in the practical implementation of these, see Yonah Ben-Sasson, 'The Philosophies of Rabbi A. I. Kook and Rabbi J. B. Soloveitchik' (Heb.), in Hayim Hamiel (ed.), *In His Light: Studies in the Thought of Rabbi Abraham Isaac Kook* [Be'oro: iyunim bemishnato shel harav avraham yitsḥak hakohen kuk] (Jerusalem: Hahistadrut Hatsiyonit Ha'olamit, 1986), 353–418, and esp. 403–8. Ben-Sasson explains the disparities as simply the need to face the gap between theory and practice in the real world.

[63] *Igerot hare'ayah*, i. 103–4. See also *Orot hakodesh*, iii. 382, where R. Kook warns against

these explanations could still allow for an attitude which takes the cognitive aspect of religious truth claims seriously.

In direct opposition to this line of explanation, another suggestion that has been raised is that even what ostensibly appears to be ordinary conservatism on the part of R. Kook (in his halakhic decisions in particular) might actually be consistent with a genuinely modern epistemology of global non-realism.[64] According to this, the true explanation for R. Kook's willingness to ignore the findings of science, and his reluctance to engage in detailed examination of scientific claims and ways of resolving them with religious ones, is the relative view he had not only of religious truth claims but even of scientific models and paradigms. If not only religious truths but even scientific perceptions are fluid and instrumental, there is really no reason, he could say, why religion has to accept individual secular theories; it may be a mark of greater sophistication to recognize the limitations of our present knowledge and to take notice of the ever fluctuating state of scientific opinion.[65] But if we bear in mind the kabbalistic underpinnings of R. Kook's thought, a final possibility is to view the contradictory options he offers for relating to conflicts between religious and scientific truth claims not as rival, mutually exclusive alternatives, but as various stages on a graded scale which all of us must traverse in order to reach final religious maturity.[66] On this understanding, all truth

---

expressing anything, even when it appears to be true, if it will lead to morally harmful influences upon the listener, whose morality is bound at the moment to other ideas which oppose that truth.

[64] See Shatz, 'The Integration of Religion and Culture'; id., 'R. Kook and Modern Orthodoxy'.

[65] Shatz, 'R. Kook and Modern Orthodoxy'. The example that Shatz cites as support for his suggestion is R. Kook's ruling in a responsum concerning the practice of sucking out blood from the wound created during circumcision, known as *metsitsah*. This responsum appears as no. 140 in *Da'at kohen* (Jerusalem: Mosad Harav Kook, 1985), 259–63. See also responsum no. 142, pp. 263–4. Here, in spite of the mounting claims from science that the Sages were wrong about its hygienic value, he refuses to take the medical evidence into account. He rejects the argument that *metsitsah* is a *mitsvah* that is independent of hygienic considerations insofar as it grants the correctness of the scientific community's claims. He also refuses to rely on the argument that *nishtanu hateva'im* (nature has changed) on the grounds that when scientists contradict the words of the Sages, their reliability is nil, and they are surely mistaken in their judgement.

[66] There is a basic structure to R. Kook's thought (similar to, but more intricate than, Hegel's dialectic scheme), which sees in every phenomenon of life (intellectual, historical, natural) an organic process that must undergo three different stages of unification between two binary principles of generality and particularity in order to reflect and embody three paradigmatic types of unification. These types represent successive stages in the Lurianic process of *tikun*, which culminates in the embellishment of a fourth and original monolithic

ultimately strives to create a perfect representation, in human terms, of a reality in which there are no 'facts of the matter', or where everything is possible because 'perhaps the phenomenon, which is beyond our intellectual comprehension, is also beyond our conditions for perfection, and all its contradictions are in harmony on some level, in no need of reasoned solutions. For reality does not fear contradictions as does science, as it is incalculably greater than science.'[67] 'When we stand in the valley of this exalted vision, we view the different principles at their roots', where all contradictions are naught.[68] From this ultimate vantage point, the interaction between religious and scientific truths is not a one-way affair leading to fixed conclusions, but rather a dynamic, dialectic process of mutual reciprocity. Just as religious truths build upon the discoveries of science, so do scientific discoveries and models of reality feed upon previous spiritual perceptions, in an ever-continuing ascent.

unity that existed before creation. (For further elaboration, see Tamar Ross, 'Myth, Structure, and Reality in the Writings of Rav Kook' (Heb.), in Haviva Pedaya (ed.), *Myth in Judaism* [Hamitos bayahadut] (Be'er Sheva: Ben Gurion University Press, 1996), 239–62.) Thus, relating to scientific and religious truth claims as complementary, separating the two realms and relating seriously only to the literal meaning of the religious truth claim, or integrating science with religion in a dialectic manner which mitigates the cognitive value of both, are progressive steps leading to the higher mystic realization that the religious message is a never-ending one, not to be exhausted by any specific ontological claim. If viewed against this background, there is no one correct response to the issue of which of the various options is to be assumed in clashes between religion and science; it all depends on one's assessment of just how far the process of unification has reached. The superior *tsadik elyon* may theoretically view the relationship of science and religion in utopian terms as worthy of inclusion in the faith dynamic (*Arpelei tohar*, 66), but in practice he must relate to more modern insights in accordance with how far the utopian ideal has been realized by the larger community in real life (*Igerot hare'ayah*, i. 103–4). Thus, R. Kook's ruling on the question of *metsitsah* (see n. 65 above) may have been governed more by pragmatic considerations of what repercussions a more liberal stance on this issue might have on the war being conducted at the time between the reformers and the Orthodox around this very issue than by a globally non-realist position. (For a brief history of this crisis and a survey of the rabbinic opinions regarding this issue, see Israel Hyman, 'The Halakhic Issues of Mezizah', *Proceedings of the Association of Orthodox Jewish Scientists*, 8–9 (1987), 17–44, and Ya'akov Katz, *Halacha in Straits: Obstacles to Orthodoxy at Its Inception* [Hahalakhah bemetsar: mikhsholim al derekh ha'ortodoxiyah behithavutah] (Jerusalem: Magnes Press, 1992), 150–84.) On this view, halakhah may sometimes take into account revolutionary developments in the real world, but only after these have become incontrovertibly established or willingly adopted by the general community of believers (*Arpelei tohar*, 15; *Igerot hare'ayah*, i. 103–4), and therefore do not pose a threat to tradition.

[67] *Igerot hare'ayah*, ii. 120.
[68] 'Exalted in Holiness' (Heb.), in *Ma'amerei hare'ayah* (Jerusalem: Mosad Harav Kook, 1984), ii. 400.

Since religious and scientific paradigms influence each other in a continually spiralling dialectic, spiritual and psychological needs do play a role in the timing and nature even of scientific discovery.[69] Not only religious, but even scientific perceptions—albeit in a more limited sense—are a function of our moral stature. In consequence, 'it is no surprise that his analyses of changes in scientific theories focus on the psychological repercussions of the old and new theories—the human self-understanding and self-image that they reflect or else engender—as distinct from their epistemological credentials'.[70]

An illustration of this psychological focus appears in a letter in which R. Kook discusses the controlling role of Divine Providence on the development of scientific discovery.[71] Two examples he offers are from the realm of cosmology: the revolutionary movement of the planet earth and the size of the cosmos. In both cases he links these discoveries to the moral state of man. In the first example he contends that had Copernicus' discovery of the earth's revolutions around the sun not been deferred until such a time when humanity had already achieved a certain measure of self-confidence, all courage for constructive activity would have been dampened. Even discovery of the laws of gravity would not have counterbalanced a fear of standing on our feet or stultification of the attempt to build, out of fear that nothing was assured of remaining where it is. In the second example, R. Kook begins with the realistic assessment that no moral system can succeed without a belief in Divine Providence. However, in the age of idolatry the Israelites had a difficult task in inculcating this belief while yet preserving the image of God's greatness (which is also a necessary component in ensuring human morality), because the human self-image was, in general, one of insignificance in the face of the vastness of the universe. What would have happened, asks R. Kook rhetorically, if people then had known what they know now about cosmic infinity? Only when man struggled with his previous conceptions and found them wanting did the new conceptions arrive on the scene.[72] Aside from the inter-

---

[69] *Eder hayakar*, 38; *Orot hakodesh*, ii. 431, 543.

[70] Shatz, 'The Integration of Religion and Culture'.   [71] *Igerot hare'ayah*, i. 105–7.

[72] Amplification on this theme can be found in *Orot hakodesh*, ii. 538–42, where R. Kook finds a parallel thrust to modern cosmological discoveries in the areas of anthropology (the new discoveries regarding the interconnectedness of societies) and biology (the interconnectedness of the various species of life in the theory of evolution), which all come to herald a new and parallel spiritual sensibility. See also Aviezer Ravitzky's comments in the symposium regarding R. Kook's contribution to the revitalization of Jewish thought, in Benjamin Ish-Shalom and Shalom Rosenberg (eds.), *The World of R. Kook's Thought* (New York: Avi Chai, 1991), 458–9, trans. from the Hebrew edn., *Jubilee of Lights: The Thought of Rabbi Abra-*

esting way in which R. Kook relates to the idea of Divine Providence (not as a fact but as a 'necessary' truth), what is remarkable in this passage is that not only religious ideas but even so-called scientific ones are transient and passing, and, just as we saw in the case of religious truths, what actually heralds their advent and their demise is the degree of their usefulness to the moral development of man. Although there is a greater influence in science than in religion from the outside in (from external experience to internal conviction) than from inside out (starting from personal feeling), on a certain level the latter has a formative influence on scientific models as well.[73]

Now if, according to R. Kook, not only religious truths but even scientific perceptions are fluid and instrumental, it would seem that there is no difference in principle in the cognitive value of scientific or religious truth formulations. Both are basically subjective and relative attempts to formulate the ineffable. The only basis for distinguishing between their rival truth claims and viewing science as subordinate lies in the scope of their vision and in the object of their endeavours. Science seeks to simply describe partial and discrete aspects of the physical world as it appears phenomenally; its vision is therefore exclusive and limited. Religion seeks to reveal the inner significance of these physical phenomena, striving to creatively encompass them within a larger metaphysical context of meaning that takes our inner feelings into account by including them in a total picture that bears a moral thrust.[74] The importance of the faith claim is in providing a controlling vision, an imagined perception through which one is to view these phenomena, rather than observing them in isolation, whereby they carry no overt and evident religious significance. The partial vision of science clearly stimulates and develops the religious formulation by providing the raw material that is required in order to apprehend the whole. It forces the comprehensive process of integration to be richer and more complete, and hence clarifies and enhances the vision of belief. But a comprehensive vision of faith can be found for any scientific model.[75] Moreover, if we add R. Kook's fluid view of science to his opinion that religious truths, too, unfold only gradually, it is even difficult to identify genuine conflicts between the two.[76] At any rate, given the dynamic nature of science, the specific propositional conclusion of the reconciliation with religious texts can only be of negligible consequence and can change with the

ham Isaac Hakohen Kook [Yovel orot: haguto shel harav avraham yitsḥak hakohen kuk z'l] (Jerusalem: Hahistadrut Hatsiyonit Ha'olamit, 1985), 358–63.

[73] Orot hakodesh, i. 58.
[74] Orot ha'emunah, 66; Arpelei tohar, 13–14; Orot hakodesh, i. 218–19.   [75] Eder hayakar, 37.
[76] This point is made by Shatz in 'Rav Kook and Modern Orthodoxy'.

times; what is important is demonstration of the sheer ability to fit any particular scientific proposition into an overall religious scheme.

R. Kook Compared to Some Contemporary Theories

In extending his elastic and tentative evaluation not only to the totalistic vision but also to the particular components which serve as its raw material, R. Kook seems to come very close to some of the more recent approaches which have become associated with the view known as postmodernism. This term is problematic and, as one exponent of postmodernism has put it, 'has something of the Yeti about it: spoken of by many, glimpsed by a few, but it is difficult to find anyone willing to give an exact description of the creature'.[77] Nevertheless, the sense that I make of it in our context is the notion that reality is intrinsically unstructured and undefined, and therefore it does not inherently mandate preference for one specific depiction or representation of itself over another. With adjustments in formulation, such a reading of R. Kook's conclusions will have a thoroughly contemporary ring to it, resembling the views of historians and philosophers such as Thomas Kuhn and Richard Rorty. Making sense of history, according to such postmodernist thinkers, is a task that requires the 'creativity of the interpretive imagination'.[78] We construct our worlds within history, out of history, and for history.

According to most postmodernist thinkers of this sort, no abiding principles are to be found behind our constructions. As Rorty memorably describes our attempts at getting at the truth, 'It is words all the way down.'[79] If we apply the postmodernist view globally, no claims can be made about the nature of reality or of God, unless such claims are acknowledged as being strictly instrumentalist. Religious models of reality as understood by this camp would be 'truer' in the sense that they powerfully encourage inclusive, life-affirming dispositions and relationships that their irreligious counterparts do not. But neither religious nor irreligious claims should be regarded as necessarily disclosing anything literally descriptive of the reality in whose terms they are phrased. Their claims are to be judged not in terms of their rendering of the nature of this reality—the ascertainment of which is impossible—but in terms of what modes of human life such visions inhibit or

---

[77] James M. Byrne, 'Foucault on Continuity: The Postmodern Challenge to Tradition', *Faith and Philosophy*, 9/3 (July 1992), 335.

[78] See William Dean, *History Making History* (Albany, NY: State University of New York Press, 1988), 6.

[79] Richard Rorty, *Consequences of Pragmatism* (Minneapolis: University of Minnesota Press, 1982), p. xxxv.

make possible. In the words of one postmodernist theologian: 'Theology, when viewed in this manner, is a thoroughly human enterprise carried out for human purposes . . . It seeks, through the critical and creative capacities of the human imagination, to contribute to the construction of interpretive worlds through which human beings can gain orientation in life and thereby pursue sustainable and humane forms of existence.'[80] Such a postmodernist would claim that this is the best that we can do.

It is important to realize that, in spite of certain similarities between postmodernism and the position adopted by R. Kook, to describe the latter as a postmodernist without qualification would be a serious distortion of his whole outlook.

1. One type of qualification to a theology that relinquishes any appeal to objective constraints appears in the passage quoted above,[81] in which R. Kook makes the distinction between the necessary truths which constitute formulated belief and the higher truth which constitutes its object. In the continuation of this passage he introduces an intermediary concept, which he equates with the necessary truths of Maimonides. As opposed to other necessary truths, which are relative and transitory, and not equally useful for all people at all times, these necessary truths are 'what determine the style', because they are 'embedded in the nature of man, so that it is impossible that a man uproot these formulations of belief from his heart without thereby uprooting the higher truths which are the basis of the absolute truth'. Because of their unique transcultural status, these well-entrenched beliefs are foundational for mankind. In fact, they serve as a basis on which other concepts must be built if they are to render the preverbal religious intuition accurately. Even these foundational beliefs, however, are not entirely fixed, for R. Kook adds: 'And after all this, in every generation many transformations take place in the relationship of these necessary truths. But the internal truth remains forever.' Presumably what he means is that the external formulae must remain, but the exact interpretation to be attributed to these is adjusted according to the needs of the time. Moreover, although he identifies these foundational formulations, in this passage, with the theological principles of Maimonides, these may not constitute the exhaustive list of those beliefs that R. Kook regards as intersubjectively necessary (i.e. as required by all human beings as such). Other passages speak of three basic beliefs that constitute everyone's *ikar ha'emunah*: God's unity, the existence of a Creator and of a divine

---

[80] Sheila G. Davaney (ed.), *Theology at the End of Modernity* (Philadelphia: Trinity Press International, 1991), 2.   [81] See p. 144 and n. 16 above.

command,[82] or the belief in a sovereign, transcendent God to whom we are subject.[83] An even more basic belief, bearing the status of a necessary truth not to be relativized, might be the very urge to view the meaning of the world in moral terms.[84] One might, therefore, conclude that there is no clear-cut transition between the area of basic religious truths and relative ones. There are many different levels of necessity and constraint between what is absolutely true from an intersubjective point of view and totally underdetermined beliefs. The lower down we go on the list of common denominators, the more 'objective' are the constraints, but as we advance upwards on the scale of particularization, we move in the direction of 'cognitive underdetermination'. The farther we enter into the specifics, the more there is room for conflict and difference of opinion and an open-ended list of formulae that we could adopt as renderings of reality in different societies in different times and places. This implies the notion of degrees of ontological commitment for human beings. There may be areas where intersubjective constraints on religious truth claims are very strong indeed, while there are other areas where the constraints are minimal. And we may suppose that between these two extremes there lie many areas where such constraints are felt more or less strongly, leaving much latitude for relativism between different societies and even, to some extent, between different individuals.

What R. Kook might be understood as saying here is that, although no formulated belief can be equated, as is, with the object it seeks to depict, and for this reason it can never be regarded as having more than relative ontological value, there are certain formulations of belief that bear constant and eternal validity—not because of their superior ontological grounding on an absolute scale, but because they are universally bound to the nature of man, regardless of his particular moral state or cultural affinities. A person may, therefore, regard some of his belief claims as not merely subjective and personal but as best for all other human beings as well, without yet being truly objective, that is, viewed, as it were, from God's non-anthropocentric vantage point. They embody, he may suppose, the best thought objects for any human being, even though they may have no straightforward ground in absolute reality. We might conclude from this that it is only because of their transcultural nature, which is not relative to any particular cultural context, that these objective truths enjoy stronger ontological status. Thus, even though they are not 'part of the furniture' of the real world, R. Kook would still feel justified

---

[82] *Arpelei tohar*, 31.   [83] Ibid. 44.
[84] *Orot hakodesh*, ii. 397–8, 481–2. See also *Igerot hare'ayah*, i. 105–7, in which R. Kook speaks of the importance of a belief in Divine Providence for any religious or moral system.

in recommending such foundational beliefs to others, and using them as criteria by which one may judge all human behaviour.

Although this view does not deny the perspectival nature of all truth claims, it does limit the parameters of religious truth claims to a degree. As such, R. Kook would be avoiding a thoroughgoing relativism or nihilism on grounds that are similar to Hilary Putnam's concept of 'objectivity for us'. So described, R. Kook's ontological claims would still remain very modest, indeed virtually insignificant. One does not know and cannot know God in himself, but only God as we experience his effects from our point of view. We do not speak of the Divine *in se* but our truth claims do reflect the presence of God as experienced in the human community. If this view were to suffice for R. Kook, all that he would be presenting us with is a kind of intermediate, 'false bottom' ontology. In other words, all that he would be claiming is that, despite his tentative view of religious statements in general, there are some which he regards as permanently more valid than others, not because he equates them with absolute truth, but because they are a universally necessary representation of it.

2. But does R. Kook indeed maintain that the only structure to be applied to infinite reality is that necessarily dictated by subjective human categories? Is there no connection between these human structures and the intrinsic nature of reality? If R. Kook were to take this track and rely on universal consensus alone, without any ontological reference, one could hardly view him as a traditionalist theologian. Since, as John Hick has argued, theology has traditionally operated out of realist epistemological assumptions,[85] such a radical postmodernism, which views language merely as a self-enclosed 'game', without some reference to a genuinely objective outside reality, would constitute a fundamental shift in the expectations surrounding traditional theological claims. But it is obvious that R. Kook does not cross that boundary.

Along with the postmodernists, R. Kook does indeed concur that it is wise to be suspicious of all claims to absolute truth, or to any direct and perfect correspondence between our perceptions and ontological reality. He accepts the fact that particular theological truth claims about reality or God are tied to perspective and historical location, and that all experiential data and criteria of judgement are paradigm-dependent. But he nonetheless makes referential claims to ontology unapologetically, because he believes that these constructions do not refer merely to people's own deepest convictions, values, and

[85] John Hick, *An Interpretation of Religion: Human Responses to the Transcendent* (New Haven: Yale University Press, 1989), 176.

visions, but also point to the transcendent, and do so truly. He thus asserts, on the one hand: 'We do not know God from the world and by means of the world, but rather from within our souls',[86] and that 'even the names of God do not signify, according to the deep meaning of Torah, God Himself, but rather the divine ideals, His ways, desires, the world of *atsilut*, the *sefirot*, the paths, the roads, the gates, and the *partsufim*, a bit of whose ideal content is engraved and embedded also in the human soul.'[87] But then he adds that man's greatest desire is 'to actualize the potential in this hidden light, and to bring these divine ideals closer and closer to that infinite perfection of those divine ideals'.[88] Our urge to reach the highest level of Divinity and to be absorbed within it can never be fulfilled. But this higher light itself sometimes descends for us into our world and allows us to draw from its light. It is then that we understand that all the phenomena of this world are not disparate sparks reflecting that light, but rather they compose one unity that includes all.[89]

In the same passage in which R. Kook compares Kant to kabbalah,[90] he also emphasizes the superiority of kabbalah on just this issue. Kantianism, which discounts any necessary connection between the phenomenal and the noumenal reality, is only a modern form of paganism, deifying the intermediary gods (the phenomenal world) out of a despair of ever reaching the Source of all Sources.[91] But it is 'Israel's majestic idea' that the name Nothingness (*ayin*), which is attributed to the highest concept of the imperceptible Divinity, and the pronoun I (*ani*), which signifies Malkhut, the lowest sefirotic emanation, are composed of the same letters, indicating their evident spiritual connection.[92] Kabbalistic teaching is not the Gentile distortion of monotheism, which proposes as its God a self-contradictory limited infinity by divorcing the phenomenal reality from it. It is *true* monotheism, which understands that every manifestation is a partial but true reflection of the infinite transcendence, as infinity must include the manifestations as well. In such a monotheism, 'where all that can be imagined does actually exist',[93] any rendition of reality must have some ontological grounding. R. Kook

---

[86] *Igerot hare'ayah*, i. 45.

[87] *Ikevei hatson* (Jerusalem: Mosad Harav Kook, 1985), 'Avodat elohim', 145.   [88] Ibid.

[89] *Orot*, 'Zaronim', 119–20.   [90] See pp. 139–40 and n. 8 above.

[91] *Igerot hare'ayah*, i. 48. This is based on a midrashic understanding of the source of idolatry. The God of Israel was called 'the God of the gods' throughout the world, but the nations chose not to worship him because of his inaccessibility. See BT *Men.* 110a.

[92] For a discussion of an interesting modern variation on this theme (i.e. the connection between 'God-talk' and 'I-talk'), see Jerry H. Gill, *The Possibility of Religious Knowledge* (Grand Rapids, Mich.: B. Eerdmans, 1971), 210–23.   [93] *Arpelei tohar*, 5.

vehemently objects to a thoroughgoing anti-realism that holds that theological discourse does not refer to transcendent reality at all, either because such a reality does not exist, or because it so transcends our limitations that talk of any such 'truth', or of correspondence between our claims and this 'reality', is empty of meaning. Unlike the epistemological sceptic, R. Kook seems to be arguing here for a form of realism which—alongside acknowledgement of the role that our immersion in history and cultural structures plays in preventing direct access to the transcendent—nevertheless insists that these structures themselves have some anchor in the reality to which our claims are directed because of its infinite nature. His view is thus realism in the sense that it still is a view that affirms that moral or theological discourse does refer, in some way, to transcendent reality. And because R. Kook's transcendent reality is also all-inclusive, it is a stronger realism than that of the usual critical realist, who will affirm that religious experience is not solely a construction of the human imagination, merely because 'to affirm the transcendent is thus to affirm that religious experience . . . is a response—though always culturally conditioned—to the Real'.[94] Hick's 'critical cognitivism' still regards the models, metaphors, and formulae that we construct as mere subjective human artifices, even though these have some indirect cognitive backing in reality itself. But R. Kook regards them as partial but true manifestations in and of themselves once they are relegated to their appointed place within the infinite reality.

R. Kook's ability to maintain some cognitive value even in our subjective, relative formulations of truth is, of course, connected with the particular panentheistic version of monotheism which he views as the unique religious insight that characterizes Judaism and distinguishes it both from the total pantheism of Spinoza and from the complete dichotomy between God and the world which typifies, in his mind, Christianity and Islam.[95] The Jewish version understands that we cannot reach the ultimate divine substance

---

[94] John Hick, 'Religious Pluralism and Salvation', *Faith and Philosophy*, 5/4 (1988), 372.

[95] The degree of R. Kook's divergence from traditional theism is a source of debate among scholars. It hinges greatly on the classic kabbalistic question of whether the relationship between the world of the *sefirot* and Ein Sof is continuous or not, and whether the *sefirot* are to be regarded as God's essence or his vessels. See Tamar Ross, 'The Concept of God in the Thought of Rav Kook' (Heb.), *Da'at*, 8 (1981–2), 109–28; *Da'at*, 9 (1983), 39–70; Yosef Ben-Shlomo, *The Song of Life—From the Teachings of Rabbi Kook* ['Shirat haḥayim': perakim bemishnato shel harav kook] (Tel Aviv: Sifriyat Ha'universitah Hameshuderet, 1988), 33–40, esp. 39; see also Tamar Ross, 'R. Kook: A This-Worldly Mystic', to be published in Steven Kepnes (ed.), *The Cambridge Companion to Jewish Theology*, in the last section, entitled 'The Spectre of Pantheism and Mystic Ascent'.

directly, but we can approach closer and closer to it via its particularized manifestations.[96] Once we begin to climb this ladder and realize that *all* substances of this world are apprehended only by means of their manifestations and their relationship to us, we finally discover in God's overriding totality the deepest and most exalted relationship of all, and thereby recognize the absolute truth of the highest form of self-effacement[97]—the realization that the substantive nature of man himself is but another manifestation of the Divine, whereas God's relationship to us is the essence and truth of reality.[98]

The Answer to Relativism

In equating absolute truth with divine infinity, and thereby attributing some degree of reality even to God's manifestations in the finite world and in the perceptions of the human soul, R. Kook may have suggested a solution to the problem of the cognitive value of truth claims in general, namely, how one can endorse the epistemic limitations intrinsic to historicism and cultural relativism and, at the same time, offer claims which purport to transcend those limitations and relate us to the Real. But even with this general assertion of some relationship between any partial renderings of reality and the infinite, R. Kook still cannot avoid the ontological question that all postmodernists face at the level of justifying their particularly favoured metaphors and models. Given his unabashed espousal of moral-spiritual instrumentalism as the final criterion for adjudicating between rival truth claims, can he avoid the conclusion that one ought to relinquish the right to make any further ontological truth claims for the superiority of any particular choice over and above another because there is no 'outside' neutral ground on which to assess this? It seems that, particularly within the monotheistic religions, there are strong barriers to completely divorcing particularist beliefs from any claim to ontologically superior grounding. Is it possible to be an ontological relativist regarding one's particular choice of religious belief (maintaining that all renditions of ultimate truth are equally limited ontologically), and at the same time be committed to those values which we regard as binding from the instrumentalist perspective (i.e. those subjective yearnings which will bring us satisfaction and fulfilment) to the degree that religious belief has traditionally demanded?

There are many indications that, although R. Kook uses moral-spiritual

---

[96] *Ikevei hatson*, 'Da'at elohim', 130–41; 'Avodat elohim', 142–56.
[97] *Ikevei hatson*, 'Avodat elohim', 146. Self-effacement (*anavah*) is one of the appellations of Keter, the highest of the *sefirot*. Keter is also known as Nothingness (Ayin). [98] Ibid.

flourishing as a yardstick for deciding between the many underdetermined options remaining beyond the universal consensus level, he is not relying on instrumentalism alone (the quality of moral-spiritual existence to which our models and metaphors direct us), without attributing a superior ontological standing to the preferred truth claim. More accurately, he sees a connection between the degree of instrumental value of any truth and the strength of its relationship to the Real. The basis for R. Kook's heightened ontological claims regarding particularist beliefs arrived at from pragmatic considerations seems threefold:

(a) The first argument is that the very success of certain truth claims on an instrumental level is an indication of their attunement to reality. Precisely because the reality to which our constructions refer is an infinite one, the only way we have of realizing it is to create multifarious versions of it. Therefore, the extent to which our religious constructions are productive of new and dynamic possibilities is the true measure of the ontological grounding upon which they are based. Successful constructions have greater ontological grounding because the versions of reality which they generate are more encompassing and vibrant, and it is for this reason too (and not only out of instrumentalist considerations) that we are entitled to believe about the Divine whatever promotes our moral-spiritual vitality, and to seek truth systems that create for us a sense of the interconnection of all beings. Whenever we experience our religious visions as bearing greater potential to better the world, we are justified in believing that these visions are rooted, however indirectly, in being and truth.

This understanding assumes that there is some ontology of right relationships of beings to one another, and that there is a prior ontological basis for preferring certain truth claims over others. Within a certain range of variability, there remain intrinsic ontological patterns of what kinds of relationality generate peace, harmony, and a prospering of life energies, and what kinds of relationality make for destructive results. It is the very success of certain visions which attests to some form of 'attunement' to reality, even if it is not one of simple correspondence with 'reality as it is'. Thus, reality-producing models are themselves attuned to the Real because of the ability of moral visions to contribute to the fulfilment of life in its many forms, and results, instrumentally appraised, become the central tool for assessing the truth value of reality-producing models.

The relationship that R. Kook stipulates between true formulations of reality and what really is is illustrated in his concept of the relationship between the revealed Torah and the primordial original, which hasn't suffered the distortions of human understanding. Since the original Torah is equated in his thought with the secrets of the kabbalah,[99] and since what he has to say about 'the language of esotericism' (i.e. the secrets of kabbalah) is that it 'speaks the absolute truth, without any backward regression',[100] it would be safe to assume that whatever is said regarding this original Torah can also be said of absolute reality. It is therefore worthwhile noting that, although this Torah, which is the first manifestation of the Divine, appears in the form of an infinite will, not every expression of that will is regarded as its legitimate reflection. Although he admits that many of our interpretations of Torah are relative to the vagaries of time and circumstances, this does not mean that there are no rights and wrongs in the matter.[101] The various constraints that R. Kook places on the interpretation of Torah testify to the fact that not every structure is

---

[99] *Orot hakodesh*, i. 135.

[100] Ibid. III, passage 98. See B. Ish-Shalom's remarks on this passage and the previous one in *Rav Avraham Itzhak HaCohen Kook*, 194, and Yosef Avivi's critique of this line of interpretation in 'History with Divine Purpose' (Heb.), in Mosheh Bar-Asher (ed.), *Jubilee Volume for Rabbi Mordekhai Breuer* [Sefer hayovel larav mordekhai breuer] (Jerusalem: Magnes Press, 1991), ii. 701–73 and n. 93.

[101] *Igerot hare'ayah*, i. 103–4. This passage was written in the context of an ongoing correspondence regarding the Torah's tacit compliance with the institution of slavery. In the previous letter (*Igerot hare'ayah*, i. 94), R. Kook justifies this compliance on the grounds that the Torah necessarily relates to a situation where people are not yet morally ready to give up this practice. Thus Torah regulations must be provided to make this institution as just as possible. Although R. Kook remarks that the institution of slavery exists in sublimated form even in our day, and that it is a law that is natural to humanity, the implication seems to be that eventually humanity will be weaned of this practice and inclined to higher levels of morality. On the basis of these remarks, his correspondent evidently drew the conclusion that R. Kook believed in an evolving Torah that changes with the times. R. Kook begins his response by vociferously rejecting this contention, making the distinction between an irresponsible, undirected form of evolution and an evolution that is already directed to a predefined goal, and asserting that his understanding of the nature of Torah attributes to it only evolutionary developments belonging to the latter category. It is for this reason that the truth of Torah can only be revealed when the People of Israel—the vessel designed for conveying Torah in this world—resides in its entirety in the Land of Israel, equipped with all of the physical and spiritual structures necessary for its existence. These include the revival of the Oral Torah in the form of a recognized Great Court (Beit Din). Under these conditions, any discrepancy between what—according to prevalent moral conceptions—should now be the understanding of any particular ruling of Torah and what had been previously accepted as the correct interpretation has every chance of being corrected. If the Great Court truly concurs that the previous ruling was intended for conditions that no longer obtain, R. Kook has no doubt that it will succeed in finding a source for this in the Torah. He then adds his belief that the convening of the external factors that prompted the new interpretation, and the re-

acceptable.[102] The intrinsic structure of reality (or Torah) is not bound by anything very specific in terms of content. Almost any truth claim will go, so long as it can be understood as serving the moral-spiritual urge, which is a reflection of the infinite will. But because the question of how any interpretation of Torah fits into the general moral scheme of things is all-important ontologically, the psychological effect of any given interpretation is a consideration that enjoys an ontological status that is stronger than mere instrumentalism. R. Kook's assertion that certain interpretations appear as a result of Divine Providence may just be his mythic way of indicating that these interpretations are a genuine perspective of ultimate reality.[103]

(b) The second argument is based on the formative influence that even our instrumentally grounded models and structures have on our felt experience. On this level, the instrumentalist test of truth claims is justified not only because of its practical benefit to human beings, but because metaphors have powerful existential value. The instrumentally successful model not only helps us to create a fuller or more multifarious reflection of the Divine from our point of view, but it also enables us to tease out of ourselves and our relationships more direct intimations of the Divine. Following this line of thought, it may be said that the religious believer may adopt certain symbols and theological visions for strictly instrumentalist reasons, but if he continues to live out these visions, he eventually will also have religious experiences which ground and affirm them. Thus R. Kook can tolerate an instrumentalist grounding for accepting the Torah and its commandments as a way of life (because of the beneficial effects upon national survival), but can nevertheless be convinced that eventually this will lead to an inner conviction of their divine nature.[104] The more successful the religious model, the more it will allow us to experience the interconnectedness of all beings, gradually diminishing the gap even between the human and the Divine. Thus, although the more prevalent eschatological model that he paints is one in which every isolated phenomenon in the world is connected to its source as graded links in an infinitely growing chain of being,[105] sometimes he describes

instatement of the power of the Beit Din and its ability to find a valid Torah source on which the revision can be based, are not a chance occurrence. This ensures that the changes to be made are consistent with the eternal goals and values of the Torah.

[102] See previous note, and the concept of *seridei hashem* in *Eder hayakar*, 38–9.
[103] *Igerot hare'ayah*, i. 20, 103–4, 123. Divine Providence also seems to be the implication in *Arpelei tohar*, 15.   [104] *Igerot hare'ayah*, i. 49.   [105] *Orot hakodesh*, i. 143–4.

the state of 'highest holiness' as a situation in which man experiences existence in its absolute totality, his private self annihilated.[106] It is because claims and commitments are also justified and tempered by the felt experience of those who adopt them and are moved by them that they are so invaluable in determining truth.

Admittedly, even a radical postmodernist could have recourse to the formative influence of beliefs as an argument for tying instrumentalism to ontology. But if religious discourse is, for the radical postmodernist, merely a self-enclosed 'language game' without reference to a reality already existing outside, this argument basically remains a form of theological idealism with a very flimsy correspondence view of truth—ontology, as it were, after the fact. Religious truth claims, on this view, are true in the ontological sense simply because outside reality is defined by those very truths themselves. R. Kook, however, uses this argument regarding the formative influence of beliefs in order to assume a connection between truth claims and their ontological grounding that is considerably more powerful, because he does assume the prior existence of an outside reality which our truth claims are striving to grasp. There is a reality already 'out there' to which we relate ourselves in various ways through our metaphors and structures. But our religious truth claims do not so much mirror that reality around us as enable more direct experience of it.

But after all is said and done, even when R. Kook reaches this more positive assertion, his instrumentalist justifications for the grounding of one's ontological claims are still relatively modest and are offered in a spirit of humility. There is, as yet, no claim made that religious truths speak of the Divine reality as such, but only as reflected and experienced in the human community.

(c) R. Kook proceeds, however, to buttress the ontological grounding of religious truth claims with reference to a third argument, which seems to have a different and far stronger epistemological status than the previous one, employing what has come to be known as the eschatological test of truth claims.[107] It has been pointed out by some philosophers that as metaphors are appropriated, lived, and shared, they structure not only our subjectively felt experience of the reality they confront, but also that very reality itself. Because the appropriation of metaphors is self-implicating, adopted metaphors can literally create worlds and determine

---

[106] *Arpelei tohar*, 16–17.
[107] See John Hick's use of this argument in *An Interpretation of Religion*, 178–80.

their nature.[108] On this understanding, R. Kook offers an option whereby it is still possible, on the one hand, to hold the post-Kantian view of truth as necessarily bound by human categories, and yet allow for the hope of a post-historical convergence of one's claims with the Real, which may be viewed as an eschatological confirmation. Here it is crucial to point out that, in R. Kook's eschatology, 'the world to come' is not merely a merging with the state of absolute perfection, which already exists from God's point of view, but rather a reconstruction of that perfection in worldly terms, within the dimensions of time and history. Thus, for example, the living out of religious constructs that affirm the interconnectedness of all of reality will lead to a conquering of death even in the physical sense,[109] and to an elevation beyond the limitations of created being to the infinite perfection of the Creator.[110] On this view, religious truths that were first justified instrumentally will eventually be confirmed by their ability to lead us to a level of experience which is recognizably beyond that which we have previously known not only on the existential and subjective level, but even in terms of the infinite possibilities capable of being realized in our external reality.

This last argument seems crucial to traditionalist theology, as it seems that in religion there are strong barriers to completely divorcing belief from the expectation of one event rather than another. So long as there is some connection of belief with testable prediction, however tenuous, it is still possible to avoid the allegation that religious statements are absolutely unverifiable in principle, and therefore have no real ontological grounding.

Conclusion

Referring back to the three quotations that introduced the subject of this essay, we may now spell out clearly the story they imply. The paradoxical proposition of the first quote is that, since the ultimate reality that any religious statement attempts to grasp is infinite and absolute, any finite and relative formulation of it equally misses the mark. There is, therefore, no difference in this respect between faith and heresy. The radical proposal

---

[108] Nelson Goodman, *Ways of Worldmaking* (Indianapolis: Hackett, 1978); see also R. Yosef Bloch's comments on the relationship between the Oral Law and the nature of reality in *Shi'urei da'at*, vol. i (New York: Feldheim, 1949), 23–5, and on the relationship between rewards of this world and the next in *Shi'urei da'at*, vol. ii (Tel Aviv: Yahalom, 1953), 12–13.

[109] See Tamar Ross, 'Immortality, Natural Law, and the Role of Human Perception in the Writings of Rav Kook', in Lawrence Kaplan and David Shatz (eds.), *Rabbi Abraham Isaac Kook and Jewish Spirituality* (New York: New York University Press, 1995), 237–53.

[110] *Orot hakodesh*, ii. 545.

posed by the second quote is that if this is the case, is it not possible to question whether there is any real difference between the religious mystic and the heretic? The answer to the riddle offered by the third passage is that, although every explanation of the ultimate reality misses the mark, all sincere explanations and formulations are valid components of its infinite character, and should be graded hierarchically in terms of their instrumental value. In this solution, it is assumed that there is, on the part both of the believer and of the sincere atheist or sceptic, an acknowledgement of the ultimate nature of that infinite and absolute reality. The religious person explicitly acknowledges it when he views his morally effective formulation as saying something true. He knows it is not the whole truth, but still there is something of the truth in his formulation. But R. Kook also maintains that the heretic, too, implicitly acknowledges the infinite and absolute reality lying beyond, even when simply denying this acknowledgement, because he correctly recognizes the insufficiency of the partial religious formulation. The heretic may not admit his implicit acknowledgement and may even vehemently contest it. But, according to R. Kook's metaphysical assumptions, any effort to embark upon the attempt to grasp the truth already evinces a reliance upon the upward spiritual pull which leads in the direction of the infinite and absolute reality. This is part of the graded realism of Neoplatonism that is reflected in classical kabbalah. R. Kook, however, dissipates to some extent this ancient model of realism in approaching it via a byway, which absorbs some of the non-realistic assumptions of modern post-Kantian idealism to a considerable degree by introducing the crucial role of 'points of view' in establishing truth.

There are certain affinities between R. Kook's view and the cognitive pluralism that seems to be advocated by several twentieth-century Orthodox theologians, who express radically new ideas regarding the grounding of religious commitment and the meaning of belief and basic religious concepts in the modern age. What appears to characterize this new wave is their common wish to minimize the reliance of religion upon very heavy ontological claims, while still maintaining complete loyalty to its normative beliefs and practices of tradition.[111] Perhaps there are grounds for viewing R. Kook, despite the vast differences in their respective theological positions, as a pre-

---

[111] See e.g. J. B. Soloveitchik, *The Halakhic Mind: An Essay on Jewish Tradition and Modern Thought* (Ardmore, Pa.: Seth Press, 1986). Comparisons may also be drawn, to a limited extent, to similar ideas in the writings of Yeshayahu Leibowitz, who was much more extreme in his attempt to create a theology based entirely on normative imperatives, devoid of almost any ontological claims (see Avi Sagi, 'Yeshayahu Leibowitz, a Breakthrough in Jewish Philosophy: Religion without Metaphysics', *Religious Studies*, 33/2 (June 1997), 203–16). A different twist can be found in the writings of Eliezer Goldman, who prefers to base religious

cursor of this new wave of twentieth-century postmodernist Orthodoxy, which consciously recognizes that in talking about God people are engaging in an activity much more complex than straightforward truth description. Such a trend to more qualified realism bears many advantages in an age when it remains unclear what strong correspondence views of truth have to offer contemporary theology, particularly when the meaning of such correspondence itself, even in the sphere of physical science, appears beclouded.

But the question still remains whether a religious world-view which is based on few, if any, ontological claims will ever have the power to match the traditional one in sustaining the emotive intensity of its models and paradigms and transmitting it for generations to come. It is not at all clear that most religious people would be capable of using this kind of language with any degree of passion and commitment if they were not convinced of the truth of the statements they made in the simplest and most straightforward sense of the term. The genuine postmodernist tends to regard his version of reality as one of any number of possibilities. But for many people, it is still much more compelling to express their moral urge by saying 'God commanded me thus' if they believe, or at least have some tendency to believe, that, as a matter of objective fact, God cares what they do and is watching over their actions than if they are motivated by some much more oblique and convoluted relationship between their image of themselves as commanded and what really is 'out there'. There are those that would claim that the radical break with realism entailed even by the milder versions of postmodernism that some contemporary Orthodox thinkers adopt leaves theology with too indistinct a voice, muted by its sidestepping of the absolute nature of religious symbols in the lives of those for whom they have meaning. As a result, such a position will make many religious adherents less inclined to take on the complex of attitudes and activities that goes along with its assertions. In bygone days, it was possible to evolve an elitist theology that could leave the masses and their simplistic views behind, and leave difficult spiritual acrobatics to the more mentally agile elite. But, given the pervasive influence

---

commitment not on any ontological, experiential claims, but rather on the conviction that observance of the Torah is a genuine method of worshipping the transcendent God (see Avi Sagi, 'Religious Commitment in a Secularized World', in id., *Tradition Versus Traditionalism: Contemporary Perspectives in Jewish Thought* (Amsterdam: Brill, 2008), 63–84). A view closer to postmodernism is the suggestion that, since the intrinsic nature of reality is inaccessible, and therefore all versions of it are equally valid, commitment to my particular version is a matter of moral choice. On this reasoning, I can prefer my choice while not delegitimizing the preferences of others (see Gili Zivan, 'Thoughts in Favour of a Bit of Scepticism in Religious Education' (Heb.), *Gilayon [Ne'emanei torah ve'avodah]* (Nisan 1996), 4–11).

of democratic education and mass communication, the residual influence of modern epistemological scepticism is widespread and wreaks religious havoc even among people who are incapable of articulating their religious difficulty. As in most sophisticated religious positions, critics of this variety of postmodernist Orthodoxy would regard the complexity and subtlety of its attachment to reality as its greatest weakness.

Yet R. Kook's personal ability to maintain his sophisticated views of religious belief statements alongside a rich and intense religious commitment in his personal life is truly remarkable and not open to dispute. In this respect, he follows a distinguished list of predecessors (starting at least with Maimonides), whose personal piety and religious commitment made them exemplars of living talmudic Judaism, even when their metaphysical views may have seemed incomprehensible, and even shocking, to their admiring but less sophisticated contemporaries. R. Kook's ability to attribute some degree of reality to any truth claim, alongside his unabashed acknowledgement of the role of historicism, and of cultural relativism in particular (which otherwise bear powerfully problematic elements for religion), in the development of religious truth claims, and his ensuing requirement that theology's claims evolve under constant scrutiny, may prove the most palatable option available to contemporary traditionalist theologians. Although this view encourages the clash of ideas and the generation of ever more comprehensive theories as a necessary tool in the advance to truth, it still emphasizes the essentialness of the simple man's belief as a stepping stone. Moreover, it is this aspect of R. Kook's thought, if it ever were to be absorbed fully into the mainstream thinking of traditional Judaism, that might provide the unexpected impetus for a new climate of discourse and for the exploration of fresh modes of accommodation, on the part of the religious camp, of the modern secular liberal outlook, on grounds that lie beyond the prudential. At any rate, it is obvious that developing the means for disseminating a theology which takes the relative nature of any truth claim into account with complete intellectual integrity, while leaving religious fervour intact and undiluted, may turn out to be the greatest religious challenge of our age.

This essay originally appeared in Yaakov Elman and Jeffrey S. Gurock (eds.), *Hazon Nahum: Studies in Jewish Law, Thought, and History Presented to Dr. Norman Lamm on the Occasion of His Seventieth Birthday* (New York: Yeshiva University Press, 1997), 479–528. It was reprinted in Tamar Ross, *Constructing Faith*, ed. Hava Tirosh-Samuelson and Aaron W. Hughes (Leiden: Brill, 2016), 41–85. It also appeared in Hebrew translation in *Akdamot*, 10 (Dec. 2000), 185–224. Some minor changes to style have been made in the present reprint.

Religious Truth
A Process Summary

ALON GOSHEN-GOTTSTEIN

THE PRESENT PROJECT was born in the interest of serving seminarians, future religious leaders, as they tackle the challenges of encounter, engagement, and collaboration with members of other faiths in their rabbinic and educational capacities. As noted in the preface, the theme was the focus of study and educational activities. It was born out of theological and educational concerns, and it remains relevant to both. The essays in this collection have grappled with the philosophical and theological meaning of religious truth. They have considered various theoretical dimensions of truth—truths of, and truths in, Judaism. In preparing the typescript for publication, I realized how rich our contribution was to the overall discussion. I realized also how much we would be asking of future and present religious leaders and educators who might turn to our collection in search of guidelines and understanding for how to consider the truth dimension of the encounter with other religions, with which they may be collaborating in various capacities. I therefore consider it both useful and true to the character and purpose of this project to translate the wisdom and insight of our authors into steps for self-examination.

The message that follows is couched in the second person. It seeks to walk the reader through the content of our book by making the issues and challenges personal. Themes are woven into and built upon one another, and the dominant note is one of questioning. What, for our authors, were statements become here invitations to think about how the reader is positioned in relation to these statements and how it is possible to move from one to another, making the entire process one of internal investigation. Questioning is crucial here, inasmuch as it forces one at every turn to identify with the process and to consider how it relates to one's previous position and how it might expand one's horizons further. I will repeatedly point back to the authors. In this way, the reader can work his or her way back to the essays on the basis of these questions. In other words, this section can function both as a summary of the project and as a kind of conceptual and practical index by means of which to turn back, to revisit and rediscover the riches of the wisdom offered by our authors.

Religious Truth and Other Religions: A Twelve-Step Theological Workshop

1. Introduction

A. The following guide for thinking about the question of religious truth in light of our collected essays is written primarily for you who are already engaged with other religions, bringing to this engagement your Jewish identity, commitment, and perspective. Your involvement may be practical, as in communal projects of collaboration; study-based, as in dialogue situations; or theoretical, as in exploring the ideas of other religions as part of your pursuit of the broader spiritual heritage of humanity, in the quest for identifying where Judaism fits in the bigger picture.

B. Depending on the activity in which you are engaged, the question of religious truth may play a more or less important role. If you follow the guidelines of many Orthodox Jews and participate in common social activities while avoiding theological dialogue, the question will be less pressing than if you are involved in the study of texts, ideas, and beliefs of different faiths. Increasingly, the boundaries between these activities are lowered and there is growing demand for thoughtful consideration of other religions from a Jewish perspective, also in theological terms. Regardless of the public activities and manifestations, it is more than likely that in your own thinking the issue of religious truth does play a role, whether this has been clearly articulated or remains implicit.

C. The perspective you take on religious truth probably does not hinder your ability to collaborate with other religions on a social basis. We can collaborate for the common good also with people we consider to be in error on various religious and even moral issues. But it certainly does impact your ability to relate to the teachings of another faith. It is likely that you yourself have posed the question of whether you must view other religions as false and Judaism alone as true. You probably know people who hold that position, which is better described as an attitude. You may share in that attitude to some extent, or you may have held it in the past. It is likely that you or others do not hold this attitude as a consequence of study and reflection, but as something inherited, a by-product of affiliation and commitment to your Jewish identity. I would like to invite you to revisit this attitude, or to critically examine it even if you do not partake of it. The essays in this book provide resources for doing so, grounded as they are in Jewish learning, precedent, and engagement. They are an invitation for you to engage in self-exploration, on a personal and communal level; to ask what truth means to you in association with your Jewish faith and commitment and what its implications are to your attitude to other faiths.

2. Taking Stock

Let us begin by taking stock for a moment. As you enter this process, try to account for how you see religious truth. Is the concept of truth important for your religious commitment and identification? If not, what plays a more important role, allowing truth to move to the back seat? If it is important, what do you mean when you relate to your Judaism or Torah as truth? Do you consider the totality of the path? A set of specific faith tenets that you uphold, and which distinguish Judaism from other faiths? Do you consider *everything* in Judaism as truth or only the totality of Judaism? Are all the historical facts recorded in tradition also true? Do you hold that tradition is always true when it contradicts not only other faiths but also science or the discoveries of history?

In all likelihood, if you are reading these words you have already developed an approach to truth that is characterized by some complexity. Examine the contours of this complexity. When do you accept truth literally? When are you comfortable relying on spiritual significance and symbolism, rather than upon a literal understanding? How does your view of truth in relation to the discoveries of science position you to view the question of religious truth in relation to other religions? These are questions that inform our essays and you may revisit them from time to time as you consider your own evolving views of religious truth.

The essays by Krajewski and Ross, as well as the challenges posed by Arthur Green in relation to traditional understandings of scriptural truths, will allow you to explore your own position on these questions. They will provide you with case studies, examples, and precedents for revisiting your own starting point. From here, you may proceed with your personal interrogation and exploration. Needless to say, this process is one that may be as relevant to your community or study group as it is to you personally.

3. Is Truth Essential?

Does truth matter? Let us begin by considering whether truth is an indispensable category in the religious life. Is religious truth really an important issue that should define your attitude to other faiths? Most people take it for granted that it is important and proceed to distinguish between faiths, viewing their own as true and the others as false. Is such a position necessitated by the Jewish tradition? Certainly, if it exists in Jewish society, it can be justified by Jewish sources. But do Jewish sources really mandate such an understanding, or do they offer us greater leeway and latitude as we ponder the subject of religious truth?

4. Can Truth Be Attained?

A. Can we construct our religious life without appeal to truth? Rabbi Nathan of Breslav certainly thinks we can. In my essay I present his view of religious truth as something that is ultimately more a social evil than a religious virtue. We cannot really attain the truth of things as they are. Holding on to our ideas of truth leads to conflict, tension, and violence. Judging by its social outcome, truth may not be a good thing. Rabbi Nathan makes the point on internal religious grounds, such as the division between hasidim and *mitnagedim*. I propose that this dynamic can be extended to other faiths as well. If the test of truth is in its social benefits, should we uphold some distinction between internal and external differences, or should the same criteria apply also to other faiths?

B. Rabbi Nathan considers that, rather than a quest for 'truth', we should focus our lives around a quest for faith. Faith should be accompanied by humility, an epistemological humility that acknowledges that we really do not know truth as it is, nor can we access it. If so, we rely on our faith experience, delivered by our tradition, or sub-tradition, and leave aside disputes. Can this preference for faith over truth translate into your circumstances? Does R. Nathan offer a meaningful spiritual justification for making religious truth less of a concern and focusing instead on our faith experience as something more central?

C. Some aspects of truth have come under scrutiny due to the state of scientific knowledge. Stanislaw Krajewski seeks to affirm something of the truth at the foundation of our approach to various historical truths, and then to adopt an attitude of 'as if' for the rest. Does this approach really uphold a sense of truth, or can it also contribute to a weakening of the sense of religious truth in relation to various religious data? If so, would this place Judaism on a par with other religions, in terms of our inability to access certain truths? Does adopting Krajewski's strategy allow us to distinguish Judaism from other faiths, or does the weakening of historical truth impact the view of Judaism and of other religions in equal measure?

D. Rav Kook holds that, on even more principled grounds, we cannot really come to the truth of religious reality in our mental formulations and concepts, even those mediated by faith. God is beyond our cognition, and therefore even what we say as part of our religious affirmation is still at great remove from the truth of God. As Tamar Ross demonstrates, from the perspective of God's truth, affirmations by the faithful and denials by heretics have the same status. How would your religious life be oriented if you lived in the realization that you cannot really possess truth as such? What implications would that have to your attitude to members of other faiths?

E. If we assume that no one really can access truth as such, does this mean that all paths are equal? Does this lead us to a position we call relativist, and would that imply that all religions have or lack an equal share of the truth? Some postmodern philosophies lead us in this direction. Tamar Ross suggests that Rav Kook does not share in such relativism. Consider her argument and consider why, if no one can really access truth, one religion would be preferable to another. Must the answer be couched in terms of truth or are there other possible criteria?

5. Truth and Human Virtues

A. If it is assumed that truth, in itself, cannot be attained, this gives room for certain qualities of the human person and of the spiritual quest to come to the fore. These are recognized as alternatives to the attainment of truth, highlighting instead the process.

B. One important virtue is intention. R. Nathan teaches us that, in the absence of truth, what counts is the proper and pure intentions of both parties. Rav Kook makes a similar point, and regards intention as that which proffers the value of truth in the absence of full cognition of the truth. Could emphasis on the purity of intention allow us to appreciate other religions? Would the equally sincere efforts made by members of different faiths also proffer upon their traditions an equal measure of truth?

C. The subject of the telos—the purpose or purposes—of the religion has come up in Gellman's presentation, as well as in how Ross reads Rav Kook. When we judge intention, how should it be seen in relation to the telos of the religion? Should we appreciate only such intention that helps advance the goals of the religion? Is there also a reciprocal perspective, wherein clear understanding of those goals conditions our intentions, thereby validating our religious lives?

D. Rabbi Nahman speaks of truthfulness as an extension of the quest for higher truth. Living in truth is a way of reflecting the higher truths that are beyond our grasp. We might refer to this as sincerity, and truthfulness can also be related to the sincerity of intention. Does shifting our attention from abstract truth to truthful and sincere living help us reframe the challenges of religious truth in relation to other faiths?

E. A further virtue that comes to light in view of the possibility that we cannot attain truth is humility. R. Nathan teaches that we must adopt an attitude of humility. Cass Fisher also highlights it as a relevant virtue in conjunction with the rabbis' understanding of truth. If we adopt a perspective of humility, rather than a certain knowledge that positions us over and against others, this will certainly lower the bar of competition and the potential social conflict that it may lead to. Is it appropriate to practise humility in relation to another faith?

F. In theory, neither Judaism nor any other religion has access to the fullness of truth. If so, humility need not open us up to receiving and learning from others. Cass Fisher suggests, however, that epistemological humility should lead us to recognize God as known by the other. Consider whether this suggestion makes sense within your understanding of faith and truth.

6. An Instrumental Approach to Truth

A. If we cannot know religious truths for what they are, what are the criteria by means of which we adopt views on various matters? Tamar Ross teaches us that for Rav Kook the criterion is instrumentality. We should adopt the views that help us advance morally and spiritually. This means that different truths will speak to different people at different times. It means that we ought to judge the positions we take in religious matters by how they help us to grow in our overall religious lives. Consider the implications of such a view to a view of other religions. Should we judge other religions on the basis of how they aid the moral and spiritual advance of these believers? If so, does such a position lead to ascribing equal value to other religions? Or are certain truths, especially faith claims, patently false, so that, regardless of their benefits, they must be declared false? Are there necessary limitations to an instrumentalist view?

B. This very issue informs Yehuda Gellman's presentation. Gellman distinguishes between classical understandings of truth and what he calls telic truths, that is, truths whose value is measured by how they lead the believer to the goal of the religion. He considers that his distillation of Jewish faith does not include any false belief, whereas all religions include at least one false belief. Nevertheless, other faiths do have telic truths; that is, they are instrumental in leading their believers to positive spiritual results. Some of their beneficial outcomes may complement Jewish aspirations and goals, and can potentially enhance them. The measure is the benefit to the spiritual or moral life. The falsity of belief is understood independently of the positive outcomes of telic truths. In this way, Gellman divorces what one typically considers the conflicting truth claims of different religions from the ability to both appreciate and draw beneficial inspiration from other faiths. His thesis is an invitation to examine various assumptions and possibilities in our view of truth. Can we, in theory and in practice, completely sidestep the issue of disagreements concerning the veracity of truth claims, only to focus on the beneficial results and the truths that give rise to them?

Maimonides' views on Christianity and Islam as teaching false beliefs but having beneficial outcomes are famous (see 'Laws of Kings', 114). In terms of the present discussion, those religions teach positive instrumental truths, or telic truths. Could an instrumentalist view of truth, echoing Rav Kook's position, also allow us to validate what we consider false beliefs, provided their moral and spiritual results were beneficial? To give an example: if the incarnation of Jesus is applied by believers as a lesson in humility, can we appreciate its benefits while bracketing the truth claim that we cannot accept?

C. Both Rav Kook and Gellman open us up to a new way of looking at truth. Truth is what we see as beneficial to the spiritual lives of believers. We know it by its results, rather than by the claims or statements made in the name of religion. We have here an epistemological claim for how truth is known and appreciated. How would this claim lead us to view Judaism and world religions? Is it the case that Judaism always produces a finer spiritual or moral life? If not, how does this lead us to think of truth in religion? Perhaps we ought to think of sections and levels of practice within religions rather than of large units such as Judaism, Islam, and so on. Some expressions of a given religion would give fuller testimony to a more exalted way of life and thereby point to truth more than others. The dividing line would then run within religions, rather than between religions, setting them apart.

D. Let us consider, following Maimonides on Christianity and Islam cited above, extending a generous hermeneutic to those religions as far as they help achieve positive goals. This instrumentalist appreciation comes against the background of recognition of falsehood in their teaching. For someone who believes that the historical foundations of Judaism have come under various critiques and therefore the 'scaffolding of Judaism' has come apart (see Green and compare Krajewski, as well as Rav Kook), does an instrumentalist validation of Judaism look any different to the possible instrumentalist validation of other religions?

7. Grounding Truth in God

A. Cass Fisher presents us with a universal dimension of rabbinic thought, wherein God's perfection necessitates his being known by others, beyond the revelation of Judaism, and having a relationship with them. To what extent are your views on religious truth conditioned by a view of Torah and Judaism, and to what extent are they drawn from a view of God? If God and his greatness shape your view of religious phenomena outside Judaism, how far can the argument be extended, without undermining Jewish particularity, mission, election, and your understanding of Judaism? How would your views of other religions change if you regarded them as points of contact with God and sought out indications for that in your encounter with individuals, ideas, and sources of other traditions?

B. There is a further possible implication to this line of thought. A way of presenting Fisher's thesis is to say that God is greater than religion, Judaism being one among many. Such a paraphrase emerges from the study of some of the figures presented in our essays. Is it the case that we can speak of God in terms of truth, while what we know in the domain of religion may not always be described in such terms? If we were to consider that God alone is true, and not any particular religion, what attitude would that generate towards other religions? Would there still be reasons for minimizing contact or for ascribing falsehood to other religions?

C. Rav Kook allows us to visit the question of truth in relation to God in another way. For him, all is God and God is found in all. The instrumentalist perspective, as well as his flexibility on matters of truth, owe in large measure to this recognition that all is God and therefore all options point to God. If God is all-encompassing, would that also make the fundamental religious truths and paths of other religions valid? What limits should be placed on this recognition? What are our criteria for deciding what is non-God or not pleasing to God within a panentheistic view? For Rav Kook, the principal criteria are moral and spiritual evolution. Do other criteria come to mind? Is there any value in internal Jewish criteria for deciding a metaphysical issue?

D. Tamar Ross suggests that for Rav Kook the truer ideas are those that lead to a greater degree of integration of the spiritual vision into one's life, and which allow one to more fully assume that vision and make it one's own. She suggests that a hierarchical view of different beliefs based on their efficacy also lends them greater ontological reality, thereby overcoming the challenge of relativism. If hierarchy of spiritual attainment is seen alongside the beneficial impact of various faiths, how does this allow us to consider the relative truth of Judaism and other religions? Rav Kook might have answered that, in its finest cases, the experience attained through Judaism approximates more closely the fullness of divine reality than those made possible by other faiths. Such a view has room for acceptance of others and their truths in instrumental terms but still privileges a Jewish perspective. Is this a position that one would wish to uphold? How can it be either proven or falsified? What is the testimony of faith experiences from other traditions that is relevant for this discussion?

8. Truth and the Testimony of the Mystics

A. One important resource for exploring the question of truth and divine reality is the testimonies of great spiritual masters and mystics. They provide us with a view of religion at its best. If truth is to be understood not simply as a series of statements but as a fuller reality that shapes the internal reality and consciousness of believers, then studying the testimonies of the finest exemplars of religion is a way of looking at Judaism and world religions in terms of the truth lived by these exemplars. Arthur Green presents us with the processes of acquisition of *da'at*, divine consciousness, in the *Me'or einayim*. Green suggests that both the testimony that is offered by the spiritual life of the religious exemplar and the very tension between the objective, concrete historical dimension and the interior mystical dimension of consciousness characterize all religions. Accordingly, we should expect to find parallel testimonies to the experience and consciousness of God in other religions. Once we find such parallels, is this where religions meet? Does that make the traditions equally true? Should truth in a religion be considered in view of the internal dimension of mystical consciousness? What other aspects of truth should balance it? Can internal, mystical truth compensate for loss of faith in external truths, the 'scaffolding of religion', as Green suggests? If truth is attained mystically and falsehood is affirmed in other aspects of the faith, we are back to the challenge presented by Gellman. Do we choose one dimension over and against another as the domain of truth? If truth is a balance between different factors, is Judaism in a privileged position, compared to other faiths, in having a higher share of the truth? Can the matter be decided in relation to any particular religion, or does conformity to higher dimensions of truth characterize some sections of a religion over and against others, so that the dividing lines run within religions, rather than between them?

B. The perspective of great spiritual masters is also the foundation for Rabbi Nahman's description of truth. For R. Nahman, truth is not a matter of a series of beliefs. It is about the totality of living and manifesting God. Truth is not a teaching. Truth is a way of being that encompasses higher consciousness, goodness, and union with God. Rav Kook and the *Me'or einayim* seem to concur. Can such a definition of truth extend beyond Judaism? Is there any importance to belief, or does the internal spiritual process provide us with the ultimate criterion and approach to truth? If so, is there anything distinctive about Jewish truth?

9. Making Truth Your Own

Cass Fisher, echoing Franz Rosenzweig, urges us to make truth more than an affirmation of objective reality. Arthur Green raises a similar point with reference to the individual owning Scripture, beyond collective historical memory and communal recitation. Truth has to be interiorized, made our own. Everyone is invited to discover his or her portion of the truth. Truth has to be moved from the domain of affirmation to a living relationship with God, to song, praise, and prayer. Does this subjective and experiential approach rely on the objectivity of truth being known? Can it compensate for our inability to know truth in and of itself? Does the interiorization of truth open us up to the recognition of other truths, interiorized by members of other faiths, or does it preclude such recognition, affirming instead greater exclusivity?

10. A Graded Approach to Truth

Tamar Ross's presentation of Rav Kook suggests a hierarchical view of truth, with some expressions of it being higher than others. Similarly, Arthur Green suggests a truth beyond truth, pointing to the internal higher truth, which is contrasted with the objective truths of the religion. A similar point emerges from the presentation of truth in the teachings of R. Nahman of Breslav. Consider the various dimensions of truth as you view the subject for yourself and as it has emerged from our essays. Can you suggest a hierarchy of truths?

Is there gradation in how truth might be applied to religion? Does gradation invite recognition of other religions or does it rather exclude it?

11. Sharing with Other Faiths

A. Arthur Green makes an argument that justifies the sharing of teaching with other religions. The teachings of the *Me'or einayim* are shared with a broader audience, offering a view of where the heart of truth and spiritual life is to be found, because this is coherent with the deeper drive of the religious system. Sharing can be based on the foundations of the common Divinity or the fullness of common humanity as these ideals exist within the Jewish tradition. If truth can be shared with others, can we also receive their truth? What kinds of truth are we open to receiving? Would it make sense that receptivity is limited to the periphery of our faith and related to various supporting features, or could it go to the heart of our faith, identifying a common spiritual reality through the examples of great individuals from whom we can learn?

B. If, as we saw in R. Nahman of Breslav, truth is understood largely as a way of being and as attachment to God, and even if it is understood largely in terms of its moral benefits, should one be receptive to truth from other faiths? If the fundamental criteria of truth concern the realm of internal transformation, can we not learn from the examples of other faiths? Gellman thinks we can. The authors who are studied in our essays all lived in an age in which the possibilities for such internal transformation were much more scarce. What does it do to our notion of truth to assume that we can be inspired and impacted in what matters most by examples outside Judaism, while other kinds of discourse (halakhic and more) are kept strictly within Jewish parameters?

C. If we consider sharing to be of value, is there a difference whether we seek to share truth as such or whether we share wisdom? Does wisdom communicate more readily across traditions and does it allow us to sidestep the conflict of competing truth claims?

12. Summary and Re-evaluation

The steps of this process have allowed us to reflect step by step on the diverse theses presented by our authors, and brought up for discussion their insights and how they may be integrated into the reader's life. Looking back at the thought process or exercise, we should now revisit that process by asking several summary questions. The purpose of these is to help identify ways in which the notion of truth has been opened up for discussion, refined, and redefined. There is not one particular answer that is true or desirable. What is desirable is to move away from a simplistic notion of truth and to cultivate a view that is thoughtful, dynamic, and able to accommodate the many dimensions of truth as well as the many challenges presented by the encounter with other religions. In summary, please reflect on the following:

A. How has your view of truth changed in the process of engaging with our essays and with the sources presented in them?

B. Are you able to find a definition of truth in Judaism? What about it makes it true and what dimensions of the tradition invite such language?

C. Are you able to suggest how moral, spiritual, and other instrumentalist dimensions come together to inform religious truth?

D. In view of this statement of truth, can the term also be applied to other religions, and in what way?

E. Does Judaism retain some unique dimension of truth, and, if so, where is it found?

F. Does the mystical association of truth, consciousness, and union with God allow us to locate truth differently than through conventional understandings? What are its implications for other religions? Can you identify with such a position?

G. What room is there for sharing with other faiths in light of the answers to the questions above? This applies to teaching as well as to learning from them.

Bibliography

ALTMANN, ALEXANDER (ed.), *Biblical and Other Studies* (Cambridge, Mass.: Harvard University Press, 1963).

AVIVI, YOSEF, 'History with Divine Purpose' (Heb.), in Mosheh Bar-Asher (ed.), *Jubilee Volume for Rabbi Mordekhai Breuer* [Sefer hayovel larav mordekhai breuer], 2 vols. (Jerusalem: Magnes Press, 1991), ii. 701–73.

BARR, JAMES, *Biblical Faith and Natural Theology* (Oxford: Clarendon Press, 1993).

BEN-AMOS, DAN, and JEROME R. MINTZ (ed. and trans.), *In Praise of the Baal Shem Tov* (Northvale, NJ: Aronson, 1993).

BEN-SASSON, YONA, 'The Philosophies of Rabbi A. I. Kook and Rabbi J. B. Soloveitchik' (Heb.), in Hayim Hamiel (ed.), *In His Light: Studies in the Thought of Rabbi Abraham Isaac Kook* [Be'oro: iyunim bemishnato shel harav avraham yitshak hakohen kuk] (Jerusalem: Hahistadrut Hatsiyonit Ha'olamit, 1986), 353–408.

BEN-SHLOMO, YOSEF, *Rabbi Mosheh Cordovero's Teachings on Divinity* [Torat ha'elohut shel r. mosheh cordovero] (Jerusalem: Mosad Bialik, 1965).

—— *The Song of Life—From the Teachings of Rabbi Kook* ['Shirat haḥayim': perakim bemishnato shel harav kook] (Tel Aviv: Sifriyat Ha'universitah Hameshuderet, 1988).

BERGMAN, SHEMUEL HUGO, 'The Theory of Evolution in the Thought of R. Kook' (Heb.), in id., *Personalities and Paths* [Anashim uderakhim: masot filosofiyot] (Jerusalem: Ha'ahim Green, 1968), 350–8.

BERNFELD, SHIMON, *Da'at elohim* (Warsaw: Ahiasaf, 1922).

BIALE, DAVID (ed.), *Hasidism: A New History* (Princeton, NJ: Princeton University Press, 2018).

BLOCH, YOSEF, *Shiurei da'at*, vol. i (New York: Feldheim, 1949); vol. ii (Tel Aviv: Yahalom, 1953).

BOYARIN, DANIEL, *The Jewish Gospels: The Story of the Jewish Christ* (New York: The New Press, 2012).

BRAITHWAITE, RICHARD BEVAN, 'An Empiricist's View of the Nature of Religious Belief', in Basil Mitchell (ed.), *The Philosophy of Religion* (Oxford: Oxford University Press, 1971), 72–9.

BRINK, DAVID, *Moral Realism and the Foundation of Ethics* (Cambridge: Cambridge University Press, 1989).

BYRNE, JAMES M., 'Foucault on Continuity: The Postmodern Challenge to Tradition', *Faith and Philosophy*, 9/3 (July 1992), 335–52.

CARMY, SHALOM, 'Dialectic, Doubters, and a Self-Erasing Letter: Rav Kook and the Ethics of Belief', in Lawrence Kaplan and David Shatz (eds.), *Rabbi Abraham*

Isaac Kook and Jewish Spirituality (New York: New York University Press, 1995), 205–36.

COHEN, ARTHUR A., and PAUL MENDES-FLOHR (eds.), *Contemporary Jewish Religious Thought* (New York: The Free Press, 1987).

COHEN, SHAYE J. D., *From the Maccabees to the Mishnah*, 2nd edn. (Louisville: Westminster John Knox, 2006).

Daily Prayer Book: Ha-Siddur Ha-Shalem, trans. Philip Birnbaum (New York: Hebrew Publishing Company, 1997).

DAVANEY, SHEILA G. (ed.), *Theology at the End of Modernity* (Philadelphia: Trinity Press International, 1991).

DAVIDSON, HERBERT A., 'Study of Philosophy as a Religious Obligation', in S. D. Goitein (ed.), *Religion in a Religious Age* (Cambridge, Mass.: Association for Jewish Studies, 1974), 53–68.

DEAN, WILLIAM, *History Making History* (Albany, NY: State University of New York Press, 1988).

DESSLER, ELIYAHU, *Mikhtav me'eliyahu*, vol. iii, ed. Aryeh Carmel and Hayim Friedlander (Benei Berak: Hapo'el Hamizrahi, 1964).

DYNNER, GLENN (ed.), *Holy Dissent: Jewish and Christian Mystics in Eastern Europe* (Detroit: Wayne State University Press, 2011).

ELIACH, YAFFA, 'The Russian Dissenting Sects and their Influence on R. Israel Ba'al Shem Tov, Founder of Hasidism', *PAAJR*, 36 (1963), 57–83.

ETKES, IMMANUEL, *The Besht: Magician, Mystic, and Leader* (Waltham, Mass.: Brandeis University Press, 2005).

FEUERBACH, LUDWIG ANDREAS, *Das Wesen des Christentums* (Leipzig, 1841); Eng. edn. *The Essence of Christianity*, trans. M. Evans [George Eliot] (London, 1854).

FISHER, CASS, 'Beyond the Homiletical: Rabbinic Theology as Discursive and Reflective Practice', *Journal of Religion*, 90/2 (2010), 199–236.

——*Contemplative Nation: A Philosophical Account of Jewish Theological Language* (Stanford: Stanford University Press, 2012).

——'Divine Perfections at the Center of the *Star*: Reassessing Rosenzweig's Theological Language', *Modern Judaism*, 31/2 (2011), 188–212.

——'The Posthumous Conversion of Ludwig Wittgenstein and the Future of Jewish (Anti-)Theology', *AJS Review*, 39/2 (2015), 333–65.

——'Reading for Divine Perfection: Theological Reflection and Religious Practice in the Exodus Commentary of *Mekhilta de-Rabbi Ishmael*', in Lucie Doleźalová and Tamás Visi (eds.), *Retelling the Bible: Literary, Historical, and Social Contexts* (Frankfurt am Main: Peter Lang, 2011), 139–57.

——'Speaking Metaphysically of a Metaphysical God: Rosenzweig, Schelling, and the Metaphysical Divide', in Martina Urban and Christian Wiese (eds.), *German-Jewish Thought Between Religion and Politics: Festschrift in Honor of Paul Mendes-Flohr on the Occasion of His Seventieth Birthday* (Berlin: De Gruyter, 2012), 151–66.

FLAVIUS JOSEPHUS, *Against Apion*, trans. John M. G. Barclay, ed. Steve Mason (Leiden: Brill, 2007).

FLEISCHACKER, SAMUEL, *Divine Teaching and the Way of the World* (Oxford: Oxford University Press, 2011).

—— *The Good and the Good Book* (Oxford: Oxford University Press, 2015).

FLUSSER, DAVID, 'A New Sensitivity in Judaism and the Christian Message', *Harvard Theological Review*, 61/2 (1968), 107–27.

FOUCAULT, MICHEL, *The Archaeology of Knowledge*, trans. Alan Sheridan (New York: Pantheon Books, 1972).

GELLMAN, JEROME, 'Beyond Belief: On the Uses of Creedal Confession', *Faith and Philosophy*, 23/3 (2007), 299–313.

—— 'Epistemic Peer Conflict and Religious Belief', *Faith and Philosophy*, 15/2 (1998), 229–35.

—— *God's Kindness Has Overwhelmed Us* (Boston: Academic Studies Press, 2007).

—— 'In Defense of a Contented Exclusivist', *Religious Studies*, 36 (2000), 401–17.

—— 'Jewish Chosenness and Religious Diversity—A Contemporary Approach', in Robert McKim (ed.), *Religious Perspectives on Religious Diversity* (Leiden: Brill, 2016), 21–36.

—— 'Religious Diversity and the Epistemic Justification of Religious Belief', *Faith and Philosophy*, 10/3 (1993), 345–64; repr. in Michael Murray and Eleonore Stump (eds.), *Philosophy of Religion: The Big Questions* (Oxford, 1999), 441–53.

GILL, JERRY H., *The Possibility of Religious Knowledge* (Grand Rapids, Mich.: B. Eerdmans, 1971).

GOLDMAN, ALVIN I., *Knowledge in a Social World* (Oxford: Clarendon Press, 1999).

GOODMAN, NELSON, *Ways of Worldmaking* (Indianapolis: Hackett, 1978).

GOSHEN-GOTTSTEIN, ALON, 'The Body as Image of God in Rabbinic Literature', *Harvard Theological Review*, 87/2 (1994), 171–95.

—— 'The Halakhah in Light of the Spiritual Life' (Heb.), in A. Berholz (ed.), *The Quest for Halakhah: Interdisciplinary Perspectives on Jewish Law* [Masa el hahalakhah: iyunim bein-teḥumiyim ba'olam haḥok hayehudi] (Tel Aviv, 2003), 257–84.

—— 'Towards a Jewish Theology of World Religions: Framing the Issues', in Alon Goshen-Gottstein and Eugene Korn (eds.), *Jewish Theology and World Religions* (Oxford, 2012), 20–33.

GREEN, ARTHUR, 'Buber, Scholem, and the *Me'or 'Eynayim*: Another Perspective on a Great Controversy' (forthcoming).

—— *A Guide to the Zohar* (Stanford: Stanford University Press, 2005).

—— 'The Hasidic Homily: Mystical Performance and Hermeneutical Process', in Bentsi Cohen (ed.), *As a Perennial Spring: A Festschrift Honoring Rabbi Dr. Norman Lamm* (New York: Downhill, 2015), 237–65.

—— 'Hasidism and Its Response to Change', *Jewish History*, 27/2–4 (Dec. 2013), 319–36.

GREEN, ARTHUR, 'Hasidism: Discovery and Retreat', in Peter Berger (ed.), *The Other Side of God* (New York: Anchor Books, 1981), 104–30; repr. in Arthur Green, *The Heart of the Matter* (Philadelphia: Jewish Publication Society, 2015), 227–53.

—— *Speaking Torah: Teachings from Around the Maggid's Table* (Woodstock, Vt.: Jewish Lights, 2013).

—— and ARIEL EVAN MAYSE (eds.), *A New Hasidism*, 2 vols. (Philadelphia: Jewish Publication Society, forthcoming).

GRIES, ZEEV, *The Book in Early Hasidism* [Hasefer bereshit haḥasidut] (Tel Aviv: Hakibuts Hame'uhad, 1992).

HALPERIN, DAVID J., *The Faces of the Chariot: Early Jewish Responses to Ezekiel's Vision* (Tübingen: J. C. B. Mohr, 1988).

HAYIM OF VOLOZHIN, *Nefesh haḥayim* (Vilna, 1874).

HERZOG, Z., 'The Bible—No Evidence on the Ground' (Heb.), *Haaretz*, 3 Nov. 1999.

HESCHEL, ABRAHAM JOSHUA, *Heavenly Torah, as Refracted through the Generations*, trans. and ed. Gordon Tucker (New York: Continuum, 2006).

HEZSER, CATHERINE, *The Social Structure of the Rabbinic Movement in Roman Palestine* (Tübingen: Mohr Siebeck, 1997).

HICK, JOHN, *An Interpretation of Religion: Human Responses to the Transcendent* (New Haven: Yale University Press, 1989).

—— 'Religious Pluralism and Salvation', *Faith and Philosophy*, 5/4 (1988), 365–77.

HIRSHMAN, MARC, 'Rabbinic Universalism in the Second and Third Centuries', *Harvard Theological Review*, 93/2 (2000), 101–15.

—— *Torah for All the World's People* [Torah lekhol ba'ei ha'olam: zerem universali besifrut hatana'im veyaḥaso leḥokhmat ha'amim] (Tel Aviv: Hakibuts Hame'uhad, 1999).

HYMAN, ARTHUR, 'Spinoza's Dogmas of Universal Faith in the Light of Their Medieval Jewish Background', in Alexander Altmann (ed.), *Biblical and Other Studies* (Cambridge, Mass.: Harvard University Press, 1963), 183–95.

HYMAN, ISRAEL, 'The Halakhic Issues of Mezizah', *Proceedings of the Association of Orthodox Jewish Scientists*, 8–9 (1987), 17–44.

ISH-SHALOM, BENJAMIN, *Rav Avraham Itzhak HaCohen Kook: Between Rationalism and Mysticism*, trans. Ora Wiskind-Elper (Albany: State University of New York Press, 1993).

—— and SHALOM ROSENBERG (eds.), *Jubilee of Lights: The Thought of Rabbi Abraham Isaac Hakohen* [Yovel orot: haguto shel harav avraham yitsḥak hakohen kuk z'l] (Jerusalem: Hahistadrut Hatsiyonit Ha'olamit, 1985).

—— —— (eds.), *The World of R. Kook's Thought* (New York: Avi Chai, 1991).

JACOB JOSEPH OF POLONNOYE, *Toledot ya'akov yosef* (Jerusalem, 2011).

JACOBS, LOUIS, *Seeker of Unity: The Life and Works of Aaron of Starosselje* (London: Vallentine Mitchell, 1966).

KAHANA, MAOZ, and ARIEL EVAN MAYSE, 'Hasidic *Halakhah*: Reappraising the Interface of Spirit and Law', *AJS Review*, 41/2 (Nov. 2017), 375–408.

KAPLAN, LAWRENCE J., 'Rav Kook and the Jewish Philosophical Tradition', in Lawrence J. Kaplan and David Shatz (eds.), *Rabbi Abraham Isaac Kook and Jewish Spirituality* (New York: New York University Press, 1995), 41–78.

KATZ, YA'AKOV, *Halakhah in Straits: Obstacles to Orthodoxy at Its Inception* [Hahalakhah bemetsar: mikhsholim al derekh ha'ortodoxiyah behithavutah] (Jerusalem: Magnes Press, 1992).

KAUFMANN, ZIPPI, *In All Your Ways Know Him* [Bekhol derakheikha da'ehu] (Ramat Gan: Bar Ilan University Press, 2009).

KEATING, THOMAS, *Intimacy with God: An Introduction to Centering Prayer* (Snowmass, Colo.: Crossroad, 2009).

KESSLER, EDWARD, *Bound by the Bible: Jews, Christians and the Sacrifice of Isaac* (Cambridge: Cambridge University Press, 2004).

KIDD, IAN JAMES, 'Beauty, Virtue, and Religious Exemplars', *Religious Studies*, 53 (2017), 171–81.

KITCHER, PHILIP, 'Challenges for Secularism', in George Levine (ed.), *The Joy of Secularism: 11 Essays for How We Live Now* (Princeton, NJ: Princeton University Press, 2011), 24–46.

KOOK, ABRAHAM ISAAC, *Arpelei tohar* (Yaffo, 1914); 2nd edn., ed. Yitshak Shilat (Jerusalem: Mahon Harav Tsevi Yehudah, 1983).

—— *Da'at kohen* [responsa] (Jerusalem: Mosad Harav Kook, 1985).

—— *Eder hayakar* (Jerusalem: Mosad Harav Kook, 1982).

—— 'Exalted in Holiness' (Heb.), in *Ma'amerei hare'ayah*, 2 vols. (Jerusalem: Mosad Harav Kook, 1984), ii. 399–417.

—— *Igerot hare'ayah*, 4 vols. (Jerusalem: Mosad Harav Kook, 1984–5).

—— *Ikevei hatson* (Jerusalem: Mosad Harav Kook, 1985).

—— *Olat re'ayah*, 2 vols. (Jerusalem: Mosad Harav Kook, 1985).

—— *Orot* (Jerusalem: Mosad Harav Kook, 1969).

—— *Orot ha'emunah*, ed. Mosheh Gurevitz (Brooklyn: Langsam Associates, 1985).

—— *Orot hakodesh*, 4 vols. (Jerusalem: Mosad Harav Kook, 1985).

—— *Selected Letters*, trans. and annotated by Tzvi Feldman (Ma'alei Adumim: Maalot Publications, 1986).

—— 'A Special Article (Against R. Zeev Yaavetz's Method in His Work *The History of the Jews*)' (Heb.), in *Ma'amerei hare'ayah*, 2 vols. (Jerusalem: Hakeren Al Shem Golda Katz, 1980), i. 105–12.

LAUTERBACH, JACOB, *Mekhilta de-Rabbi Ishmael*, 2 vols. (Philadelphia: Jewish Publication Society, 2004).

MAIMONIDES, MOSES, *Guide of the Perplexed*, trans. M. Friedländer (New York: E. P. Dutton, 1904).

MARMORSTEIN, ARTHUR, *The Old Rabbinic Doctrine of God* (Oxford: Oxford University Press, 1927).

MCCAIN, KEVIN, 'The Virtues of Epistemic Conservatism', *Synthese*, 164 (2008), 185–200.

Mechilta d'Rabbi Ismael cum variis lectionibus et adnotationibus, ed. H. S. Horovitz and I. A. Rabin (Frankfurt: J. Kaufmann, 1931).
MENAHEM NAHUM OF CHERNOBYL, *Me'or einayim*, 2 vols., ed. Y. S. Oesterreicher (Jerusalem, 2012).
MENDELSSOHN, MOSES, *Jerusalem; or On Religious Power and Judaism*, trans. Allan Arkush (Hanover, NH: Brandeis University Press, 1983).
MILL, JOHN STUART, *On Liberty* (London: Longmans, Green, 1913).
MURRAY, MICHAEL, and ELEONORE STUMP (eds.), *The Big Questions* (Oxford: Blackwell, 1999).
NEHORAI, MICHAEL ZVI, 'Halakhah, Meta-Halakhah, and the Redemption of Israel: Reflections on the Rabbinic Rulings of R. Kook', in Lawrence Kaplan and David Shatz (eds.), *Rabbi Abraham Isaac Kook and Jewish Spirituality* (New York: New York University Press, 1995), 120–56.
NEUSNER, JACOB, *The Mishnah: A New Translation* (New Haven: Yale University Press, 1988).
PACHTER, MORDECHAI, '*Katnut* and *Gadlut* in Lurianic Kabbalah' (Heb.), *Jerusalem Studies in Jewish Thought*, 10 (1992), 171–210.
Pesikta derav kahana, ed. Bernard Mandelbaum, 2 vols. (New York: Jewish Theological Seminary, 1987).
POLEN, NEHEMIA, 'Why Would Someone Cut Plants in Paradise? "Four Entered Pardes" in Light of 1 Enoch 6–8' (forthcoming).
RAWIDOWICZ, SIMON, 'Philosophy as a Duty', in I. Epstein (ed.), *Moses Maimonides, Eighth Centenary Memorial Volume* (London: Soncino Press, 1935), 177–88, repr. in Simon Rawidowicz, *Studies in Jewish Thought*, ed. N. Glatzer (Philadelphia: Jewish Publication Society, 1974), 305–16.
RORTY, RICHARD, *Consequences of Pragmatism* (Minneapolis: University of Minnesota Press, 1982).
ROSENAK, AVINOAM, 'Hidden Diaries and New Discoveries: The Life and Thought of Rabbi A. I. Kook', *Shofar: An Interdisciplinary Journal of Jewish Studies*, 25/3 (Spring 2007), 111–47.
ROSENZWEIG, FRANZ, *Der Mensch und sein Werk: Gesammelte Schriften*, 4 vols. (The Hague: Martinus Nijhoff, 1976).
—— 'Das neue Denken', in *Der Mensch und sein Werk: Gesammelte Schriften*, 4 vols. (The Hague: Martinus Nijhoff, 1976), iii. 139–61; Eng. trans., 'The New Thinking', in *Philosophical and Theological Writings*, trans. and ed. Paul W. Franks and Michael L. Morgan (Indianapolis: Hackett, 2000), 109–39.
—— *Philosophical and Theological Writings*, trans. and ed. Paul W. Franks and Michael L. Morgan (Indianapolis: Hackett, 2000).
—— *The Star of Redemption*, trans. Barbara Galli (Madison: University of Wisconsin Press, 2005); trans. William Hallo (New York: Holt, Rinehart, and Winston, 1970).
ROSKIES, DAVID, 'Memory', in Arthur A. Cohen and Paul Mendes-Flohr (eds.), *Contemporary Jewish Religious Thought* (New York: The Free Press, 1987), 581–6.

ROSS, TAMAR, 'The Concept of God in the Thought of Rav Kook' (Heb.), *Da'at*, 8 (1981–2), 109–28; *Da'at*, 9 (1983), 39–70.

—— 'Immortality, Natural Law, and the Role of Human Perception in the Writings of Rav Kook', in Lawrence Kaplan and David Shatz (eds.), *Rabbi Abraham Isaac Kook and Jewish Spirituality* (New York: New York University Press, 1995), 237–53.

—— 'Myth, Structure, and Reality in the Writings of Rav Kook' (Heb.), in Haviva Pedaya (ed.), *Myth in Judaism* [Hamitos bayahadut] (Be'er Sheva: Ben Gurion University Press, 1996), 239–62.

—— 'R. Kook: A This-Worldly Mystic', in Steven Kepnes (ed.), *The Cambridge Companion to Jewish Theology* (forthcoming).

—— 'Two Interpretations of the Doctrine of *Tsimtsum*: R. Hayim of Volozhin and R. Shneur Zalman of Liadi' (Heb.), *Jerusalem Studies in Jewish Thought*, 2 (Jerusalem, 1982), 153–69.

SACKS, JONATHAN, 'The Binding of Isaac: A New Interpretation' (2010 [5771]), Covenant and Conversation website (accessed 24 Oct. 2010).

SAGI, AVI, 'Religious Commitment in a Secularized World', in id., *Tradition Versus Traditionalism: Contemporary Perspectives in Jewish Thought* (Amsterdam: Brill, 2008), 63–84.

—— 'Tolerance and the Possibility of Pluralism in Judaism' (Heb.), *Iyun*, 44 (Apr. 1995), 175–200.

—— 'Yeshayahu Leibowitz, a Breakthrough in Jewish Philosophy: Religion without Metaphysics', *Religious Studies*, 33/2 (June 1997), 203–16.

SCHATZ-UFFENHEIMER, RIVKA, *Hasidism as Mysticism: Quietistic Elements in Eighteenth-Century Hasidic Thought* (Princeton, NJ: Princeton University Press, 2015).

SCHECHTER, SOLOMON, *Aspects of Rabbinic Theology: Major Concepts of the Talmud* (London, 1901).

SCHOLEM, GERSHOM, *Major Trends in Jewish Mysticism* (New York: Schocken Books, 1946).

Sefer ba'al shem tov al hatorah (Jerusalem: Nofet Tsofim, 1997).

SEGAL, ALAN, 'Universalism in Judaism and Christianity', in Troels Engberg-Pedersen (ed.), *Paul in His Hellenistic Context* (Minneapolis: Fortress Press, 1995), 1–29.

SEPTIMUS, BERNARD, 'What Did Maimonides Mean by Madda'?, in Ezra Fleischer et al. (eds.), *Me'ah She'arim: Studies in Medieval Jewish Spiritual Life in Memory of Isadore Twersky* [Me'ah she'arim: iyunim be'olamam haruḥani biymei ha-beinayim lezekher yitsḥak tverski] (Eng. and Heb.) (Jerusalem: Magnes Press, 2001), 83–110.

SHATZ, DAVID, 'The Integration of Religion and Culture: Its Scope and Limits in the Thought of R. Kook', in Y. Elman and J. S. Gorock (eds.), *Ḥazon Naḥum: Studies in Jewish Law, Thought and History Presented to Dr. Norman Lamm on the Occasion of His Seventieth Birthday* (New York: Yeshiva University Press, 1997), 529–56.

SHATZ, DAVID, 'Rav Kook and Modern Orthodoxy: The Ambiguities of "Openness"', in Moshe Sokol (ed.), *Engaging Modernity: Rabbinic Leaders and the Challenge of the Twentieth Century* (Northvale, NJ: Jason Aronson, 1997), 91–115.

Sifre on Deuteronomy, ed. Louis Finkelstein (New York: Jewish Theological Seminary, 1969),

SLIFKIN, NATAN, 'Was Rashi a Corporealist?', *Ḥakirah, the Flatbush Journal of Jewish Law and Thought*, 7 (2009), 81–105.

SOLOVEITCHIK, JOSEPH B., *The Halakhic Mind: An Essay on Jewish Tradition and Modern Thought* (Ardmore, Pa.: Seth Press, 1986).

STRAUSS, DAVID FRIEDRICH, *Das Leben Jesu Kritisch Berbeitet*, 2 vols. (Tübingen, 1835–6); Eng. edn. *The Life of Jesus Critically Examined*, trans. George Eliot (London, 1848).

Tanakh: The Holy Scriptures (Philadelphia: Jewish Publication Society of America, 1978).

TILLICH, PAUL, *Dynamics of Faith* (New York: Harper and Row, 1957).

TISHBY, ISAIAH, and YERUHAM FISHEL LACHOWER, *Wisdom of the Zohar*, 3 vols. (Oxford, 1989).

TOUROV, IGOR, 'Hasidism and Christianity of the Eastern Territory of the Polish–Lithuanian Commonwealth: Possible of [sic] Contacts and Mutual Influences', *Kabbalah*, 10 (2004), 73–105.

URBACH, EPHRAIM, *The Sages: Their Concepts and Beliefs*, trans. Israel Abrahams (Jerusalem: Magnes Press, 1975).

WASKOW, ARTHUR, and PHYLLIS BERMAN, 'Relearning and Rethinking the Passover Saga', Jewish Telegraphic Agency website (accessed Apr. 2011).

WILLIAMS, BERNARD, *Truth and Truthfulness* (Princeton, NJ: Princeton University Press, 2004).

YSANDER, T., *Studien zum Bestschan Hasidismus* (Uppsala, 1933).

ZELIGMAN, NAFTALI, 'Letter to My Rabbi' (2005), Talk Reason website (accessed Jan. 2010).

ZIVAN, GILI, 'Thoughts in Favour of a Bit of Scepticism in Religious Education' (Heb.), *Gilayon* [*Ne'emanei torah ve'avodah*] (Nisan 1996), 4–11.

Notes on the Contributors

◆

CASS FISHER is an associate professor in religious studies at the University of South Florida. He received his Ph.D. from the University of Chicago. His research focuses on rabbinic theology and modern Jewish thought, to which he brings resources from both continental and analytic philosophy. His first book, *Contemplative Nation: A Philosophical Account of Jewish Theological Language* (2012), presents a new model for understanding Jewish theology that emphasizes the multiple forms and functions of Jewish theological language and grounds theological reflection within religious practice. He is currently working on a second book, *As If It Could Be Said: Realism and Reference in Jewish Theology*, sections of which have appeared in *Harvard Theological Review* and *AJS Review*.

JEROME YEHUDA GELLMAN has written seven books and over 110 articles on the philosophy of religion and Jewish thought. He is a past Fellow at the Harvard Center for the Study of World Religions and past Alvin Plantinga Fellow at the Center for the Philosophy of Religion, Notre Dame University. He was also a Fellow at the Advanced Institute of the Shalom Hartman Institute, Jerusalem. He edits a series for Brill in philosophy of religion and is an editorial board member of four philosophy journals. His forthcoming book, *The God of the Jews and the Jewish God*, is the last in a trilogy on contemporary constructive Jewish theology.

ALON GOSHEN-GOTTSTEIN is the founder and director of the Elijah Interfaith Institute, and lecturer and director of the Center for the Study of Rabbinic Thought, Beit Morasha College, Jerusalem. Ordained a rabbi in 1977, he holds a Ph.D. from the Hebrew University of Jerusalem in the field of rabbinic thought. His publications are divided between the areas of interreligious dialogue, theology of religions, Jewish spirituality, and rabbinic thought, and he is editor of the series Interreligious Reflections (Wipf & Stock), where the work of the Elijah Think Tank is featured. He has published fifteen books in the field of the theology of religions and interfaith relations, including *Jewish Theology and World Religions* (edited with Eugene Korn; Littman Library, 2011) and his most recent monograph, *Luther the Antisemite: A Contemporary Jewish Perspective* (2018).

ARTHUR GREEN is Irving Brudick Professor of Jewish Philosophy and Religion at Hebrew College, where he also serves as rector of the Rabbinical School, which he founded in 2003. A historian of Jewish mysticism as well as a theologian, he is co-editor of *A New Hasidism* (2019). His annotated translation of *Me'or einayim* is forthcoming.

STANISLAW KRAJEWSKI is Professor of Philosophy at the University of Warsaw. He has published papers and books in the fields of logic and the philosophy of mathematics, as well as on the philosophy of dialogue, Jewish experience, and Christian–Jewish dialogue. He has been the Jewish co-chairman the Polish Council of Christians and Jews since 1991, and is co-author of the post-war section of the exhibition in the POLIN Museum of the History of Polish Jews in Warsaw.

TAMAR ROSS is Professor Emeritus of the Department of Jewish Thought at Bar-Ilan University. She has taught in many academic and religious settings in Israel and abroad, and publishes widely on various topics relating to Jewish philosophy. Her particular areas of interest include contemporary challenges to traditionalist Jewish theology (including feminism, historicism, biblical criticism, and postmodernity), concepts of God, divine revelation, religious epistemology and hermeneutics, the philosophy of halakhah, the nineteenth-century *musar* movement founded by Rabbi Israel Salanter, and the writings of Rabbi A. I. Kook.

Index

A
Aaron (biblical figure) 69
Abraham (biblical figure) 53–4, 58–9, 69, 79n.
Abrahamic religions 1, 14, 18
acceptance:
  and belief 30–1
  of other religions 11, 185
  of science 54
  and tradition 153
Akedah 11, 53–5, 57–9
Akiva, R. 5In., 74, 77, 79, 113
Altmann, Alexander 144n.
Anselm of Canterbury 36
anti-realism 8, 167
  see also non-realism
Avivi, Yosef 170n.
avodah begashmiyut 92n.
  see also devotion

B
Barr, James 12, 66–7, 76n.
Batsheva (biblical figure) 134
belief:
  and biases 44
  and book of Job 50, 52
  and constructivism 42
  and content of truth 115, 130
  and divinity 62–3, 76, 81
  and eternal essence 48–50
  and expressionism 36–7
  false belief 32, 131, 183
  and historical truth 55
  and interreligious understanding 29–35, 58, 131–2, 178, 185
  R. Kook on 149–57, 160–5, 174, 176
  and mysticism 84
  R. Nahman on 186
  and nativity objection 38–40
  necessary and true beliefs 144–5
  and postmodernism 41, 172
  and relativism 168–9
  and spirituality 23–4
  and telic truth 9–10
  see also Kook, R. Abraham Isaac: on belief; truth
Ben-Amos, Dan 104n.
Ben-Sasson, Yonah 157n.
Ben Sirah 76–7
Ben Zakai, Yohanan 77
Bergman, Shemuel H. 148
Bernfeld, Shimon 88n.
Bethar, capture of 56
Biale, David 85n.
biasism 41, 44–5
Bible:
  Bultmann's interpretation of 137
  and creation 76n.
  Deuteronomy 35, 72, 74, 77–8, 87, 96
  emet in 110n.
  Exodus 69, 74–5, 79
  Hebrew Bible 66–7
  Isaiah 88, 92, 95, 109
  Kings 73–4, 89
  Proverbs 73, 78, 92, 94–5, 109
  Psalms 66, 73–4, 78, 93, 96, 103, 112, 115, 120, 123, 135, 140
  Samuel 134
  and spiritual nature of God 135
  and universal and particular truth 73
  Zechariah 73, 77, 109
Bloch, R. Yosef 173n.
Boyarin, Daniel 48n.
Braithwaite, R. B. 36–8, 137–8
Breslav theology 7, 18–22
  see also Nahman of Breslav: *Likutei moharan*
Brink, David 151n.
Buddhism 30, 39, 105
Bultmann, Rudolf 137–8

C

Carmy, Shalom 155n.
Christianity 31–2, 37, 39, 57–9, 61, 64, 66n., 85, 136
  see also Jesus
Cohen, Shaye D. 65n.
coherence theory 10, 13, 19, 21, 24, 134, 146
constructivism 41–3
Copernican revolution 32, 139, 152, 160
core beliefs 9, 29–30, 34
correspondence theory:
  Fisher on 13
  Gellman on 9
  and reality 24
  and telic truth 32, 38–40, 45
  and theology 134
  and truth 5, 9–10, 16, 20–1, 29–30, 55, 172, 175
Creation:
  biblical account of 54, 87, 125–6, 152n.
  and *da'at* 95, 104
  and divine perfection 12–14, 23, 66, 70, 76–7
  explanations of 146
  and free choice 111
  and God's providence 72–4, 150
  and interreligious relations 127–8
  man's relation to 149
  Primal Word 18, 106
  and Torah 104
  and truth 20, 110–21, 130, 132, 135
  and wisdom 93
Cupitt, Don 138

D

da'at:
  and correspondence theory 21
  creation and 95, 104
  explained 15–16
  and identity 96
  language of religious awareness 87–91
  in *Me'or einayim* 6–7, 17, 91–7, 185
  midot 97–102
  and mystical consciousness 14–17
  and religious truth 6–7, 22, 24
  universalist truth 83–6
  see also Bible; hasidism; truth

David, king of Israel 134
devotion:
  devotional praxis 105–6
  and divinity 95, 101n.
  and faith 83–4, 86, 102
  and kabbalah 90–1, 93
  and prayer 92n., 98
  and Torah 80
  and truth 2, 4, 8, 14
divine–human relationship 62, 65, 77, 79–80
divine perfection:
  and concept of truth 62–3
  and creation 12–14, 23, 66, 70, 76–7
  and God's eye 72–80
  Mendelssohn on 61–2
  as metaphysical 80
  problem of universal and particular truth 68–72
  and rabbinic theology 64–7
  in *Sifrei Deuteronomy* 72–3
  universal truth derivative of 12–14
divine providence 96, 112, 120, 138, 160–1, 171
Dynner, Glenn 85n.

E

Eid al-Adha festival 59
  see also Islam
election 10, 184
Eliach, Yaffa 85n.
emet 110n., 113, 116–17, 144–5
  see also truth
epistemological framework conservatism 9, 33–6, 42, 45
eternal essence 11, 48–50
Etkes, Immanuel 100n.
exegetical encounters 57, 77
exemplars 9, 31, 176, 185
exile 51, 87, 100
Exodus from Egypt 52, 54, 69, 74–5, 79, 83, 87, 97, 100n.

F

falsehood 1, 107, 109–13, 121–2, 131, 184–5
Feuerbach, Ludwig Andreas 137

Fisher, Cass 6, 12–14, 62n., 68n., 81n., 182, 184, 186, 197
Flavius Josephus 76n.
Fleischacker, Samuel 29n.
Flusser, David 65n.
Foucault, Michel 43
free choice 111, 117–18, 121

G
gadlut sheni 95, 101n.
Gamaliel, R. 69, 75–6
Gellman, Jerome Yehuda 5, 8–10, 13, 24, 181, 183, 186, 197
Gill, Jerry H. 166n.
Goldman, Alvin 41–2, 44
Goldman, Eliezer 174n.
Goodman, Nelson 173n.
Goshen-Gottstein, Alon 1–28, 107–32, 177–88, 197
Grand Narrative 44
Green, Arthur 6–7, 14–19, 21–2, 92n., 179, 184–7, 198
Gries, Ze'ev 86n.

H
halakhah lemosheh misinai 154
Halperin, David 88n.
Hartman, David 2–4, 27
hasidism:
 and acquisition of consciousness 14
 Breslav theology 7, 18–22
 and divine providence 96–9
 and kabbalah 90
 key writings 84–6
 and *mitnagedim* 125, 127, 180
 perceived inconsistencies 17
 and truth 7, 124–5
 view of pleasure-seeking 101–2
 see also *da'at*; Menahem Nahum of Chernobyl; *Me'or einayim*
Heidegger, Martin 137
Heschel, Abraham Joshua 51n., 88n.
Hezser, Catherine 78n.
Hick, John 39, 165, 167, 172n.
Hirshman, Marc 65, 66n.
historical fact 5, 53–5, 58, 179
human reason 61–2, 65, 82

humility 7–8, 12, 14, 21, 28, 32, 82, 123, 127–8, 172, 180, 182–3
Hyman, Arthur 144n.
Hyman, Israel 159n.

I
identity:
 construction of 27
 da'at and 96
 Judaism and 178–9
immanentism 17
infinity 133, 137, 140, 160, 165–6
instrumentalism:
 and pantheistic mysticism 21–7
 and postmodernism 162
 and relativism 168–9
 and truth 8, 147–8, 171–2, 182–4, 188
interfaith relations 57–60
interreligious understanding 29–35, 58, 131–2, 178, 185
Ish-Shalom, Benjamin 157n., 160n., 170n.
Ishmael (biblical figure) 58–9
Ishmael ben Elisha, R. 5n., 65–6, 74–5
 Mekhilta of Rabbi Ishmael 64, 68–71, 74–5, 77
Islam 32, 58–9, 82–3, 167, 183

J
Jacob Joseph of Polonnoye 91n., 100n.
Jacobs, Louis 141n.
Jerusalem 56, 154
Jesus 2, 32, 59, 83, 136, 183
 Toledot yeshu 11, 59
Job (biblical figure) 50–3
Joshua ben Korha, R. 79–80, 82
Judah, R. 74–5, 77–8

K
kabbalah 90–1, 140–1, 150n., 166, 170, 174
 see also mystical/mysticism
Kahana, Maoz 85n.
Kaplan, Lawrence J. 149n., 155n., 157n., 173n.
katnut 95, 100
Katz, R. Elijah, of Yurewicz 86
Katz, Ya'akov 159n.
Kaufman, Zippi 92n.

Kessler, Edward 57
Kidd, Ian James 31n.
Kitcher, Philip 39
Kook, R. Abraham Isaac:
   on belief 149–57, 160–5, 174, 176
   compared to contemporary theories 162–8
   on constraints of science 154–62
   metaphysical assumptions 25–7, 174
   R. Nathan and 119n.
   on necessary vs. absolute truths 143–8
   on non-realism 8, 139–43, 158, 159n., 167
   on non-theological truths 151–4
   and relativism 168–73
   on theological truths 148–51
   and truth 21–7
Krajewski, Stanislaw 5–6, 10–11, 15, 179–80, 184, 198

L

Lauterbach, Jacob 68n.
Levinas, Emmanuel 97
literary fiction 51, 53

M

McCain, Kevin 33n.
Magid of Mezhirech 86, 90n., 91n., 96n.
Maimonidean terminology 123n., 144
Maimonides:
   on belief 144, 163
   and *da'at* 89, 91
   on faith 149
   on incorporeality of God 48
   on Job 51–2, 54, 57
   on 'necessary beliefs' 32, 144
   on truth 163, 176
   views of other religions 183
Malkhut 90, 103, 140, 166
Marmorstein, Arthur 64
Mekhilta of Rabbi Ishmael, see Ishmael ben Elisha
Menahem Nahum of Chernobyl 6, 14, 16–17, 85, 86n., 91n., 94n., 99, 103
Mendelssohn, Moses 6, 61–2, 70, 73, 77, 80–2
   on divine perfection 61–2
   Jerusalem; or, On Religious Power and Judaism 61
   'The New Thinking' 62
Me'or einayim 6–7, 17–18, 85–7, 90–106, 185–7, 198
   see also hasidism
Merton, Thomas 31
metaphysics 130, 136, 138, 161
midot 97–102
midrash 69, 78, 115–16, 126, 129n.
Mill, John Stuart 38, 39n.
mitnagedim 125, 127, 180
modernism 48, 106
monotheism 62, 65, 70, 73, 82, 150, 166–7
moral/religious urge 145, 154–6, 171, 175
Moses (biblical figure) 51, 55–7, 69, 74, 98–9, 103, 128, 154
Muhammad 32, 83
Murray, Michael 33n.
mystical/mysticism:
   in cross-traditional context 102–6
   and *da'at* 6–7
   and interreligious understanding 130
   and knowledge of God 89–91
   R. Kook on 139, 150, 174
   mystical ethos 97–102
   R. Nahman on 108, 111, 113–14
   R. Nathan on 123, 127
   and pantheism 21–7, 83–4, 86
   and religious truth 14–18, 20, 133, 138, 188
   truth and testimony of mystics 185–6
   and universal truth 83–4
   see also kabbalah; Merton, Thomas
myths 10, 18, 57, 105, 136–8

N

Nahman of Breslav:
   on falsehood/lies 108–14
   on impossibility of religious truth 114–22
   Likutei moharan 108–14
   relevance of teachings to interreligious relations 127–32, 187
   on spiritual virtues 122–7, 186
   on truth 7, 19–22, 127, 182
   see also Nathan of Breslav

Nathan (biblical figure) 134
Nathan of Breslav:
  on humility 182
  on impossibility of religious truth
    114–22
  Likutei halakhot 108, 114–22
  relevance of teachings to interreligious
    relations 19, 127–32
  on spiritual virtues 122–7, 186
  on tolerance 20
  on truth 7–8, 19–21, 180–2
  see also Nahman of Breslav
natural theology 12, 64–8, 76n.
necessary beliefs 32, 144–5
  see also Maimonides
Nehorai, Michael 157n.
Neoplatonism 88, 136, 140–1, 174
Neusner, Jacob 78n.
'Nishmat' 71–2
non-realism 8, 22, 24, 26
  R. Kook on 139–43, 158, 159n., 167
  and non-theological truths 151
  in theology 134–9
  see also realism

O
Oral Law 154, 173n.
Orthodoxy 22, 96, 159n., 174–6, 178

P
Pachter, Mordechai 95n.
paganism 25, 98, 166
particularism 62–3, 66, 76, 78n., 91, 146
paytanim 82
peace 20–1, 28, 75, 108, 115, 123, 126–32,
  149, 152, 169
perfection, *see* divine perfection
Pesikta derav kahana 71n.
pharaoh 54, 97
Phillips, D. Z. 137–8
pleasure 92, 100–2, 129, 150
plurality 19, 25, 82, 115–16, 118, 123, 125,
  127, 174
polemics 11, 27, 59
Polen, Nehemia 88n.
polytheism 39

postmodernism:
  biasism 44–5
  constructivism 42–3
  R. Kook on 8, 23–4, 162–3, 165, 168, 172
  Orthodoxy 175–6
  problems with 41
  repressionist 43–4
  and truth 29, 36, 181
pragmatic contradiction 41–3
Pragmatism 141
prayer 13, 32, 35–6, 62, 68, 71–2, 76, 92,
  98–9, 104, 128, 139–40, 186
priestly heritage 65
prophecy 134–5, 154
providence 63, 70, 72, 76n., 77, 83, 96,
  103, 112–13, 120, 160–1, 171

Q
Quran 58
  see also Islam

R
realism 151, 167, 174–5
  see also non-realism
redemption 82, 119, 125
repressionism 43–5
revelation:
  communal revelation 82
  and faith 10
  and Judaism 88, 98–9, 184
  and natural theology 66–7
  revealed theology 66–7
  revealed truth 61–2, 81, 118–21, 128–9,
    135–6
  and Torah 92, 96, 98–9, 124, 170
  and universal truth 12–13
Rorty, Richard 182
Rosenak, Avinoam 144n.
Rosenzweig, Franz:
  on divine perfection 70, 77
  on faith 49
  on Judaism's relationship to God 80–2
  The New Thinking 62–3
  The Star of Redemption 62
  on truth 6, 14, 186
Roskies, David 56
Ross, Tamar 7–8, 21–2, 24–6, 159n., 179,
  181–2, 185–6, 198

S

Sacks, Jonathan 53, 57
Sages of Israel 51, 69–70, 78, 89n., 93–4, 113, 154, 158n.
Sagi, Avi 174n.
salvation 1–2, 6, 61, 70, 81
scepticism 18, 22, 70, 133, 139, 143, 152, 167, 174, 176
Schatz-Uffenheimer, Rivka 86n.
Schechter, Solomon 87n.
Scholem, Gershom 85n., 141n.
Septimus, Bernard 89n., 97n.
sexuality 87n., 94–5, 100–1
Shatz, David 151n., 155n., 156, 158n.
Shekhinah 69, 75–6, 90, 93n., 94, 96
Shema 68
Shulḥan arukh 108
Sifrei Deuteronomy 70, 72–3, 75, 78
sin 51, 152n.
Sinai, revelation at 52, 74, 77–8, 83, 87, 135, 154
Slifkin, Natan 48
Smith, Huston 16
Solomon's Temple 74, 87
Strauss, David Friedrich 136
subjectivism 151

T

Talmud 22, 89n., 97n., 104, 109, 126n., 134–5, 154, 176
telic truth:
    and biasism 44–5
    and constructivism 42–3
    epistemological framework conservatism 33–5
    explained 29–31
    expressionist objection 36–8
    and interreligious engagement 9–10, 31–3, 183
    nativity objection 38–40
    and postmodernism 41
    recognition of 31
    and religious truth 24
    and repressionism 43–4
    and *temimut* 35–6
telos 9, 24, 116, 181

temimut 35–6
Temples 55, 74, 87
Thich Nhat Hanh 31
Tillich, Paul 57
Tishby, Isaiah 90n.
Toledot yeshu, see Jesus
Torah:
    and belief 144
    and book of Job 50–3
    compared to Bible and Quran 57–8
    compared to Christian and Islamic texts 57–8
    and creation 92–3
    and *da'at* 87, 89, 94–5, 98–9
    on divine perfection 68–70, 153–4, 166
    and faith 103–4
    R. Gamaliel on 69
    on God's nature 48–9
    hasidic homilies on 86
    and history 34, 152
    R. Ishmael on 75
    Israel's receiving of 77–80, 83
    R. Nahman on 115
    R. Nathan on 121, 124–5, 128–9
    and Oral Law 154
    and prayer 104–5
    and religion 128–9
    and revelation 12–13, 61–2, 81, 118–21, 128–9, 135–6
    and truth 108, 110–12, 124–5, 156, 170–1, 179, 184
    truth vs. fiction in 53–4, 56–7
torah shebe'al peh 15
Tourov, Igor 85n.
traditionalism 52, 138–9, 141–3, 148, 165, 173, 176
truth:
    attainability of 180–1
    and correspondence theory 5, 9–10, 16, 20–1, 29–30, 55, 172, 175
    and devotion 2, 4, 8, 14
    graded approach to 186–7
    grounding truth in God 184–5
    and history 10–11
    and human virtues 181–2

importance of 180
instrumental approach to 8, 147–8, 171–2, 182–4, 188
making truth one's own 186
as metaphysical concept 1, 3, 7, 18–21, 109–14, 118,
and mystical consciousness 14–18
pragmatic theory of 134
re-evaluating 187–8
religious truth and other religions 178–88
Rosenzweig on 6, 14, 186
sharing with other faiths 187
subjective 6–7, 14–15, 22, 139, 142–3, 155, 161, 164–5, 167–8, 173, 186
and testimony of mystics 185–6
and Torah 108, 110–12, 124–5, 156, 170–1, 179, 184
unattainability of 18–21
universal and particular truth 68–72
universal truth and divine perfection 12–14
see also telic truth
Tsadok, R. 69

U

universalism 64–7, 71, 73, 114n.
Urbach, Ephraim 64, 70n., 88n.
Uriah (biblical figure) 134

W

wilderness Tabernacle 54, 87, 89
Williams, Bernard 47
wisdom:
    compared to truth 16–17
    and faith 84
    R. Nathan on 117
    in religious texts 105–6
    and revelation 93, 98
    sharing of 17–18, 187
    and Torah 98–9
Wissenschaft des Judentums 80

Y

yoga 87n.
Ysander, T. 85n.

Z

Zeligman, Naftali 52n.
Zivan, Gili 175n.
Zohar 98

www.ingramcontent.com/pod-product-compliance
Lightning Source LLC
Chambersburg PA
CBHW070825250426
43671CB00036B/2153